JOHN SCOTT
OF AMWELL

By Lawrence D. Stewart

UNIVERSITY OF CALIFORNIA PRESS

BERKELEY AND LOS ANGELES · 1956

JOHN SCOTT OF AMWELL

THE
POETICAL WORKS
OF
JOHN SCOTT ESQ.

of Amwell near Ware Herts

Hanned pinx.t   *J.Hall sculp 1782*

Ware   **LONDON**
Printed for J. Buckland ,
MDCCLXXXII.

John Scott at 47; from a copy owned by the author. "My own Portrait ... though executed by the Most Eminent Artist in that Line, might have been better, it conveys the idea of a lustier heavier person." This remains the only extant portrait of the poet.

JOHN SCOTT OF AMWELL

By Lawrence D. Stewart

UNIVERSITY OF CALIFORNIA PRESS

BERKELEY AND LOS ANGELES

1956

UNIVERSITY OF CALIFORNIA PUBLICATIONS

ENGLISH STUDIES: 13

EDITORS (LOS ANGELES): LEON HOWARD, J. J. ESPEY,
ADA NISBET, H. T. SWEDENBERG, JR.

Submitted by editors January 10, 1955
Issued April 25, 1956
Price, $3.50

UNIVERSITY OF CALIFORNIA PRESS

BERKELEY AND LOS ANGELES

CALIFORNIA

◇

CAMBRIDGE UNIVERSITY PRESS

LONDON, ENGLAND

FOR LEON HOWARD

—forsan et haec olim meminisse iuvabit.

PREFACE

How many readers of poetry in the present day are conscious of the existence of John Scott?" With such a rhetorical question, Charles Knight began—around 1840— his brief study of the Quaker poet and man of affairs which he included in his *Glimpses of the Past*. If the ordinary readers of poetry in Knight's day had difficulty remembering John Scott of Amwell, eminent scholars ever since have been ignoring him. And even when he is mentioned in such a splendid work as Mr. R. W. Chapman's edition of Johnson's *Letters*, the only footnote discussing him is misleading: the date of Scott's major publication, his poem *Amwell*, has been overlooked.

Although John Scott of Amwell is an eighteenth-century figure who is today all but completely forgotten, he was not always so ignored. He was an exposer of the Rowley forgeries, an employer of the young William Blake, and a friend of Dr. Johnson and James Beattie. In his lifetime he was closely associated with the most brilliant and memorable people of a noteworthy era; and, therefore, even if he had never written a line, he should not have passed from literary and historical memory. Scott, however, should not have had to rely on his associates in order to be remembered. He devoted his life to works which would benefit his society, and he labored assiduously in his endeavors. He wrote two political pamphlets, a tract on poor relief, two volumes on highways and turnpikes, a volume of literary criticism, and five pamphlets and volumes of poetry—all of which were intended to keep him from evanescing into the mists of literary oblivion. And, in the beginning, this intention seemed to stand a good chance of being fulfilled: the young Wordsworth published *An Evening Walk* in 1793, and a footnote acknowledged his indebtedness to Scott's *Critical Essays*.

Many of Scott's writings have deservedly sunk beyond present sight, but the almost total neglect which the man and his career have received is one of those historical curiosities which can never be satisfactorily explained. It is true that no account of his life appeared between its own covers but only in rather unselective compilations of eighteenth-century poetical works. Had Dr. Johnson lived to fulfill the last of his contemplated literary tasks, he himself would have prevented this inattention, for he, late in 1784, began to gather materials for a biographical essay on the Amwell poet whom he stated he had loved. What was to have been a notable life of Scott was scarcely undertaken, however, when the death of the good doctor canceled his literary obligations; and the task fell to another. When Boswell failed to mention this projected work in his famous biography, the best opportunity of linking Scott's name with Johnson's inevitably passed, and Scott was already gravitating toward oblivion. John Scott should have been remembered, however, for two important reasons: he was frequently the percipient commentator on and reflector of a magnificent age, and he was a sensitive man who made substantial contributions to his society and our heritage.

There exists today no biography of Scott which is satisfactory, either in its scope or its accuracy. The first detailed sketch of his life appeared with a review of Scott's *Poetical Works* in the *European Magazine* for September, 1782. Earlier mention had been made of Scott's benevolent character, but this was the first account which attempted to give a complete picture of the poet's life; and it is significant as being the only version which Scott himself approved as accurate. Whether this biographical essay was written by John Hoole is unknown, but the phraseology of the piece is much the same as that used in Hoole's acknowledged life, and if Hoole did not write the original, he certainly relied upon it considerably and without admitting it. The standard biography of John Scott was what the *Monthly Review* called the "sensible and well written account" by Hoole, prepared as a preface for Scott's posthumously published *Critical Essays on*

Some of the Poems, of Several English Poets. Although it will be seen that in several places this account, too, is inaccurate, it is the most trustworthy single record we have and derives its authenticity from several causes: it was the only essay on his life written immediately after the death of the poet when all of Scott's letters and manuscripts were intact and could be used. Most of these materials have since disappeared, and all that we know of them is what is given here. Hoole was also fortunate in that his study was made with the help and assistance of Scott's friends, who were anxious to lend their materials and their memories to that effort. Samuel Scott, the poet's brother, was read the biography on April 25, 1785, while it was still in manuscript, and there is an implicit suggestion that the account met with his approval. Because of these facts, the Hoole essay is of basic importance in any biographical study of Scott.

But while we use Hoole's work for its facts, we must not deceive ourselves about its merits. It is frequently vague and confused. The chronology can be disputed on many points, and it is apparent from reading the account that Hoole did not make satisfactory use of many of his materials. The discovery of new documents and papers has aided immeasurably in our knowledge of Scott's activities and has made the Hoole account obsolete.

In the twenty-seven years following Hoole's work, six other accounts of the poet appeared. In 1795 Robert Anderson prefaced his printing of Scott's poems in his edition of *The Works of the British Poets* with a life of the poet. This was but a recasting of Hoole, interspersed with some of the magazine reviews of Scott's works. In 1808 appeared the shortest of the six biographical sketches, written by S. J. Pratt for his *The Cabinet of Poetry*. In 1810, Alexander Chalmers rewrote the material used by Anderson and Hoole, but he also included in its entirety *Some Memoirs of the Last Illness of John Scott* which had been written

by Samuel Scott, the poet's brother, and published anonymously
in 1785. This appeared in Chalmers' *Works of the English Poets,
from Chaucer to Cowper.* In 1819, Thomas Campbell made some
brief observations on Scott when he included him in his *Specimens of the British Poets,* but it is clear that he made no search
for new materials: he even refused to see whether Scott's grotto
still existed, being content to say only that it had been still at Amwell in 1785 when Hoole had made his study. In 1822 two biographies of Scott came out, one by R. A. Davenport in his *The
British Poets,* and one by Robert Walsh, Jr., in his *The Works of
the British Poets, with Lives of the Authors.* Neither of these
contributes anything factually to our understanding of Scott's
life, although the Davenport account is significant for showing
the genuine appreciation which some held for Scott as long as
forty years after his death. The most recent—and certainly the
most pleasant—account of Scott's life and works was compiled
in 1948 by Herman Liebert in his *Johnson's Last Literary Project.*
None of these biographical essays is thoroughly accurate; each
only restates what had been said before—often without accuracy.
The result is that a biographer must ignore all of these later
accounts and return to Hoole to see the basic facts.

My life of Scott has been based upon Hoole and is supple-
mented with those letters by or about Scott which Hoole did not
print and which I have been able to obtain; those critical contemporary reviews of Scott's works which Hoole did not mention; *Some Memoirs of the Last Illness of John Scott,* which was
used by Chalmers, but inaccurately and with too much emphasis,
there being no attempt made by him to relate this document to
the religious aspect of Scott's life; the journals of James Beattie,
which help to establish the dates of the philosopher's visits to
Scott; and the histories of Hertfordshire and the archaeological
explorations of Scott's grotto, all of which documents tell us
much about the man and his relationship with the Amwell area,

which he so deeply loved. It must be admitted immediately that this life of Scott will be complete only in the sense that it will tell all that is now known; the discovery of new documents may someday lengthen and fill it out. To locate more of the poet's papers is, unfortunately, essential before a proper biography can be written and the vague contour of John Scott can be rounded into the substantiality of a man.

In making my study of John Scott, I have been generously helped by many people: Professor Z. S. Fink of Northwestern University suggested the topic to me; and he, as well as Professors Wallace W. Douglas and Robert D. Mayo of Northwestern and Mr. Leland H. Carlson, president of Rockford College, have read parts of the work in its earliest form. Professors Donald A. Bird, Hugh G. Dick, John J. Espey, Ada Nisbet, and H. T. Swedenberg, Jr., of the University of California, Los Angeles, and Mr. James Kubeck of the University of California Press have read the final work. To all of these scholars I am indebted for valuable and perceptive criticisms. Three residents of John Scott's Hertfordshire have also, across so great a distance, kindly extended suggestions and information to a stranger: the detailed engraving of Scott's grotto was made by R. T. Andrews for the *East Herts Archaeological Society. Transactions* and appeared in the first (1899) issue of that publication; it is reproduced here by courtesy of Gordon Moodey, Esq., the honorable secretary of the society. To Colonel W. Le Hardy, County Archivist of Hertfordshire, and to John C. Hanbury, Esq., present owner of Scott's Grotto, I shall always be obligated. Finally, I owe more than I can possibly express to Professor Leon Howard of the University of California, Los Angeles. The faults of the book cannot be attributed to him; but its virtues can.

L. D. S.

Los Angeles, California
    October 16, 1955

CONTENTS

CHAPTER I

THE CONVENTIONAL YOUTH

I

IN HIS seventy-fifth year, Dr. Samuel Johnson continued to be a paradox: long an opponent of a country manner of living and a climatic theory of composition, he nevertheless arranged to leave London for the country in pursuit of the health which continually eluded him in the city. Boswell and Reynolds were making plans for him to spend the winter in Italy, but by July of 1784, Johnson was determined not to wait but to leave London immediately "to try the air of Derbyshire."[1] He left the city behind him on the thirteenth of July and, after a five-day visit in his beloved Lichfield, arrived in Ashbourne on the nineteenth "to try what air and attention can perform."[2]

He went to Ashbourne in a depressed mood, because he had learned that three old friends had died since he had last been at Lichfield. Furthermore, his old schoolmate Dr. John Taylor, the strongest tie with the past, had become adapted to a routine of going to bed nightly at nine, a habit which did not at all accord with the doctor's own. In Ashbourne, where he lived in despondency with dropsy and asthma as his only companions, Johnson stayed for two months, leaving there on the twenty-seventh of September. It was "a gloomy frigid ungenial Summer,"[3] in Ashbourne; lacking even the most minor materials from which to weave the fabric of a letter to London, he wrote, "I am now reduced to think, and I am at last content to talk of the weather."[4] After this lonely existence, which cured the dropsy and alleviated the asthma at the expense of his spirits, Johnson rejoiced to flee

---

[1] For notes to chap. i, see p. 201.

back to his beloved London, being more convinced than ever that "they who are content to live in the country, are *fit* for the country."[5] And yet, it was in the country that Johnson made arrangements for his last literary project.

By 1784, Johnson's literary career seemed over, as far as the creation of new works was concerned. Though he turned his hand to an occasional Horatian ode or wrote a minor article, he had done nothing noteworthy since the appearance of the last of his *Lives of the Poets* series in 1781. He seemed to have directed his thoughts increasingly toward death, and in June of the year he died he was contemplating the publication of some of his prayers and meditations. In view of this lessening of his literary output, it is significant to see that in his most depressed state of mind he still was willing to write when an appealing subject was offered him: for at the end of his life, he undertook to write the life of John Scott of Amwell, the Quaker poet, critic, road builder, political writer, humanitarian, and general country gentleman and grotto builder who had been one of his circle of friends.[6]

Scott had died in London on December 12, 1783, leaving in the press, on the eve of their publication, a volume of literary essays: *Critical Essays on Some of the Poems, of Several English Poets.* Friends decided to append a biographical sketch of the author to this production and further determined to approach the most eminent of English biographers for the study. Consequently, David Barclay, the grandson of the writer of the great Quaker apologia *An Apology for the True Christian Divinity,* wrote to Johnson, who was also his old friend. By this time, the doctor was in Ashbourne and his depression was at its most intense. His short reply to Barclay revealed his state of spiritual exhaustion and also his genuine affection for the dead Quaker, as he was drawn again to the pen and the evaluation of a friend's life and creations.

SIR

As I have made some advances towards recovery, and loved Mr.
Scot, I am willing to do justice to his memory. You will be pleased to
get what account you can of his life, with dates, where they can be
had, and when I return, We will contrive how our materials can be
best employed.

I am Your humble Servant
Sam: Johnson

Ashbourn in Derbyshire Sept 16. 1784[7]

On the sixteenth of November Johnson returned to London
and, in his rooms one day, was called upon by Barclay who by
then was beset with considerable doubts. He was alarmed by
Johnson's continued poor health and felt that it was unreason-
able to ask him to undertake another biography. More embar-
rassing, however, for Barclay was his discovery that John Scott
would have been a trying subject for the doctor, even had he
been in the best of spirits. In gathering his materials, Barclay
realized what he had not known before (though it could hardly
have been a revelation to Johnson): that although Scott liked
Johnson personally, he had seldom agreed with him, had published replies to two of the doctor's political tracts, and had been
inspired to write his *Critical Essays* by what he considered were
the injustices done by Johnson in his *Lives of the Poets*. Therefore, Barclay found himself in the awkward position of asking
the doctor to write a tribute to one of Johnson's harshest and
most annoying critics. The only solution for the dilemma,
thought Barclay, was to abandon the project and forget even
about publishing the *Critical Essays*. It could easily have been
done; Scott's family seemed to take little interest in the post-
humous reputation of the poet, and they were independently
wealthy and needed no additional royalties.[8] Furthermore,
though Scott himself had hungered after a literary reputation,
it was pretty well agreed by this time that he would be remembered more for his personality and benevolence than his miscel-

laneous publications.⁹ To Johnson, however, who felt that all
writing was the product of much pain and more effort, the suggestion of abandoning a completed manuscript was not to be
considered casually. He asked Barclay to read him some of the
passages which Barclay thought were personally offensive.
Barclay did this dutifully, and Johnson replied:

> That he differed from Mr. Barclay respecting the publication, as from
> what he had then heard, he believed the book would do credit to their
> late friend, and as to Mr. Scott's dissenting from him, he observed,
> that authors would differ in opinion, and that good performances
> could not be too much criticised.

Johnson then considered the biographical materials which
Barclay had brought him. Although he thought they, such as
they were, were acceptable, he insisted that many more would
be needed if this was to be a suitable biography; and he, expressing his anxiety to begin the life of Scott, urged Barclay to gather
more anecdotes and facts. Johnson had long believed that "no-
body can write the life of a man, but those who have eat and
drunk and lived in social intercourse with him";¹⁰ since his relationship with Scott had begun in 1766 and had been a somewhat
intimate one, he felt qualified to speak of his old friend. At the
same time—following his conception of biography—he insisted
that anecdotes and personal eccentricities, other than those observed by him, should be included. "Beside the common inci-
dents of life, it [the ideal biography] should tell us his studies,
his mode of living, the means by which he attained to excellence,
and his opinions of his own works."¹¹ But though a true picture
of Scott would be his aim, he realized that he would be betrayed
by his own delicacy and sensibility. As he had written in his life
of Addison:

> The necessity of complying with times and of sparing persons is the
> great impediment of biography. History may be formed from perma-
> nent monuments and records; but Lives can only be written from

personal knowledge, which is growing every day less, and in a short time is lost forever. What is known can seldom be immediately told, and when it might be told it is no longer known. The delicate features of the mind, the nice discriminations of character, and the minute peculiarities of conduct are soon obliterated; and it is surely better that caprice, obstinacy, frolick, and folly, however they might delight in the description, should be silently forgotten than that by wanton merriment and unseasonable detection a pang should be given to a widow, a daughter, a brother, or a friend.[12]

And yet, strongly motivated as he was by feelings of sympathy for one's associates, he wrote to Dr. Burney on November first of 1784,

Of the caution necessary in adjusting narratives there is no end. Some tell what they do not know, that they may not seem ignorant, and others from mere indifference about truth. All truth is not, indeed, of equal importance; but if little violations are allowed, every violation will in time be thought little; and a writer should keep himself vigilantly on his guard against the first temptations to negligence or supineness.[13]

How Johnson planned to solve this dilemma is unknown. Struggling between desires to be kind and desires to be truthful, he might have left the life of Scott as unrevealing as his immediate successor did. Whatever the theories, however, Johnson was never able to demonstrate them with a life of Scott. After Barclay's visit, Johnson's illness became worse by the day, and when Barclay returned to London with additional materials, Francis Barber met him at the door of Johnson's house and said the doctor had grown so ill he could have no visitors. But a few days before his death, Johnson sent word to Barclay "that he had not forgot his engagement; and that, if it should please God to restore him, he would certainly perform it, for he loved Mr. Scott." The Life of Scott remained only a project, but for Johnsonians it has had a special significance: it was the last literary project that the doctor had. Some years later, Boswell wrote of Johnson,

Volumes would be required to contain a list of his numerous and various acquaintance, none of whom he ever forgot; and could describe and discriminate them all with precision and vivacity. He associated with persons the most widely different in manners, abilities, rank, and accomplishments.[14]

This might explain the scant mention Scott received in Boswell's *Life of Johnson,*[15] but it would not account for the especial affection with which Johnson spoke to Barclay about Scott after the poet's death; and it seems unwise to attribute Johnson's repeated compliments about Scott only to "the venerable graces of decay."

After Johnson died, the collected materials for Scott's biography were turned over to John Hoole, the translator, playwright, and glorified hack writer, who had also been a friend of both Johnson and Scott. Although the account which he wrote remains a basic source of materials for a life of Scott, it is pedantic, dull, wearisome, and generally uninformative. The facts which Johnson himself would have used would not perhaps have differed measurably from those employed by Hoole, but the expression of his judgments at least would have been interesting. There is much that he would have disapproved of in Scott: the principles of the Whig could not have found sympathy with him, nor could he have accepted many of the attacks leveled at his own critical position. Scott's Quakerism would also have annoyed Johnson, even if this is not the first Quaker who, despite his reason, had won his heart. But in having loved the man, Johnson had been particularly impressed by the character of Scott, his benevolence, his social interest, and a gentle humanity which, paradoxically, was always demonstrated with force and emphasis. The fact that we may deduce the general tenor of what he would have said does not compensate for his not having said it. For had he lived to say it, he would have preserved the memory of a friend, John Scott of Amwell.

II

John Scott's father, Samuel Scott, was a linen draper[16] and citizen of London, a man who was described as having plain and irreproachable manners and who was a preacher in the Society of Friends. Married to Martha Wilkins, he was the father of several children, all except two of whom died in early childhood. Though the rate of infant mortality nowadays frightens few parents, in the early eighteenth century the rate was terrifying to most. The Scott family had suffered too much illness to regard health as anything except of supreme importance, and the basic desire to stay alive shaped their entire life. Smallpox was the symbol of disease for the family, and from their concern solely with it, one cannot help assuming that it must have caused the deaths of some of the other children. The two surviving boys were to be hoarded like jewels, and nothing was to be spared in protecting them from the world of predators into which they had been born. The older of the two sons was Samuel Scott, who had been born March 21, 1719, in Gracechurch Street, London, and who, for reasons unexplained but probably related to those of health, had spent his early childhood living with his aunt in the neighborhood. The second son was the poet, who was born January 9, 1730, in the Grange-walk, in the parish of St. Mary Bermondsey, Southwark. The boys were descended from ancient families of York and Warwick, but it is not known which parent came from which county.

The two boys apparently were never close companions, perhaps because of the considerable difference in their ages. Although they later went walking through Amwell together, and although his brother was the one person whom John Scott called for when on his deathbed, there remains no testimony of any great affection between them. No poem is inscribed to Samuel Scott; and in the diary of Samuel, there is scant mention made of John.[17] Samuel later wrote that he "was, in the seventeenth year of his age [*ca.* 1736], remarkably favoured with a divine visitation; by which his understanding was enlightened, and the great beauty, heavenly order and economy of a truly religious life, at seasons even ravished his soul."[18] He entered the ministry of the Society of Friends about 1753. On October 3, 1754, he married and moved to Hertford.[19] Samuel later became a gloomy man, so obsessed with his own sense of sin that he believed silence was the greatest virtue, and he would go for long periods of time without speaking in Quaker meetings. Comforting as this may have been for his own soul, it probably did little for those who worshipped in meeting with him. He had begun his ministry, however, as an enthusiastic preacher, so he may have got to Hertford meeting before his evangelistic fires burned themselves out; "...manifold were the errors, even of my religious youth, seeking the praise of some good men, but despising others, and smiting them with the tongue."[20] Though this introspection and alienation from others increased with age, at the same time he developed considerable interest in, and derived satisfaction from, several curious and fascinating things: the fragrance of his garden, the fidelity and attendance of his spaniel, the pleasure of his rural, solitary, and evening excursions, and the gratification (in strict moderation) of his palate.[21] He hastily confessed in his diary that these were all vanities of vanities and he regretted being interested in them; but there is no indication that he, even in most introspective moments, ever gave them up. Samuel's biographer said that the natural abilities of Samuel were above the common rank, and he was versed in literature. "Yet," as his biographer pointed out, "these he counted but as dung."[22] Temperamentally, therefore, Samuel was quite different from his brother John, and this fact was to be significant in the poet's development; he was compelled to turn to friends for the advice and encouragement in his poetry and writings which it was obviously impossible for him to receive at home.

At the age of seven, Scott began his formal education when his father engaged John Clarke, who kept a small school in Barnaby Street in London, to come to the Scott home and tutor the boy in the fundamentals of Latin. Of this man, Scott later wrote:

... he was, I believe, a native of the Shetland-Islands; he was ingenious and learned, but rather a severe pedagogue; yet, spite of the domination which he exercised over his pupils, I respected him, and there was something in the man, and in his manner, that I even now faintly recollect with pleasure.

Clarke tutored the boy for three years, always apparently at home and never at his school. The location of Scott's training is significant: it indicates how early began the family's obsessive fear of smallpox which determined the poet's educational and geographical background; and it also shows to what lengths they would go to prevent his contamination by the disease-ridden world of London. Although the training received from Clarke could hardly have been extensive, it was to be especially valuable to the boy since it was, with a slight exception, the only formal education he ever received. He never learned French or Italian, and although he became a devoted admirer of Virgil, he never was at ease with any language other than English. Only once in his writings (and then it was in the *Critical Essays,* his final publication) did he make learned allusions to Virgil and quote from the original Latin with deceptive ease. Johnson once said, "Not to name the school or the masters of men illustrious for literature, is a kind of historical fraud, by which honest fame is injuriously diminished."[23] But Scott was no illustrious pupil; he gave no promise of talent or ability, and there is no indication that students were dispatched to John Clarke merely because Scott had studied under him.

In 1740, when the poet was ten, his father withdrew from business in London and, taking his wife and two sons with him, moved to the small village of Amwell in Hertfordshire—not

quite twenty miles north of London and only two miles from
the town of Ware. In Amwell, the father entered into the malt-
ing trade and he soon became prosperous.

Foreigners are not a little amazed when they hear of brewers, dis-
tillers, and men in similar departments of trade, held forth as persons
of considerable consequence. In this great commercial country it is
natural that a situation which produces much wealth should be considered as very respectable; and, no doubt, honest industry is entitled
to esteem. But, perhaps, the too rapid advance of men of low extrac-
tion tends to lessen the value of that distinction by birth and gentility,
which has ever been found beneficial to the grand scheme of subordination.[24]

In such a tone, a judicious mixture of admiration and contempt,
did Boswell begin his discussion of Mr. Thrale; it is clear that he
might have said much the same sort of thing about the senior
Scott. The Scotts were Quakers, however, and were less concerned with social structure than was the lord of Auchinleck.
Hertfordshire began to fill with Quaker maltsters and brewers,[25]
and though the trade may not have increased their social stature,
it did much to improve their economic standing. It is not difficult
to see why a prosperous London merchant would look toward
Hertfordshire with financial and not social aspirations. Another
attraction for the Scotts was the wonderful pure air of Hertfordshire, free from the contaminations of the city. Fuller had talked
in his day of those who paid two years' purchase for the air
when they settled in that county, and as late as the nineteenth
century, people were still saying, "Time out of mind, Hertfordshire has been famous for the finest roads and the worst coachmen, the richest soil and the worst crops, the happiest poor and
the worst servants, the best malt and the worst ale, of any shire
in England."[26] This move from the city to the country was to
have a profound effect on Scott's life; for Amwell grew to
epitomize all that he loved in life, and the London that he had

left gradually evolved into the symbol of all that was evil in his world.

After the family had settled at Amwell, Scott was sent daily to Ware to a private school which was kept there by a Mr. Hall. Hall had but one talent, evidently, and that was the ability to write a clear hand and to interest his pupils in the rudiments of penmanship. John Scott's own clear hand may have been a product of this early training, but that was to be the only benefit derived from the school, as Hall knew nothing of languages and was only a simple teacher, who could not provide the advantages for what Hoole called "classical improvement." Meanwhile, there increased that fear of smallpox, which had doubtless helped to motivate the family's moving to Amwell; the poet was soon withdrawn from Hall's school and his formal education came to a quiet end. The rest of his training was the result of self-discipline and the encouragement of better-educated friends; it was also the result of being under a Wordsworthian ministry of nature and of natural beauty. Despite the peculiar irregularity of his academic training (indeed, perhaps because of it) Scott did not find his childhood unpleasant. The exceptional nature of his education—certainly, the freedom of it—gave him uncommon pleasure when he was a boy.

> CHILDHOOD! happiest stage of life,
> Free from care and free from strife,
> Free from Memory's ruthless reign,
> Fraught with scenes of former pain;
> Free from Fancy's cruel skill,
> Fabricating future ill;
> Time, when all that meets the view,
> All can charm, for all is new;
> How thy long-lost hours I mourn,
> Never, never, to return!
>
> Then to toss the circling ball,
> Caught rebounding from the wall;

Then the mimic ship to guide
Down the kennel's dirty tide;
Then the hoop's revolving pace
Thro' the dusty street to chace;
O what joy!—it once was mine,
Childhood, matchless boon of thine!—
How thy long-lost hours I mourn,
Never, never, to return![27]

It was in the Amwell countryside that Scott grew up a lover
of nature and the country which, he felt, was alone free from that
evil which infected city life. The Amwell region was particularly
suited to the young boy's love for gentle hills and clear streams,
and he roamed the days over the hills of Hertfordshire, develop-
ing a love for all sorts of physical activity and, especially, walking—a love which he never outgrew. Piscator, of Izaak Walton's
Compleat Angler, had a century earlier met Venator on Amwell
Hill before sunrise, and they had drunk a cup of good barley
wine and sung "Old Rose" and rejoiced together before they had
wandered along the banks of the Lea to Ware. Piscator said it
was the best place in the world to "sit on cowslipbanks, hear the
birds sing, and possess ourselves in as much quietness as these
silent silver streams, which we now see glide so quietly by us."
The reverential attitude which Scott had for the Amwell region
was caught earlier by Walton, too, who found those meadows
"too pleasant to be looked on, but only on holy-days." So it was
in these same regions of benign spirits and gentle ghosts that
Scott as a boy fished and hunted. Later, in a manner which
seemed more suited to the melancholia of his brother than to his
own rationality, he got to brooding over his childhood pleasures,
and he ended by discarding his weapons as he developed theories
about the humane treatment of animals:

The amusement of angling has been generally regarded as a diver-
sion, not only inoffensive in itself, but also favourable to the meditations of the philosophical and religious. Perhaps, however, it might

be difficult to reconcile with the idea of moral rectitude, the idea of pleasure obtained by the punishment of innocent beings. The attention of an angler will also be too anxiously employed on the object he is endeavouring to procure, to admit the exercise of his mental powers on dissimilar subjects.[28]

This later attitude, however, was not a reversal of his earlier position: it was the inevitable result of an increasing love of natural things and creatures, a love which had been fostered by his life in the village of Amwell. Such a sensitivity to the plight of animals would have pleased Johnson who "would not sit at table, where a lobster that had been roasted alive was one of the dishes," and who on his visit to Wales had released a captured hare so it could not be eaten for dinner.[29] In his attitude toward animals, Scott came the closest he was to come to that unrealistic sentimentality which he, in his most rational moments, detested and lambasted with stern Quaker wrath.

About 1747 or 1748, when he was in his late teens, Scott became acquainted with Charles Frogley, a bricklayer, who had been hired by the poet's father to do some work on the Amwell estate. Until that time, Scott had apparently read only at random: neither his father nor his brother, though kind and retired men, living their quiet lives in Hertfordshire, was inclined toward reading poetry or classical literature. The Quaker faith had encouraged silent meditation and separation from the concerns of the world. Well indeed might Samuel Scott, the elder brother, say, "I have little judgment in poetry, or propensity to peruse it,"[30] when his concern was only with his own salvation. But this sort of attitude could not be helpful to the education of a younger brother and aspiring poet. It is for this reason particularly that the meeting with Frogley was a propitious one, since Frogley had a great love for literature. A self-educated man, Frogley had enthusiastically read those books which had come into his hand, and he had rigorously developed and disciplined what is re-

ported to have been a "natural taste for metrical composition."
When he first entered the Scott home, he saw "some little
poetical essays" of John Scott, and he recognized, evidently, an
ability which was as untutored as it was genuine. Frogley, in a
pattern which would later have won the approbation of Warton,
immediately showed the boy Milton's *Paradise Lost,* giving him
his first great model for imitation and creating for him a personal hero. Frogley's attentions to the young boy were repaid
with constant devotion, and Scott later in life told Hoole "that
he seldom found reason, in his advancing state of judgment, to
dissent from the opinion of his friend Frogley." Frogley insisted
on a program of intensive reading, and he early instilled in
Scott's mind a fundamental theory: the difference between men
can largely be measured by the length and degree of their education. It was the fortunate meeting with Frogley which began an
important phase of Scott's career as a man of letters; and years
later, when he had achieved intellectual independence and a
moderate degree of literary fame, he testified to his constant
friendship for Frogley in his "Ode XI. To a Friend Apprehensive of Declining Friendship," a poem which revealed Frogley's
wistful speculation that his student would someday outgrow
him. The significance of the poem lies in its biographical motivation and, unfortunately, not in its intrinsic merits. It probably
deserves its present fate when it is reprinted only in *The Stuffed
Owl* as an example of unfortunate poetry, primarily because
Frogley's name was used and was not transmogrified into something less grinding on the ears.

In 1753 or 1754, Scott met a second person who was to have
considerable effect upon his poetic development. This was the
divinity student John Turner, who lived at Ware and was introduced to Scott by Frogley. Four years the poet's junior and a
fellow-dabbler in criticism and poetry, Turner was easily Scott's
superior in a knowledge of literature. In 1767, he was described

as being "not only master of the Hebrew, but of several other oriental languages; he has devoted part of his time to natural and experimental philosophy and the mathematics."[31] Turner had been trained in the London dissenting academy of Dr. Jennings, and he further encouraged and directed Scott's reading by lending him several books, including Glover's *Leonidas,* Thomson's *Seasons,* and Pope's works and translations. From London, where he was staying, he also sent Scott a telescope with directions how to use it; and he seems responsible for helping to develop that scientific eye which Scott would later believe made his poetic images unique.

> Pleas'd with the scene, I range from field to field,
> Till loftier lands remoter prospects yield;
> And there the curious optic tube apply,
> Till a new world approaches on the eye;
> Till where dark wood the hills slope surface shrouds;
> Or the blue summit mingles with the clouds;
> There fair inclosures lie of varied hue,
> And trees and houses rise distinct to view.
>   But this too oft th' inclement clime denies,
> Involv'd in misty or in watery skies;
> And yet ev'n then, with books engag'd, I find
> A sweet employment for th' exploring mind.[32]

The telescope never lost its allure for Scott, and the *Critical Essays* stated that only by examining the Welsh mountains through a glass had he been able to distinguish the mountains from the clouds which covered them; to the end of his life, he retained this basic notion which Turner had helped inculcate in him and which the Amwell poet in turn may have passed on to Wordsworth: only a precise observation could create a precise image. And false though the notion may have been, Scott certainly believed that he saw things better through Turner's telescope than through his own unaided vision. His dependence upon Turner was not only scientific. In the same way that he apparently allowed Frogley to influence him, so he was willing to see theories of poetry through Turner's eyes. The fact that it took him the larger part of his life to outgrow his teachers, who themselves were not outstanding intellectuals, reveals much about the pace of his intellectual development.

III

Scott's close friendship with Frogley continued, and the brick-layer was accustomed to visit the poet during the evening of the day. Scott's poetry was the usual subject of discussion, and the two would pass the hours criticizing Scott's poems and talking about literature. Because of his father's financial position and his family's consuming fear of smallpox, Scott did not take a job in the city or mingle with the society of London; in fact, he visited the English capital only once in the twenty years between 1740 and 1760, even though he lived no more than a few miles away. The young man therefore became accustomed early in his life to leisurely isolation; concerns were developed in benefactions and local government, in letters and the arts. Scott's verses were also sent to Turner, who was then in London; but though Scott's enthusiasm for writing increased, both Turner and Frogley kept him from publishing any of his works. They urged upon him a policy of caution, with the result that Scott published nothing until he was almost twenty-four. It was also a policy of disaster, since this hothouse air of pseudo intellectualism in which he spent his formative years did nothing to develop anything orig-inal or creative. The genius which developed at Amwell was completely imitative.

On December 18, 1753, Scott wrote to the editor of the *Gentle-man's Magazine:*

Accidentally looking over your Magazines for July and August 1752, I was agreeably entertained with a critical dissertation on that beautiful description in the 12th chapter of Ecclesiastes. I thought your correspondent's explication was just, and having a mind to see how the passage would look in a modern poetical dress, I attempted the following version of it, on his plan; to which if you please to allow a place in your next Magazine, you will extremely oblige

Your friend and constant reader,
R. S.

The casual tone of the letter does not reflect the earnest young man and his first published poem, "Epidemic Mortality, from Eccl. xii," a poem written in heroic couplets to hammer down the moral, "Thy Maker God in early time revere!" Only one image—and it is conventional, to be sure—suggests that a poet and not a preacher wrote the lines: "Death's in the house and Silence in the street!"

On November 15, the following year (1754), the *Gentleman's Magazine* published Scott's "Verses occasioned by the Description of the AEOLIAN HARP, in February Magazine, 1754," also under the signature of R. S. The Aeolian harp interested many poets of the time: Gray, Smart, and Mason all wrote about it, but it was an unusual subject for a member of the Society of Friends. Also written in heroic couplets, this poem describes the Aeolian harp and then suggests how it led Scott's imagination to conjure up delightful and deleterious scenes: "To fancy'd sighs I real sighs return, / By turns I languish, and by turns I burn." Coming from a twenty-four-year-old Quaker, such lines must have been astonishing indeed. Scott never was able to reconcile himself to the notion that a Quaker should not like organs or worry about strange and modern musical instruments. Though he later said, "My knowledge of musick is but superficial,"[33] he once composed an ode to the organ; the Aeolian harp itself fluttered through his poetry until the end of his life. This was a trivial matter, in which his own ideas differed from the dogma of his faith, yet it marked the beginning of a schism which was to set him apart from the prescribed doctrine of the Society of

Friends. That he, when living in the center of the most pious Quaker community, should develop ideas of his own revealed for the first time that he possessed individuality. Whether other verses of his appeared during this period is unknown, as only these two were traced by Hoole.

By January of 1755, Scott had written at least six pastorals, four of which, years later, were revised to appear as *Moral Eclogues* (1778). In 1755, he also wrote an "Ode to Fear" and sent it to Turner. In the July, 1758, issue of the *Gentleman's Magazine,* a poem entitled "To Fear" was published, but it is impossible to tell if this is the earlier poem, a reshaping of it, or an entirely new work. None of these earlier poems was reprinted by Scott. There was nothing about them, perhaps, which a beginning poet, reared on minor early eighteenth-century poetry, need acknowledge with shame; but there was nothing about them either which made them seem memorable. The imagery was in a common tradition, and the precision of meaning which the heroic couplet originally had served to emphasize in the form itself, had given way to a rather verbose and uncompressed idea of occasional verse. The most significant work of that year was reported in a December, 1755, letter to Turner, when Scott said, "... he hopes, when he comes next to Ware, he shall have the pleasure of seeing the scenes which had so often entertained him, described in verse, that would never decay." This was the genesis of *Amwell: A Descriptive Poem,* which did not appear until 1776, and which remains one of Scott's finest and most important poems. Scott's conception of *Amwell* as something which not willingly would be let die, emphasizes the continual influence of Milton on him, particularly with the notion that he must write a long poem of lasting value to justify his claims as a poet.

Turner was generally absent from Ware, but he corresponded regularly with the poet and was taken into Scott's confidence about the poet's first love, an affair with a girl we know only as "Sylvia." Hoole suggests that some of the shorter poems in Scott's *Poetical Works* (1782) may have been a product of this attachment; but this is only a speculation, for by 1763, "Sylvia" had been replaced in Scott's affection by "Delia." The "Elegy in the Manner of Hammond; Supposed to Have Been Written in the Author's Garden, During a Storm. 1756," may have resulted from the earlier affection, although the images are so conventional and the diction so stereotyped, it is difficult to say whether it proceeded from one of the poet's emotional involvements or from a desire to imitate a poetic genre. This choice of imagery could also be explained by the object of his imitation. Johnson said later of these elegies of Hammond, "He that courts his mistress with Roman imagery deserves to lose her; for she may with good reason suspect his sincerity."[34] The same charge could be made against Scott's poem.

Besides this elegy, Scott, in 1756, wrote "Winter Prospects in the Country"; he addressed this to Turner and had intended it for the *Gentleman's Magazine,* but the poem did not appear until 1770, when it was printed by George Pearch in his supplement to Dodsley's collection of poetry. Later, this same poem was considerably revised for inclusion as an epistle in the *Poetical Works.* In the same year (1756), Scott began writing critical letters to Turner and to Joseph Cockfield, his Quaker Whig friend at Upton, who was a poet and contributor later to the *Christian's Magazine,* and a friend of Hoole, Langhorne, and Mrs. Anna Williams. In the letters he discussed Denham, Pope, and Thomson with observations which were to culminate nearly thirty years later in his *Critical Essays.*

In 1757, Turner, who had been preparing under Dr. Jennings for the ministry, left London because of some disagreement in theological matters and went to Taunton in Somerset, where he completed his studies and began officiating as a dissenting min-

ister. Sometime around 1758, he went to settle at Lympstone in
Devon; and about 1762, he joined with the Reverend Mr. Hogg
and another gentleman as tutors and managers of an academy
at Exeter. Seldom with Scott after he left London, Turner nevertheless corresponded regularly with the young poet and visited
him occasionally during the summer vacations. Scott's affection
for the friend of his youth never diminished, however; "To an
Absent Friend" was a poem he addressed to his old acquaintance, and "The Shepherd's Elegy" suggests strongly that it was
written to commemorate Turner's death in 1769.

About 1758, Scott decided that he had made sufficient preparation to be a poet, and he began readying for the press four elegies
and a poetic adaptation of the eighth Psalm, which he would
publish in a small quarto. Though in the same year, he wrote
an ode, "Occasioned by Reading Dr. Akenside's Odes," this did
not appear until 1782 when it was included in the *Poetical
Works*. The only one of the four published elegies which can be
dated even approximately is the second, which was written in
July, 1757.

By the time *Four Elegies: Descriptive and Moral* issued from
the press in the spring of 1760, Scott's early life and basic training had come to an end. The virtually complete withdrawal
from London stopped, and the young poet began to make tenta-
tive gestures toward joining the more glamorous and exciting
society of his fellow artists. He and his parents still had a consuming fear of smallpox, however, and it was to be some time
before any of them could mingle in London society without fear
of physical contamination. As for John Scott, he never lost the
fear of spiritual contamination, and he always regarded London
life as basically evil, even though he maintained a London home
in Ratcliff and spent much time there. Ever the opposite of Johnson, who "thought worse of the vices of retirement than of those
of society,"[35] Scott was to be happiest in Amwell; and the study

of his later years is the study of a man who invariably champ-
pioned the life of the country over that of the city:

> I shun the scenes where madd'ning passion raves,
>   Where Pride and Folly high dominion hold,
> And unrelenting Avarice drives her slaves
>   O'er prostrate Virtue in pursuit of gold.
>
> The grassy lane, the wood-surrounded field,
>   The rude stone fence with fragrant wall-flow'rs gay,
> The clay-built cot, to me more pleasure yield
>   Than all the pomp imperial domes display.[36]

CHAPTER II

THE TIMID POET

I

IN APRIL, 1760, the *London Magazine* listed in its monthly catalogue the publication of *Four Elegies: Descriptive and Moral,* and it seems likely that this first quarto of Scott's poetry appeared late in that month. Scott's initial and, significantly enough, anonymous publication did not limp bedraggled into the arena of poetic quartos. Nor did it rely on the extensive ornamentation which, years later, was to aid the *Poetical Works,* a volume in which the poetry itself found difficult going.[1] Instead, this twenty-four page quarto, printed in the customary large type and with the usual typographical presentation, came from the best-known publishers of the time. Seven publishing firms had undertaken the work, and they included the most eminent: Buckland, the Dodsleys, and Dilly. In an age when such quartos plopped unsolicited into the hands of an unsuspecting public, this had unusually good fortune in receiving an extensive review from James Kirkpatrick in the *Monthly Review.* The second of the four elegies was singled out as having Virgilian power and giving the reader

almost a sensation of the Poet's corporeal heat while he wrote it, and naturally [it] reminds us of Virgil's wish in the like situation [*O quis me gelidis sub montibus Haemi / Sistat, et ingenti ramorum protegat umbra!*]; and to which, abstracted from the veneration which antiquity and death (those Mitigators of Envy) have superadded to the real merit of deceased Poets, we think it very little, if at all, inferior.[2]

Being compared, even in the smallest amounts, with Virgil (the one Latin poet he seems to have had even a passing acquaintance

---

[1] For notes to chap. ii, see p. 202.

with) doubtless affected Scott. And even though a comparison of one line of Virgil with the effect of his elegy should not have implied that the Quaker poet was a genius, it must have encouraged him and led him to believe that he could, if only for short amounts, summon up the highest degree of poetic inspiration. It may well have been this early review which gave Scott the firm conviction that he had poetic ability, and no later critical attack could make him question this assumption on which he operated.

Several fairly eminent people in London literary society also seem to have taken a fancy to the poems, and Catherine Talbot and Elizabeth Carter, both famous bluestockings, praised them, and Anna Seward later ranked them second only to Gray's churchyard elegy.[3] On August 11, 1760, Shenstone wrote to Thomas Percy and urged him to read the poems.[4] Meanwhile, Edward Young, author of *Night Thoughts*, received a complimentary copy of the elegies from his bookseller and replied: "Sir, I thank you for your present; I admire the poetry and piety of the author, and shall do myself the credit to recommend it to all my friends." When these words were relayed to Scott, they doubtless further encouraged him, although in later life he contemned Young and the school of poets his verses had started; Scott's later contempt of the Batheaston set suggests he held small regard for bluestockings either. Hoole himself found the elegies to be the finest of all of Scott's productions, whether one considers "the liveliness of the painting, the harmony of the verse, or the amiable strain of benevolence and piety that runs through the whole." Despite this encouragement, the young poet apparently wrote little and printed nothing more until 1769. And he did not present himself to the world as a self-acknowledged poet until 1776, sixteen years later, when *Amwell* was finally issued under his own name.

Only a theory of poetic composition which emphasized the

usual and the conventional—both in the subject and the language used—justifies Scott's earlier poetry, for he seems to have
been reluctant to deal with the personal or the immediate.
When, therefore, he published his *Four Elegies,* he was presenting himself to the world as a poet who wished to conceal himself
and his personality from the world. That he should have published the volume anonymously emphasizes also that he was not
yet willing to assume a critical responsibility for what he had
written. It also lays stress upon the rather innocuous quality of
the poems themselves. Though in these elegies he dealt with his
own life and stated that he had lived in London before having
moved to the country, he managed to disclose these facts in such
a way that one thought of the author not as an individual but as
one of a large group of persons who had also lived in London
before having moved away. The poems revealed a person who
disliked the city and lamented the state of man, finding that man
was born to die, alas! a slave to mutability. Each of the elegies
closed with the same moral reconciliation, however: from present distress might stem happiness and the fulfillment of a divine
plan. In brief, the "poet" who emerges from these poems pre-
sents himself as the idealized latter-day eighteenth-century youth,
melancholy and mannered, who moves in a world of decay but
responds to it with formalized, conventional gestures. He was
the Byronic hero without the bleeding heart; indeed, there was
no heart at all.

> Who dreams of Nature, free from Nature's strife?
>   Who dreams of constant happiness below?
> The hope-flush'd ent'rer on the stage of life;
>   The youth to knowledge unchastis'd by woe.
>
> For me, long toil'd on many a weary road,
>   Led by false Hope in search of many a joy;
> I find in Earth's bleak clime no blest abode,
>   No place, no season, sacred from annoy:

For me, while Winter rages round the plains,
  With his dark days I human life compare;
Nor those more fraught with clouds and winds and rains
  Than this with pining pain and anxious care ...

There is, who deems all climes, all seasons fair;
  There is, who knows no restless passion's strife;
Contentment, smiling at each idle care;
  Contentment, thankful for the gift of life!

She finds in Winter many a view to please;
  The morning landscape fring'd with frost-work gay,
The sun at noon seen thro' the leafless trees,
  The clear calm ether at the close of day:

She marks th' advantage storms and clouds bestow,
  When blust'ring CAURUS purifies the air;
When moist AQUARIUS pours the fleecy snow,
  That makes th' impregnate glebe a richer harvest bear:

She bids, for all, our grateful praise arise,
  To Him whose mandate spake the world to form;
Gave Spring's gay bloom, and Summer's chearful skies,
  And Autumn's corn-clad field, and Winter's sounding storm.[5]

If the resolution to the laments of man seemed overly simple and uncomplex, it could probably be explained only by the nature of the problem. The problem in the poems was conventional; the solution was equally convenient. The philosophy of the poet did not seem complex, unusual, or thought out; it could be explained in one phrase: there is a divine reason for all things. This commentary was merely a framework and structure for the work, and there is no indication that Scott himself actually believed this. (Indeed, his political convictions would suggest quite the opposite attitude.) Therefore, in his earliest poems, Scott's notions about poetry as a genre were clearly implied: one used poetry for the impersonal, for the conventional. Feeling, conviction—indeed, all of those emotions which we normally believe must rise to an intense state to result in poetic expression—these were dismissed as not only unimportant but frequently destructive to the poetic disposition. Cold, intellectual perception was the basis of poetic expression, and the creation of a poem became analogous to the solving of an algebraic equation.

Even with the regularity of the thought, however, there were some slight and rather interesting peculiarities in these poems. In the first place, for a poet who appeared to love regularity— and a belief in regularity underlay Scott's critical system and theory of composition—it is curious that though there should be one elegy for each of the four seasons, they were not all of the same length. Second, although the same stanza form was used consistently throughout, the last verse in the last two quatrains of the fourth elegy was an alexandrine, rather than the expected pentameter. (This, incidentally, was one of the earliest illustrations of Scott's fondness for an elongated final line in his poetry, a device which he used on at least thirteen other occasions.) These would be trivial objections to make against the works, were it not that they are an indication that Scott had neglected to see the total implications of his intention. Presumably the final alexandrine of the final poem could be justified as a conclusion. But it is difficult to see the purpose of the first alexandrine, and it is equally difficult to account for the varying lengths of the poems. These elegies also demonstrated the poet's unfortunate tendency to invert the natural order of words whenever he encountered trouble in making the rhyme and rhythm consistent. Scott later objected to such distortions of sense, and in revising the poems for inclusion in his *Poetical Works,* he seems to have labored to remove these more obvious faults. As a result, by the time the *Poetical Works* appeared, sixty-six of the elegies' 332 lines had been revised. Scott took the quatrain

> But why these Plaints?—Amid his Wastes of Sand,
> Far more than this the wand'ring Arab feels;

> Far more the INDIAN in COLUMBUS' Land,
>   While Phoebus o'er him rolls his fiery Wheels:

and altered it to

> But why these plaints?—reflect, nor murmur more—
>   Far worse their fate in many a foreign land,
> The Indian tribes on Darien's swampy shore
>   The Arabs wand'ring over Mecca's sand.

This, doubtless, was done to avoid a mixture of images. Scott had objected to inconsistencies of imagery in others, and here he avoided it by canceling the classical reference and retaining those drawn from his reading of travel books. He chose to retain the true rather than the mythological. Since the revision was made to bring the poem into conformity with his critical standard, which he called "classical simplicity," it shows the peculiar meaning he attached to the expression "classical simplicity." Actually, to have been *classical* in matter would have been to contradict the basic idea of the theory. This emphasis on the specific and the particular was not always fortunately employed. It led him to change the verses

> He, whom the dreaded Rage of Fever burns,
>   Or slow Disease leads ling'ring to the Tomb—

to

> He, whom fell Febris, rapid Fury! burns,
>   Or Phthisis slow leads ling'ring to the tomb—.

Even constant revision could not have saved the elegies, however, for they were cut according to an old-fashioned and rather uninteresting pattern. Scott would not have admitted it, since he was reluctant to admit on any occasion that any of his poems were faulty, but these elegies are excellent illustrations of poetry born of the judgment rather than of the imagination.

In his first publication, Scott had followed the tradition of

Pope:

> Soft were my numbers; who could take offence
> While pure description held the place of sense?

And Johnson, following Warton, said of such phenomena:

It seems natural for a young poet to initiate himself by Pastorals, which, not professing to imitate real life, require no experience, and, exhibiting only the simple operation of unmingled passions, admit no subtle reasoning or deep enquiry.[6]

If there is any one of Scott's early poems which deserves some consideration, it is his short adaptation of the eighth Psalm, which he printed with his elegies, a Psalm which had already been translated into quatrains some years earlier by Christopher Pitt. Scott's composition, in the tradition of the Augustan lyric, seems within its ordered form to show an ability at compression and structure; elements appear in mathematical precision, and the conclusion of the poem, with its reiteration of the introduction, completes the balanced equation. There is no emotion here—nor was any intended—but the conception of a mathematical universe, which was such a comfort to many of Scott's contemporaries, is expressed pleasantly in lines which themselves seem but poetic equivalents of algebraic formulas.

> Almighty Pow'r! amazing are thy Ways;
> Above our Knowledge, and above our Praise!
> How all thy Works thy Excellence display!
> How fair, how great, how wonderful are they!
> Thy Hand yon wide-extended Heav'n uprais'd,
> Yon wide-extended Heav'n with Stars emblaz'd,
> Where each bright Orb, since Time his Course begun,
> Has roll'd a mighty World, or shin'd a Sun:
> Stupendous Thought! how sinks all human Race!
> A Point an Atom in the Field of Space!
> Yet ev'n to us, O Lord, thy Care extends,
> Thy Bounty feeds us, and thy Pow'r defends;
> Yet ev'n to us, as Delegates of Thee,

> Thou giv'st Dominion over Land and Sea;
> Whate'er, or walks on Earth, or flits in Air;
> Whate'er of Life the wat'ry Regions bear;
> All these are ours, and for th' extensive Claim,
> We owe due Homage to thy sacred Name!
> Almighty Pow'r! how wond'rous are thy Ways!
> How far above our Knowledge and our Praise!

For once, the matter and the manner had begun to merge to form that amalgam which is poetry.

Though the *Monthly Review* would later complain because this poem was omitted from Scott's *Poetical Works,* the reasons for its omission seem clear. Despite the fact that this was an acceptable poem in terms of the Augustan conception of simplicity, it was not in conformity with what became Scott's own notions of "classical simplicity." Nor could the poem be revised and made "natural" without destroying its structural conception. The poem also attempted to define the powers of God in a rational fashion; Scott later felt with Johnson and Beattie that any attempt to speak of the Godhead was a futile and disastrous one, since God and His powers were, by definition, beyond the comprehension of man. Scott would have agreed with Johnson's observation on Denham: "... he consecrated his poetical powers to religion, and made a metrical version of the psalms of David. In this attempt he has failed; but in sacred poetry who has succeeded?"[7] The reasons for failure were also apparent, as Johnson noted on another occasion: "All amplification is frivolous and vain: all addition to that which is already sufficient for the purposes of religion seems not only useless, but in some degree profane."[8] Although an interesting poem, therefore, this translation could not meet with its author's approval two decades later. As it is one of the few of Scott's poems, however, which were excluded from the *Poetical Works,* it is an excellent illustration of two of Scott's earlier theories about the subject matter and the

form of poetry, two theories which the Quaker poet later rejected. And it is ironic that in one of the few areas where Scott
formulated a definite poetic theory, the theory was not understood by his friends or literary executors, since they reinstated
the poem in the second edition of his *Poetical Works,* brought
out three years after his death.

II

In 1761, when the smallpox broke out in the town of Ware,
Scott moved to the village of St. Margarets, only two miles from
Amwell; there he found another friend who would have a profound effect upon his literary career. This was John Hoole, who
was to be his most famous biographer. Hoole had married into
the Society of Friends in 1757, when he had become the husband
of Susanna Smith of Bishop's Stortford;[9] he met Scott through
James Bennet, who had been Hoole's tutor and was master of
the grammar school at Hoddesdon, where Scott and Hoole accidentally met. Evidently the friendship was a striking one, for in
their first conversation Scott showed Hoole the early draft of
Amwell, which was then called *A Prospect of Ware and the
Country Adjacent.* In the course of their future conversations,
Scott showed Hoole many of his manuscript poems, some of
which finally appeared in the *Poetical Works.* In the same year
he met Hoole, he wrote an "Ode to Hospitality," perhaps influenced by his treatment at St. Margarets. In the following year,
impressed by Milton's octosyllabics,[10] he wrote his "Ode to Leisure," and by 1764, he was writing to a friend that "a variety of
avocations, very different from literary, had so engaged his attention, that he had scarcely time to put pen to paper, but upon
occasions that could not be dispensed with."

These new occupations may have included road building and
attending to the general welfare of the Amwell community, but
the most interesting, which particularly engaged his interests at

that time, were gardening and building a grotto. Like Thomas Warton, John Langhorne, Matthew Green, and an interminable list of poets from Pope downward, Scott too yearned to contemplate his lot in a grotto. This was doubtless part of the motivation in an age gone mad with excavating and grotto building. Hoole conjectured that it was in 1765 or 1766 that Scott began his extensive work on his lands, although some of Scott's earlier poems would suggest that he had been active in embellishing the estate at Amwell as early as 1756, when he had written the "Elegy in the Manner of Hammond." In July, 1757, Scott had complained of the heat and had written in his second elegy:

> O for some secret shady cool recess,
>   Some Gothic dome o'erhung with darksome trees,
> Where thick damp walls this raging heat repress,
>   Where the long aisle invites the lazy breeze!

Perhaps this is the genesis of the grotto, though it was always popular to include this sort of poetical lamentation. Scott's much-admired Warton had written, "Complaints of immoderate heat, and wishes to be conveyed to cooling caverns, when uttered by the inhabitants of Greece, have a decorum and consistency, which they totally lose in the character of a British shepherd."[11]

The building of grottoes had been an approved leisure activity for the English country gentleman since the seventeenth century.[12] The desire for this sort of decorative and interesting ruin was doubtless influenced by the paintings of Claude and Salvator Rosa, but it was not without its religious stimulus as well. Bishop Thomas Burnet's propagation of the increasingly fashionable doctrine that the world itself was a ruin, the remains of the Flood, drew to an interest in ruins many who would not have felt an aesthetic appeal for them alone. In the eighteenth century, grottoes flourished, and when they were not conveniently placed in recesses of the earth they were, as at Richmond and Stowe, placed above ground. From 1644 on, shells were their chief decoration, and it became a common practice to make pebble, stone, and shell mosaics on the walls. The purist Sir John Chetwode attempted, on his estate, Oakley, to separate Greek and Gothic decorative devices by building two grottoes—one in each school. The 1740's were perhaps the period of most intensive interest in this architectural activity. Significantly, when the Scotts left their London quarters for the spacious lands of Amwell and undertook the labors of country gentlemen, the grotto was becoming one of the most popular of such suggested "improvements" for estates. It is quite understandable that they, too, should have tried their own as well as their hired hands at it.

The precise date on which Scott began building his grotto may never be known, since his poetic themes are frequently conventional rather than autobiographical; however, we do know that the excavations were completed by the summer of 1773, and it has been suggested that a minimum of fifteen years was occupied in building the grotto, although legend states that thirty years were required for the task.[13] In the same manner, it is alleged that £10,000 were spent on the project, though a later critic suggests that half this amount would be more accurate. Because so little is known of the building of the grotto, and no one has been able to determine the reason it was built, innumerable speculations have arisen about it. Certainly the grotto was well on its way to being constructed in the middle 1760's, for Scott wrote to his friend Turner, while the latter was at Exeter (where he had gone in 1762), and asked him to gather shells and fossils for the completion of the work. In the same manner, it is not clear whether the grotto was first conceived and begun by Scott's father or by the poet himself. But it is certain that John Scott took an active interest in the project and spent his own time and manual labor in carrying it into effect. He later told Hoole, "... in making the excavation under the hill, for the subterraneous passage, he marched first, like a pioneer, with his pick-ax in his hand, to encourage his rustic assistants." In 1766, he also wrote in a sonnet that he was having financial difficulties since the range of his desires was being confined by the limits of his purse.

> On the high hill to raise the higher tower,
> To ope wide prospects over distant plains,
> Where by broad rivers towns and villas rise;
> Taste prompts the wish, but Fortune bounds the power.

In his enthusiasm he had quite forgot Pope's own advice on this matter:

> Something there is more needful than expense,
> And something previous even to task—'tis sense.

Scott's sonnet "After Reading Shenstone's Elegies" shows that he was obviously thinking of the Leasowes and attempting to emulate Shenstone's success in his own works. Johnson did not share Scott's high opinion of this sort of endeavor. Of the Leasowes, he later wrote:

Whether to plant a walk in undulating curves, and to place a bench at every turn where there is an object to catch the view; to make water run where it will be heard, and to stagnate where it will be seen; to leave intervals where the eye will be pleased, and to thicken the plantation where there is something to be hidden, demands any great powers of mind, I will not enquire: perhaps a sullen and surly speculator may think such performances rather the sport than the business of human reason. But it must be at least confessed that to embellish the form of nature is an innocent amusement, and some praise must be allowed by the most supercilious observer to him who does best what such multitudes are contending to do well.[14]

Johnson was a great investigator of grottoes and once toured Scott's gardens and later arranged to take other visitors through the estate, but he clearly did not have much admiration for this sort of expenditure of time, artistic impulses, and money. Scott himself professed to grow weary of his gardens and the grotto,

and, like Pope's Villario, having spent his life building an artificial garden, ended by preferring an open field. The estate, originally, was probably influenced by a poetic tradition which was
best seen in John Pomfret's *The Choice,* in which an eighteenth-
century gentleman of leisure and substance attempted to make
his estate conform to the inspiration of poetry. It is significant
that the basic assumption in this architectural plan never
changed for Scott. When he renounced his gardens and his artificial estate, it was only because his theory of poetry had changed.
He had rejected Augustan notions of beauty and had come to
adopt a curious notion of "classical simplicity" which shunned
ornamentation, elaboration, and artificiality. So in the *Poetical
Works,* he wrote:

> For me, my groves not oft my steps invite,
> And far less oft they fail to offend my sight ...
> These neat-shorn hawthorns useless verdant bound,
> This long straight walk, that pool's unmeaning round,
> These short-curv'd paths that twist beneath the trees,
> Disgust the eye, and make the whole displease.
> "No scene like this," I say, "did Nature raise,
> "BROWN's fancy form, or WALPOLE's judgment praise;
> "No prototype for this did I survey
> "In WOOLLETT's landscapes, or in MASON's lay."

It is clear that Johnson was well aware of Scott's intention in his
project, even though he did not approve of grottoes as such and
attributed them to a curious psychological motivation in an
Englishman

who has more frequent need to solicit than exclude the sun. ... It may
be frequently remarked of the studious and speculative that they are
proud of trifles, and that their amusements seem frivolous and child-
ish; whether it be that men conscious of great reputation think
themselves above the reach of censure, and safe in the admission of
negligent indulgences, or that mankind expect from elevated genius
an uniformity of greatness, and watch its degradation with malicious
wonder.[15]

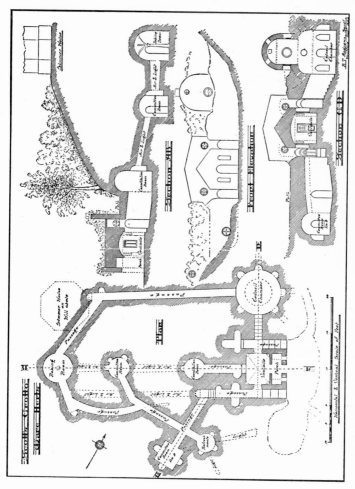

R. T. Andrews' survey of Scott's grotto; reproduced by courtesy of the East Herts
Archaeological Society, Gordon Moodey, Esq., the honorable secretary.

Scott's grotto was dug into a chalk hill in his garden, and by the time work was abandoned on it, it consisted of seven chambers of various dimensions, all connected by passages, with walls covered with pebbles, ore, and fossils, all intricately arranged in strange and curious patterns which were supposed to have been especially beautiful when lit by a chandelier. Meanwhile, on top of the chalk hill which houses the grotto, Scott constructed a summerhouse, but there is no connection between it and the grotto itself. The ornamentation of the various rooms gives no indication of Scott's purpose. In one chamber, the ceiling is covered with white flint, and designs of a triangle (over the entrance) and two hearts and a crown (over the niches in the wall) have been created by black flints. The grotto extends 67 feet into the hill, and the lowest room is 34 feet below the surface of the earth. Some idea of the extent of the grotto may be gathered from the accompanying plate, but no one has been able to determine the grotto's purpose. Some critics suggest that it was built in connection with Freemasonry, but there is no evidence to link Scott to the Masonic Order, and what is most likely is that he began by deciding to construct an English grotto in the tradition of Pope's Twickenham; and once he began, he moved in the direction his inclination led him. Since he presumably had not traveled extensively when he began his project, the grotto is not an imitation of other English garden grottoes but is unique in its design and execution. Some of the rooms, with their more elaborate patterns, reveal an initial enthusiasm for the project which gradually diminished, and there is no suggestion of a consistent motif in the project. What is most likely is that Scott build one room at a time and did not conceive of the entire work as having a unified theme. As he wrote of such activities in his *Critical Essays,* "The proprietors of these improvements, as they are called, even if they are innocently obtained, seldom derive much satisfaction from them. The pleasure

they afford chiefly results from making them; when they are
completed, few objects sooner produce satiety." And in the same
volume, he included an even more puzzling observation:
"Riches are not guilty for what they consist in, but for the mode
in which they are acquired, or the use made of them."

When Thomas Gray wrote to Norton Nicholls, "...how
charming it must be to walk out in one's own garding, & sit on a
bench in the open air with a fountain, & a leaden statue, & a
rolling stone, & an arbour!"[16] he was merely expressing a wish
which determined the activity of more than one affluent eighteenth-century gentleman. To build a garden and a grotto, however, was a labor which not only required wealth: it required
taste as well. Despite his published protests about this sort of
enterprise, Scott himself apparently always nourished a secret
fondness for this labor of his, since he threw it open to the public
and it was a fashionable visiting place for London society on
week-end excursions.[17] But Scott's artistic talents outgrew this
initial display, and he later concerned himself with improving
his world rather than working over the chalk mounds in his own
yard and garden. Even the sympathetic Hoole admitted that
the best that could be said of the gardens and grotto was that
they "are thought not unworthy the attention of strangers, who
come accidentally into the neighborhood."

III

In 1766, Scott evidently took up his poetic pursuits again and
wrote five of six published sonnets, all of which reveal much of
biographical interest: they disclose a man who was happy in his
retired life and who delighted in gentle poetry and the pleasant
scenery of his neighborhood. They also suggest that the author
was again in love—this time with "Delia," with whom he apparently fell in love in 1763. They reveal further much of interest
about Scott's theory of the sonnet. He never mentioned the son-

net form in his criticism and did not later in life consider the
genre as of especial importance, since he listed his sonnets in the
category of miscellaneous pieces; but he did have certain notions about it. Invariably he thought of a sonnet as having two
parts: an octave and a sestet. However, this was not the Italian
sonnet, because the rhyme patterns themselves were varied and
inconsistent; like most of his contemporaries he showed little
interest in regular sonnets which followed traditional practices.[18]
The subject matter was so disorganized and the style itself so un-
distinguished, it seems clear that Scott saw the sonnet's principal
characteristic to be a poem of fourteen pentameter lines. (But
even here, he was not always consistent: the sonnet "To Delia"
concludes with an alexandrine.) He never employed enjambment, and he made no use of his octave-sestet division. Apparently he wrote in the form because it had long been recognized
as suitable for expressions of the personal and the lyrical; though
he reworked his sonnets for publication in his *Poetical Works,*
he altered them merely to accord with his theories of "classical
simplicity," and there was no change in the use of the form itself. To be sure, the revision of the fifth sonnet, "To Britain,"
resulted in a changed rhyme scheme in the second quatrain; but
this was caused by inverting two lines to improve their logical
meaning. That it should not have occurred to him that there was
a metrical effect also to be considered, again shows that he attributed no special rules to the genre. In 1766 Scott also wrote "Stanzas on Reading Mrs. Macaulay's History of England," in which
he showed his enthusiasm for personal liberty—as opposed to
"kings, and courts, and courtly slaves"—and this narrative of
seventeenth-century British history. Mrs. Macaulay, whose notions of leveling were cordially detested by that "friend to subordination" Samuel Johnson, ever remained one of Scott's hero-
ines and he once entertained her at Amwell when she came to
visit him.

Of more consequence to his literary development was Scott's meeting Johnson for the first time in 1766. This was especially important, as Scott's later career was to pivot around Johnson's: Scott wrote on the same subjects that the doctor did, and he tried to emulate the doctor's success, by correcting those faults—both political and literary—which he felt the doctor had committed. Hoole states that

notwithstanding the great difference of their political principles, Scott had too much love for goodness and genius, not to be highly gratified in the opportunity of cultivating a friendship with that great exemplar of human virtues, and that great veteran of human learning; while the Doctor, with a mind superior to the distinction of party, delighted with equal complacency in the amiable qualities of Scott, of whom he always spoke with feeling regard.

We do not know precisely how this introduction came about, but Hoole arranged it, since he was a mutual friend. Boswell states, however, that Johnson was always easy of access to those who wished to meet him and came properly recommended. And since Johnson had a high regard for Hoole and even wrote a dedication for Hoole's translation of Tasso, it would not have been difficult to bring about this meeting, even though it was to be with, for Johnson, that most impossible of combinations, a Whig who was a member of the Society of Friends!

The constraining influence upon Scott's life which had been exerted by a consuming fear of smallpox had never been irrational. In the period from 1758 to 1767, within the bills of mortality alone, 23,308 persons perished from the disease, and this one illness accounted for 10 per cent of the deaths during that time. In the first decade of the eighteenth century, only 5 per cent of the deaths were attributed to smallpox: there was cause, therefore, for the increasing terror of the people and the mounting hope that inoculation could stop the disease.[19] Inoculation itself was a dangerous operation, however (Joseph Warton had lost one of his children through it), and only the greater fear of the disease drove people to this remedy. It was with such a motivation that Scott in April of 1766 put himself into the hands of a Quaker physician, Thomas Dimsdale, to be given the preventative by the man who was famous for his successful inoculations. Scott did not undergo injections unaccompanied, for his friend Joseph Cockfield had also resolved to submit to the operation with him. On April 15, 1766, Cockfield wrote:

I set out for Hertfordshire to-morrow, in order to be inoculated by Dr. Dimsdale. I hope however, if the disease proves favourable, to return in a fortnight.... The Doctor has at present amazing success with persons of all constitutions and degrees. I have observed an exact regimen for some time past, and have taken the powders he gives usually to patients preparing for inoculation.[20]

Scott later wrote to a friend that "they had not one day's confinement, though sufficient tokens to secure them from future fear or danger"; at the time of the operation, however, he was more apprehensive. Cockfield wrote to a friend, during their confinement:

I have left my friend [Scott] below, and must not much longer be absent from him. He has got on his table several new publications,— Hasselquist's Travels into the East (which, notwithstanding the solecisms and inaccuracies of the translator, is a curious useful work), Timberlake's Journal, Dr. Warburton's and Dr. Lowth's Second Correspondence, Major Rogers's Account of North America, and Denville's Maps, engraved for Rollin's Ancient History; he needs not want more entertainment, but he thought last evening that he felt a slight attack of the eruptive fever. When we expect illness we attend to every trivial tremor and every unusual symptom of disorder.[21]

The interest in travel literature and history, expressed this early in his career, resulted later in a large body of poems in the *Poetical Works* which dealt with Mexico, China, Arabia, and India. Despite his apparent difficulties, Scott was pleased with the success of the operation and he later became an outspoken advocate of inoculation.[22]

On December 14, 1766, Scott's mother died at the age of eighty. He seems to have been especially fond of her, and a sonnet to her memory is said to have been among his manuscripts, but it was never published and no copy of it exists. By March of the following year, 1767, Scott asked Cockfield for criticisms of some of his poems—the early pastorals of 1756, evidently—and Cockfield wrote to a friend that

> they are in a manner fit for publication, but he seems not to be in any great haste to publish. The second Pastoral on Benevolence, and the third on Resignation to the Divine Will, are very fine ones. I long to see them printed, and hope, if nothing intervenes, they will be put to the press next winter.[23]

Another decade was to pass before these poems finally were published; for in 1767, Scott turned his thoughts to marriage when, at the age of thirty-seven, he married Sarah Frogley, the daughter of his old friend and teacher Charles Frogley. It is a testimony to Hoole's general disregard for dates that we know nothing about this marriage, except that Sarah Frogley was not reared a Quaker. She was admitted to the Society of Friends before the wedding, and the ceremony was held at the Quakers' meeting house at Cheshunt in Hertfordshire.

Toward the middle of January in 1768, Scott spent a week in London, visiting booksellers and other friends. Cockfield wrote:

> My friend Scott is giving a revisal to a long descriptive Poem he wrote about ten years ago, which he intends to commit to the press. A large number of the edition of the Elegies yet remain unsold, a proof that a piece of intrinsic merit often lies neglected on the bookseller's shelf, whilst obscene novels, temporary political pamphlets, and useless plays, find a rapid sale; a proof, however unpleasing, of the dissipated spirit of the times.[24]

If *Amwell* was to be published, Scott was determined it should not meet with the same reception, and he called upon J. Buckland and Edward Dilly, both of whom were responsible for the publication of *Four Elegies*. Cockfield apparently did not have a high regard for Dilly's literary standards, as he referred to him as a "dealer in literature 'of inferior stature, but superior loquacity.' "[25] Scott does not seem to have shared this opinion, for Charles Dilly was an occasional visitor at the Amwell estate, and when *Amwell* finally appeared in 1776, it was published only by the Dillys. In 1768, meanwhile, Cockfield's poem "Written at the Hermitage at Aldersbrook, MDCCLXI"—which appeared later in Pearch's supplement to Dodsley's collection—was being revised. "Most of these corrections were made by the advice of my poetical friend at Amwell, whose good taste and fine genius are equalled by few, but whose extensive benevolence must entitle him to the praise of all his acquaintance."[26] This was the first time of which we have a record, when Scott's poetical powers were explained away in terms of his universal benevolence. This was to become a general attitude toward his work, however, when his artistic achievements were to be defended because of his character, humanitarianism, and general integrity.

The domestic happiness and poetic activity which began in 1768 were short-lived. Scott's father died in February at the age of eighty-four, and by the following August, both Scott's wife and infant child were dead; *Amwell* had again been laid aside, and a year of anticipated pleasure concluded as a year of consummate pain. The death of Scott's wife on the twenty-sixth of June[27] shattered the isolated peacefulness which had characterized the poet's life, and when their only child died the following August, the circle of his closest relatives had been fragmented in the space of only twenty months. Scott, living the removed sort of life he did, had been especially close to his parents, and their devotion to him and his health had dictated the course of their lives, contributing to their moving to Amwell and their breaking off their London affiliations. The relationship with his wife had not only constituted the greatest of marital felicity; it had also symbolized a union with his oldest friend and the person who, more than any other, had been responsible for the poet's intellectual development.

When his wife was dying, Scott wrote Cockfield, and his friend, who had just recovered from an illness himself, went to Amwell to find her still alive but near death. Late in July, Cockfield returned from a second visit with Scott, observing with true Quaker piety that he had

had the satisfaction to find my valued acquaintance at Amwell more resigned to the late melancholy event that has happened in his family than I suspected. Happy those who study the science of dying, and by every dispensation of this awful kind are made sensible of their extreme imbecility, and taught to contemplate with unremitted diligence the scenes of immortality.[28]

On September 10, 1768, Cockfield wrote of Scott:

The sudden demise of his amiable wife has made impressions on his mind which will not be soon erased, and he has now fresh cause of affliction; his poor infant lay (when he last wrote) at the point of death. "I never," says he in his letter, "had any extravagant fondness for this child, being well apprised of the uncertainty of its life; but I was taught to love it as my own, and the thought that it was a pledge of love left me by the dearest and best of women increased my attachment to it, more, I believe, than otherwise would have been the case; but I am like to lose it, and hope I shall be enabled to bear the loss with patience and resignation, and only say with the good old Patriarch, after many afflictions, 'If I am bereaved of all, I am bereaved.'"[29]

Early in November, Scott visited Cockfield at Upton for a couple of days;[30] it was not a long visit, but its effect upon him was ever remembered by Scott with affection; he later wrote, paying tribute to all the joys drawn from this friendship:

> 'Twas when Misfortune's stroke severe,
> And Melancholy's presence drear,
> Had made my Amwell's groves displease,
> That thine my weary steps receiv'd,

And much the change my mind reliev'd,
And much thy kindness gave me ease;
For o'er the past as thought would stray,
That thought thy voice as oft retriev'd,
To scenes which fair before us lay.

  And there, in happier hours, the walk
Has frequent pleas'd with friendly talk;
From theme to theme that wander'd still—
The long detail of where we had been,
And what we had heard, and what we had seen;
And what the Poet's tuneful skill,
And what the Painter's graphic art,
Or Antiquarian's searches keen,
Of calm amusement could impart.[31]

IV

No one knows precisely how long Scott neglected his poetry; but by the fifth of December, Cockfield believed he had still not come to terms with his grief and begun to mitigate his sorrow in that most acceptable fashion for promising poets: by writing an elegy to the memory of his wife. Johnson once encouraged such creative expression at a time of sorrow as a way of assuaging grief and preserving the memory of a beloved one,[32] and in the few weeks remaining in December of 1768, Scott wrote his *Elegy, Written at Amwell, in Hertfordshire, MDCCLXVIII,* which was printed in the following year, 1769.[33] 1768 was the *annus mirabilis* of such elegiac verses: Cuthbert Shaw wrote his *Monody to the Memory of a Young Lady Who Died in Child-bed,* John Langhorne inscribed his *Verses in Memory of a Lady Written at Sandgate Castle,* and Edmund Cartwright also lamented Mrs. Langhorne's death in his *Constantia, an Elegy to the Memory of a Lady Lately Deceased.* John Nichols, the editor of the *Gentleman's Magazine,* later suggested that these elegies be collected together with Scott's poem and Lyttelton's

To the Memory of a Lady Lately Deceased. A Monody (1747) and be published as *The Nightingale,* an uninspiring title for such a dreary collection.[34] Fortunately, such a volume was not published. Scott's elegy itself was never published for sale, and it was distributed only among close friends of the author. Scott had Hoole give a copy to Hawkesworth, whose *Almoran and Hamet* Scott particularly liked, and the author of the *Adventurer* highly praised Scott's poem. It was first available to the public when it was included in George Pearch's collection for 1775, where it was listed as the work of John Scott. Later, the elegy was considerably revised for inclusion in the *Poetical Works* of 1782.[35] The need for revision, however, had been felt much earlier, for Cockfield had written on December 26, 1769:

> I am glad, for the sake of my friend, that the Elegy has its admirers; the two last stanzas he does not deem equal to the rest, and therefore proposes to omit them in a second edition. He has been a pretty liberal contributor to Dodsley's additional volume, which will ere long appear in public. We have a work in meditation, which will be published, if we pursue our design, late in the winter or early next spring.[36]

What this contemplated joint literary endeavor was to be, we do not know. But in the December, 1769, issue of the *Monthly Review,* the elegy was reviewed as containing in it "that beautiful strain of genuine simplicity, which is nature's truest elegance." We do not know precisely when the revisions of the elegy were completed, for by January of 1771, Scott was still reworking the poem with a view toward publishing it.[37]

Of all of Scott's early poetry, the elegy seems the most autobiographical and came the closest yet to reflecting a genuine emotion in its description of his life in the idyllic countryside of Amwell.

> A few choice volumes there could oft engage,
>   A few choice friends there oft amus'd the day;
> There his lov'd Parents' slow-declining age,
>   Life's calm unvary'd ev'ning, wore away.

Foe to the futile manners of the proud,
 He chose an humble Virgin for his own;
A form with Nature's fairest gifts endow'd,
 And pure as vernal blossoms newly blown;

Her hand she gave, and with it gave a heart
 By love engag'd, with gratitude imprest,
Free without folly, prudent without art,
 With wit accomplish'd, and with virtue blest.

Swift pass'd the hours; alas, to pass no more!
 Flown like the light clouds of a summer's day!
One beauteous pledge the beauteous consort bore;
 The fatal gift forbad the giver's stay.

Ere twice the Sun perform'd his annual round,
 In one sad spot where kindred ashes lie,
O'er wife, and child, and parents, clos'd the ground;
 The final home of Man ordain'd to die!

So personal were these lines, that the casual reader, unfamiliar with Scott and his life, could not, perhaps, have understood their full meaning. But this poem was not written for the public; it was written for the poet's friends and the immediate circle of his acquaintances who, themselves, doubtless had known the gentle Sarah Frogley Scott, who had died in childbirth. After these personal remarks, however, the elegy turned into the conventional elegiac form where the grief was deplored and resolved. Actually, the grief here was so personal and immediate that Scott was incapable of resolving it. What we have, therefore, is a personal feeling which was placed in the conventional elegiac form. And though there was a final two-stanza resolution—in which it was stated that affliction is only the minister of pain, which, in turn, makes man virtuous—the poet does not seem to have been convinced by it. His attempt to cheat the reader into believing this is true only emphasizes the cheapness of the poem and Scott's reluctance to portray his undisciplined emotional state realistically.

This poem is of considerable importance in a study of Scott's development, as here the poet was meeting a basic conflict between conventional forms and attitudes, and his own convictions. Having begun his career by attempting to adapt his own thoughts and attitudes to what were the uncertain poetic norms in an age of transition, he was to end by evolving his own poetic theories, which would assume that his own feelings were sincere and valid, and the forms should be constructed so as to embody and express them. In the monody on his dead wife, he had come to the transitional point in his development.

V

Scott had addressed a sonnet to John Langhorne in 1766, expressive of the pleasures Scott had received from Langhorne's poetry, but Scott's personal friendship with the poet did not commence until 1768 or 1769. He seems to have regarded this friendship as one of his most fortunate literary associations.[38] It was Scott's fate that, with the exception of Dr. Johnson, he moved in a morass of mediocre minds. Langhorne's wife had died in the same month and year as had Scott's, and the "muse of Blagdon" had also expressed his feelings in an elegy. Scott was familiar with it when he wrote his poem, for he alluded to it and called Langhorne his friend. When Scott finally sent his poem to Langhorne, that poet remarked to an acquaintance: "Mr. Scott's poem came so near my own feelings, that it hurt my peace of mind; and while I admired the writer, and pitied the man, I saw my own miseries in the strongest point of view." The close nature of this friendship between the two poets was expressed in Langhorne's "A Monody, Inscribed to My Worthy Friend John Scott, Esq. Being Written in His Garden at Amwell, in Hertfordshire, the Beginning of the Year 1769."

> FRIEND of my genius! on whose natal hour
> Shone the same star, but shone with brighter ray;

Oft as amidst thy Amwell's shades I stray,
And mark thy true taste in each winding bower,
From my full eye why falls the tender shower,
  While other thoughts than these fair scenes convey,
  Bear on my trembling mind, and melt its powers away?

Hoole said that the two poets seldom met and rarely corresponded; yet this poem would suggest that Langhorne's affection for Scott was a real one, and Langhorne's son also stated
that the friendship continued uninterrupted until Langhorne's
death, April 1, 1779.[39] When Scott in later years revised his elegy,
he in no way minimized the respect and tribute paid to his old
acquaintance, and the "Ode XXI. Written after a Journey to
Bristol" testified to the friendship, even after Langhorne's death;
and the *Critical Essays* repeatedly mentioned Langhorne as a
poet of "superior rank," a judgment which is understandable because of Scott's friendship but indefensible critically.

In view of the three tragedies which came into his own life
in 1768, it seems incredible that Scott should, in the same year,
have found time or inclination to supervise the building of the
main thoroughfare between Ware and Hertford. It is asserted
by all his biographers, however, that he undertook this road-
building activity in 1768, so we are forced to assume that it was
begun before the death of his wife and yet sometime after the
spring rains, as Scott was most emphatic in his refusal to build
roads on wet ground. Such a road could scarcely have been created within a matter of two or three months, however, and it
was probably not completed until the following year, at the
earliest. If Scott was solely responsible for the building of this
road (and no one has suggested that someone else may also
have helped), it seems highly unlikely that he built it entirely in
1768. To have done so, he would have had to have been present
to watch the work, and for a large part of 1768 his cast of mind
was such that road building must have been impossible. His

education, which trained him to lead an indolent life, had not prepared him for seeking forgetfulness in activity. It is clear that throughout his life he was inclined to take refuge in retreat, and when he did succeed in forcing himself to do battle with the world's problems, he was often so slow in doing it that the battle was over and he alone was on the plains, charging at an enemy who already lay on the ground.

VI

The year 1769 marked the end of the second period of Scott's life—his literary apprenticeship. The people who had filled his early days and influenced his career—his parents, his wife—all were gone now, and only Frogley remained at home, being in himself the rather somber memory of past happiness which had ended in death. Turner had been in Essex for seven years, and all that was heard from him was in his letters and infrequent visits. The first poetical endeavors of the poet had met with approval, and now the years of discipline were to receive their trial. When news reached Scott that his old friend, Turner, had died in his thirty-fifth year on June 30, 1769, at Colliton in Devonshire, he realized that the end of one part of his life had come. It took him longer than almost any other poet to mature, but once he had developed self-confidence he never retreated, slow though the progress might be at times. When he turned forty on the ninth of January, 1770, Scott turned also from retirement and was ready at last to do battle with the world—for even in his retreat, there had been no security. "The Day that centers in Eternal Spring"[40] could not be created even at Amwell. The Quaker faith, which had encouraged silence and withdrawal, was therefore to be modified to include a militant belief in good works and the building of the kingdom of God on earth, as well as in the heaven of our minds and religious philosophies. He had come to share his friend Cockfield's conviction that

It is indifferent to me whether a person hears organs or refrains from hearing them, repeats a form of prayer every day or uses an extemporaneous one, kneels or sits at the communion-table, believes seven sacraments or only two, if his heart is not regenerated by the Divine Spirit and rendered a habitation of holiness! This is the only religion which is essential, and its increase and diffusion upon earth ought to be the frequent subject of our petitions to the throne of divine grace.[41]

The John Scott who was to emerge in London society as a man of action was not to be regarded by anyone as a simple country Quaker. He obviously thought of himself as a man of considerable worldly merit, and whenever he published anything under his own name, it appeared as John Scott, Esq.; yet he later said in his *Critical Essays,* "The adjective *great,* applied to any particular person, as expressive of military, political, literary, or moral eminence, for some reason or other, mostly disgusts." There was to be humility even in the Quaker who was a self-acknowledged country squire. Cockfield, who was certainly not a reactionary Quaker, requested that he be given no title of "esquire,"[42] and Samuel Scott, in strict accordance with Quaker doctrine, opposed the use of such titles, and once cautioned a friend against addressing him in such a manner.[43] Similarly, Samuel attacked "hat honour," calling it "the most unmeaning ceremony, the merest phantom that ever pride and folly obtruded on their deluded votaries";[44] but his brother John did not share this conviction, and when he had his portrait painted, he wore simple garb, but there was no evidence of a hat anywhere. But removing a hat and assuming a title were minor infractions of Quaker belief compared to the basic violation which was Scott's, as Samuel saw it. Samuel once wrote in his diary:

I was much solicited to engage in a conference, between two friends, respecting misconduct during the town election, but found no freedom to intermeddle with strife; my principal business at present being in the vineyard of my own heart.... Many of our society have suffered loss by hastily engaging in supposed services, both in the

ministry and discipline, at the instigation of others, without duly
waiting to feel their own way.[45]

This concept of "feeling one's own way" was basic to the
Quaker belief. Quakers, who emphasized seeking God within
the soul, were led to a great faith in sensation and a distrust of
logic or external reasoning. God, to them, was known by sensation and not by speculation. As a result, what would appear in
the world as good works was not to be considered as good works
by them, unless they had been motivated by an inner light. If a
work was the product of reasoning and not sensation, then it
was not capable of pacifying a guilty conscience. A work, however, could be good in itself, though the members of the Society
seldom mentioned this possibility.

One of the most radical departures Scott would make from his
faith would be in his concern with good worldly works. As a
result of his continual benevolence, he was admired by all men
and frequently referred to as a latter-day Man of Ross. Like
Charles Churchill in *Independence,* he was not afraid to oppose
the general public and defend his own ideas and beliefs; he had
courage enough to be different. But because this obsession with
good works in and of themselves often led Scott to ignore his
Quaker faith as such, and because by the very act of action he
was shown to be thinking of the world rather than the state of
his own soul, he was always regarded by his Society as a religious
deviate; the truth is that the Quakers of Scott's time did not have
their procedures of conduct clearly defined for them. Barclay's
Apology gave basic principles, but it was distressingly uninformative on how much the benevolent man should be concerned
with the world. Scott therefore probably found much comfort
in Cockfield's belief, although it was a belief which it might be
difficult to defend theologically: "It is in the sphere of active life
that the true Christian must move. . . . the sweet and social pre-
cepts of Christianity . . . command us not to bury ourselves alive

in deserts and forests, but to be useful to our fellow creatures in our generation, feeding the indigent, aiding the sick, and keeping ourselves in the world unspotted."[46] Johnson would have praised Scott's attitude, since he once stated, "It is our first duty to serve society, and, after we have done that, we may attend wholly to the salvation of our own souls."[47] John Scott's turning his deathbed thoughts to theology was a great comfort to Samuel, as he saw this as a repudiation of his brother's concerns and, in some fashion, a justification of his own rather narrow and introspective life. It is clear that Samuel was never capable of deciding whether his brother set an admirable pattern of conduct, or whether he was a worldly man who had fallen away from religion. But when Samuel came to publish the deathbed scene of his brother, his action strongly suggested that he was not totally concerned with his brother's pattern of conduct but partly with a justification of his own. It is important to remember, however, that Samuel's was not the only belief held by a devout Quaker. In March, 1769, when Cockfield visited Amwell and wrote four poems on the Amwell estate, he concluded his cycle with the poem:

> Think not religion to the cell confin'd,
> And banish'd from the dwellings of mankind;
> She loves not always the monastic gloom,
> The silent cloister, and the mouldering tomb,
> Where vestals plaintive o'er their kindred dead
> Oft at lone eve their heart-felt sorrows shed:
> No! where society refines the soul,
> There best is felt pure piety's control.[48]

CHAPTER III

THE QUAKER LIBERAL

I

URING THE 1760's, while Scott was still spending most of his time in Amwell but was venturing occasionally into London, the domestic political concerns of the British government centered largely on the deeds of John Wilkes, who, in the forty-fifth issue of his *North Briton,* had given what the government thought was cause sufficient for his arrest. The expulsion and exile of Wilkes were matters of more than passing importance to the common British citizen, and Wilkes became a popular hero.[1] When, with a background of such injuries from the Crown, Wilkes was elected to parliament and then refused a seat, there arose a considerable fear throughout the nation over the constitutional rights of the individual—rights which it was thought were rapidly evaporating.

It was in the midst of this concern that, on January 16, 1770, Samuel Johnson published *The False Alarm,* the first of his four political tracts, and with Olympian disdain, showed what he thought about the nonsensical rumpus being raised by the miscreants. Dealing with the Wilkes affair and the contested Middlesex election, the essay interested everyone, and so much was it read and in demand that it went through a second edition on the sixteenth of February and a third edition on the twelfth of March of the same year.[2] Although the work appeared anonymously, everyone seemed certain from the first that only Johnson could have written such a defense of the government, and all three rebuttals to his pamphlet attacked him as a hireling. That one of the replies should be a vituperative letter from Wilkes sur-

---

[1] For notes to chap. iii, see p. 205.

prised no one. But two other supporters of Wilkes appeared—
one in the writer of *The Crisis;* and one in the retiring Quaker
of Amwell, John Scott himself, who brought out his *The Constitution Defended, and Pensioner Exposed; in Remarks on The
False Alarm.* Beattie wrote on May 4, "Nothing, I think, is stir-
ring in the literary world. All ranks are run mad with politics."[3]
Scott's pamphlet probably appeared during the madness between
April 28 and May 1, as it was given a full first-page review in
that issue of the *London Chronicle* and was also mentioned in
the May numbers of the *Critical Review,* the *Monthly Review,*
and the *London Magazine.*

The appearance of this pamphlet marked the entrance of Scott
into an area which was customarily avoided by Quakers. The
exemplary Quaker attitude was later to be explicitly delineated
by Samuel Scott in his own reflections on September 1, 1780:

The parliament being dissolved, a general election is coming on;
the devil cometh forth, and hell from beneath; the heart of man will
be moved for him, to meet him at his coming. The present period is
important and interesting beyond many others; but if it pleaseth
infinite Wisdom to punish a people for their iniquities, it mattereth
not whether it is done by one man or by many: but it becometh not
the members of our society to meddle much in those matters, or to be
active in political disquisitions. Our duty and felicity consists in peace-
ably acquiescing in the all-wise determinations of Him, who ruleth in
the kingdoms of men. In respect to elections, we ought to go no
farther than voting for the candidates we best approve, and declaring
our preference of them, without endeavouring by any other means to
influence others. "Israel is to dwell alone, and not to be mixed with the
people."[4]

Therefore, when he entered the ranks of the political pamphlet-
eers, Scott violated one of the basic teachings of a faith which—
paradoxically—he always devoutly espoused. That he should
have attacked Johnson, his friend of some four years, and have
also violated the doctrines of his religious belief, can be explained

only by a devotion greater than either of these—a devotion which Scott paid to truth and the principles of right as he saw them. The Quakers, in their concern with the inner light, sometimes acted as though it could not be the same light which shone among men. Scott, however, seems to have felt that the basic light of truth must be made manifest to all men, and it was not enough if it lighted only the soul of the individual. For these reasons, he took up a course of action which was deplored by many of his acquaintances and his religious friends who mistook impassioned devotion to truth for personal vituperation; being more conservative men, they did not see that when Scott replaced a life of contemplation with one of action, he was following his inner light in the best way he knew how, and making the truth that he saw within demonstrable to all men. The paradox of this man was, perhaps, not to be unique within the Society of Friends. Only the most simple and the most conservative of the Society would find that the inner light could exist apart from the external world. Even Samuel Scott condemned Johnson's "strong attachment to an exterior establishment, and an hireling and sin-soothing ministry,"[5] and said, regarding elections, that "in those cases, it is almost impossible to avoid being, in some degree, interested; although the preference may seem slight, and without any culpable interference."[6]

John Scott's resolution of the problem did not give him the self-assurance he needed in the face of death, but it will be significant to notice that his mental anguish on his deathbed rose from this fundamental conflict which bothered all liberal Quakers, and especially those who were altruistic; it was not a product of any personal moral decay. Although charity was advocated by the Society of Friends, such charity acknowledged the existence of an external world which the Society wished to ignore. The religious dilemma of John Scott, therefore, was to be a product of his religious faith itself—a faith which embodied within itself a paradox which seemed incapable of solution. And yet there was to be a final and personal irony here. For what drew Scott from a life of isolated contemplation was the gigantic issue of the Wilkes affair, which apparently was to him a clearly cut and sharply delineated contrast between black and white, virtue and vice; to succeeding generations it has seemed to be only a study in ordinary political chicanery and various shades of gray.

The Constitution Defended, and Pensioner Exposed; in Remarks on The False Alarm was like both of the other replies to Johnson's pamphlet, in that it was a careful appraisal and criticism of Johnson's remarks; it differed from the other replies in its tone, and there was no suggestion made that Scott expected any reward or favors for this pamphlet or merely desired to join the Whigs in their unending fight against the Tories. Though he did not hesitate to assail Johnson for his faults, there was less an air of vituperation about Scott's pamphlet. "The note of Wilkes was savage abuse; that of Scott was respectful regret."[7]

TO substitute sophistry for truth is often unhappily the task of genius and learning, this must be obvious to every intelligent reader....

The advancement of political knowledge, this author observes, has by no means kept pace with that of natural; but in this he may possibly be mistaken.

The doctrines of divine hereditary right, and passive obedience to the will of kings, were doctrines readily adopted by those who believed the comet and the eclipse, prognosticks of publick calamity: but to the honour of this nation, the gloom both of philosophical and political prejudice, has been long since dissipated.

In these, his opening remarks, Scott revealed his basic philosophical difference with Johnson. Johnson had almost implicit faith in an enlightened monarchy, whereas Scott believed in a limited monarchy which approached a democracy. Well indeed

might Johnson, in view of his attitude, print six years later on
the title of his *Political Tracts:*

> *Fallitur egregio quisquis sub Principe credit*
> *Servitium; numquam libertas gratior extat*
> *Quam sub Rege pio.*[8]

Scott never shared this adulation of the monarch—even when
the monarch was one favorable to Whig principles. In criticizing Denham's *Cooper's Hill,* he said it was a ridiculous notion
to assume a stag would die contented if it were shot by a king;
the one thing for which he gave Denham credit was his "manly
boldness in praise of civil liberty" when he described the signing
of the Magna Charta at Runnymede.[9] Johnson's entire argument
proceeded from his assumption of the virtues of enlightened
monarchy, and because of his belief in the pious king, he felt it
wrong to question the authority of the king's ministers when
acting at the command of their sovereign; particularly was this
true when one examined the character of the "abused," John
Wilkes.

Scott's reply to Johnson's pamphlet stressed the constitutional
privileges which were the right of every freeborn Englishman,
and it attacked Johnson for having treated lightly those preroga-
tives which had descended to the common people only through
years of perseverance in the cause of liberty and freedom. Scott's
approach would suggest that he would be a defender of Wilkes
against the injustices done that man by the government, but
actually he was not a prejudiced adherent to Wilkes's cause. He
was more interested in the constitutional issues involved, and
while he was perhaps mistakenly inclined—as were most Englishmen at the time—to regard Wilkes as a popular champion
of those principles, he did not become so blind to personal defects that he also championed Wilkes's vices.[10] That Scott should
have distinguished between Wilkes as a man and Wilkes as a
symbol of principle, set this tract apart from the others in the

controversy. Though Johnson himself pretended to be dealing solely with the constitutional issues involved, he was never reluctant to use the known imperfections of Wilkes as a man, to suggest that something was equally deficient with Wilkes as a symbol of a constitutional principle. But Scott recognized Johnson's rhetorical trick and condemned it.

> But, by your leave, good Dr. J——n, the subject of our dispute is not a criminal in a gaol, but a much more glorious object, an object more glorious than all the crowns of all the Kings in Europe or Asia. An object for which the best blood of Greece, of Rome, and of Albion has been effused. An object as important to the Clown and the Pedlar, as to the Gentleman and the Philosopher: and that object is LIBERTY.[11]

It was in making this distinction that Scott developed an idea which would be consistent in his political writings:

> To exculpate the entire character of this man, were a task as impracticable as unnecessary. Vice and virtue may surely exist together in one subject. An immoral man may love and serve his country, and assist in the construction of laws, of which he may prove no very strict observer.[12]

This seems closely related to the well-known Miltonic concept, here given a somewhat different practical application: "Good and evil we know in the field of this world grow up together almost inseparably." As Scott himself said later in his pamphlet, "If a nation be saved or ruined, it is quite immaterial whether it be saved or ruined, by a profligate Lord or an illiterate Mechanick." This idea would be expanded in his second political pamphlet.

To Johnson, the House of Commons was a select body which ruled English affairs, and it did not represent the constituents of the members of the House; rather, it represented right principles as the members saw them. Therefore, the House of Commons owed its devotion not to its electors but to the higher principles of truth and justice which, presumably, were mirrored in

the character of a benevolent and pious monarch. This basically
aristocratic theory of government under monarchy was opposed
by Scott, who believed in the principle of representative government under which the legislature was merely the spokesman for
the constituents electing it. Scott said that the legislature had
only those powers which the people gave it and could draft only
that legislation which the people themselves desired and approved. Any bills which did not arise at the request of the people
but from a notion on the part of the legislature that such a statute
was good for, or was needed by, the people, was invalid and not
binding upon the electors. Scott did not say what was to be done
when there was an inevitable conflict between the opinions of the
electors, but he presumably (with his support of the majority
vote as being the only one proper for consideration by the legislature) felt the utilitarian principle of the greatest good for the
largest number was to be followed. He would never, however,
have given unlimited power even to a parliamentary majority,
for such an action would eventually have destroyed the liberty
of the subject.

    Johnson's famous attack on petitions horrified Scott, who felt
the petition was the fundamental check on the powers of the
legislature. Realizing that Johnson attacked the character of the
petition only by ridiculing the characters of the petitioners, Scott
pointed out that these signers of petitions

are not all pedlars and the meanest and grossest of the people: They
[the petitions] are signed by the middle gentry, yeomanry and substantial traders, who are sensible, if not learned, who can feel when
they are oppressed; and can think more consistent, though perhaps
they cannot write like Dr. J——n.

What was particularly offensive to Scott was Johnson's choice of
words, which seemed to imply that mankind consisted only of
two classes: the nobles and the slaves. Hearing the doors of the
Bastille about to clank shut on English liberties, Scott took alarm

and he excoriated Johnson.[13] He saw that Johnson was propagating through his scorn and vituperative language, through his innuendo and implication, a doctrine of class supremacy and aristocratic monarchy which violated all of the principles embodied in the British constitution. Though "surrounded with a complicated system of law, designed for its preservation, English liberty seems silently hastening to its period,"[14] and it was essential that enlightened people should turn against unreasoning acceptance of governmental encroachments upon their liberty. For these reasons, Scott used every means available to reveal Johnson's motivations and to bring before the public the total implications of the doctrines of *The False Alarm*.

> Your polite epithets of profligate and dissolute, your plebeian grossness and savage indecency, but very indifferently supply the place of argument, and might perhaps be retorted with much more propriety, than they are bestowed. Your charge of malignity in the mean, against the great, discovers only your own malignity against the mean. You once discovered as much malignity against the great, but you were then one of the mean. You must now be allowed to think differently.[15]

Unlike Johnson, who believed in a class society, Scott believed that the only difference between men was one of education. His democratic principles were nowhere revealed with more telling force than in his observation:

> Ignorance is a misfortune, not a crime, and cannot intitle to slavery. The man who cannot write or read, has the same right to Liberty as he that can. The doctrine, of submission the duty of the ignorant, and content the virtue of the poor, might have become the mouth of an emissary of the church of Rome, whose power is well known to be founded on the ignorance and implicit submission of the vulgar.

Scott's pamphlet appeared anonymously, and it was largely fragmentary in its structure; it seems to have been a product of much haste, and Scott evidently was not anxious to claim it as his own. Occasionally it referred by page number to *The False*

Alarm without quoting Johnson's particular argument that was
being refuted at the moment. The main body of the pamphlet
carried Scott's arguments and theories; but in a set of footnotes
to the argument, he made more personal references to Johnson's
own character and the contradictions which were implicit in the
tract and in the relation of that tract to the corpus of Johnson's
writings.[16] Scott did this to emphasize that the arguments of
The False Alarm were not the product of sincerity or of a serious
consideration of English constitutional principles. He wished to
stress that Johnson was writing as a pensioner and was here pen-
ning an apologia for the government. This was not done solely
to attack Johnson's character. Indeed, one could almost say this
was done in defense of Johnson's well-known character of virtue
and probity. By proving that any principles of aristocratic monarchy—such as those given here—were logically indefensible and
that Johnson himself, in the corpus of his writing, had proved
conclusively that democratic processes were best, Scott relied on
the well-known Johnsonian doctrine to disprove this new Johnsonian heresy. Scott drew his material from Johnson's *Dictionary* and poetry, and from the *Rambler*. In all of these works he
found abundant defense for his own beliefs, and he was able to
defeat Johnson's arguments largely by quoting the old Johnson
against the new. These footnotes, signed by Martinus Scriblerus
and written in a quasi-Elizabethan and pseudo-biblical language,
sometimes seem humorous in their exposure of Johnson's contradictions, but they always served a more serious purpose in
making the reader aware of Johnson's inconsistencies and the
philosophical weaknesses of his political argument.

If one were to examine Scott's first prose tract as a work of
art, he would find it lacking any structural unity; though it is
interesting for its rebuttal of Johnson's arguments, the tract cannot stand independent of the pamphlet which was its motivation. There are many themes casually introduced here—the no-

tion of avarice being the dominant English vice because it caters
to luxury, the theory that the deeds and institutions of our ancestors cannot be defended solely for their antiquity, and the belief that dissenters and sectarians are not politically abnormal
people but share eagerly the responsibilities of citizenship—
which, expanded and developed, occur in Scott's later writing.
The philosophical notions, which emerge here in a singularly
uncomplicated form, were also to be enlarged afterward and
the implications of them were to be discussed in greater detail.
Though *The False Alarm* was, with its gusto and pontifical observations, to be Johnson's finest political tract, Scott's reply to it
was the weakest of his prose writings. When, five years later, he
came to do battle with Johnson over *The Patriot,* he was to have
more to say about man's position in the world and the system of
government which best fitted his philosophy and his needs.
Johnson, in commenting on Lyttelton's *Persian Letters,* had said
they "have something of that indistinct and headstrong ardour
for liberty which a man of genius always catches when he enters
the world, and always suffers to cool as he passes forward."[17]
Johnson's observation may be applicable to Lyttelton, it would
not serve for Scott as an observation on universal human conduct. There is nothing to indicate that Scott's fervor diminished;
it was consistent, while his eloquence increased in its effectiveness. Nowhere was this distinction between Scott's two pamphlets better emphasized than in the *London Magazine*'s reviews
of them. Of the first, they wrote: "The frog in the fable, whose
ambition to rival the ox, proved fatal to him in the end, would
be no bad lesson for the present author to read; he may swell, as
much as he can, but it is much more probable he will burst, than
appear any thing like an equal competitor for the Rambler." But
the second pamphlet was accorded quite a different reception:
"These remarks are very sensible, judicious, and spirited, and
the pensioned author of the Patriot is laid very low."

II

On November 1, 1770, two and one-half years after the death of
his first wife, Scott married for a second time; the woman was
Maria De Horne, daughter of Abraham De Horne. The ceremony was performed at the meeting house in Ratcliff in London, where Scott had a town house and where he was accustomed to spending a large part of the winter each year.[18] In 1770,
Scott also bought the manor of Halfhide, or Westmill, in Ware,[19]
but it is not clear that he ever lived in it, because in November,
1770, he took a house at Amwell—this being, it seems certain,
his father's house, in the park of which the grotto and gardens
had been built.[20] Nothing is known of Scott's activities during
the next two years, although he seems during that time to have
made frequent visits to London where he met Mrs. Montagu
and—at her home—Lord Lyttelton. He also became acquainted
with John Hawkesworth, Sir William Jones, James Boswell, and
William Mickle; he also became a correspondent of Dr. John
Lettsom[21] and a close friend of the Reverend Mr. Robert Potter
and of John Payne, the publisher, who was an old friend of Johnson and the "Esteemed friend" of Samuel Scott.

One of the most fruitful of the friendships of his later years
was begun June 3, 1773, when Scott was introduced to James
Beattie, who had come to London and, on that June day, had
gone to dine with the publisher Charles Dilly and Dilly's sister.

There were present also two Quakers Mr. Beesley (who bids me dine
wt. him tomorrow) and Mr. Scot a man of a considerable fortune at
Ware, and an ingenious poet, who has long wished to see me, and
who is anxious that Mrs. Beattie and I should visit him at his Country
house and stay some time with him. He is a chearful, affable, well-
bred man, of very good taste, and competent learning.[22]

Hoole says this friendship was begun about 1771, but Beattie's
entry in his diary strongly suggests this was his first meeting with

Scott. The next day, Beattie went to dine with Beezley, Scott, and five other Quakers at Beezley's house at Bridewell dock.

The conversation decent, chearful, and literary. *Thee & Thou* much used, though not constantly. No drinking of healths; nor the word *Sir* once mentioned by the brethren. We sate till four o'clock, when I came home.[23]

In the same summer of 1773, Hoole paid a "family visit" to Amwell, accompanied by Johnson and Mrs. Anna Williams. Mrs. Williams was in her late sixties at the time and was totally blind, so it is questionable whether she appreciated the gardening project and the grotto which by then had been completed. As for Dr. Johnson,

He was now in his sixty-fourth year, and was become a little dull of hearing. His sight had always been somewhat weak; yet, so much does mind govern, and even supply the deficiency of organs, that his perceptions were uncommonly quick and accurate.[24]

Despite the fact that he was blind in his left eye, Dr. Johnson had enough visual powers left to give him the basis for a critical judgment: he smiled when he saw the grotto, termed it Fairy Hall, and said that "none but a poet could have made such a garden." Johnson's comment was judicious, in that it has a pleasing ambiguity which leaves some doubt whether he approved of what he saw. He once said, "Having a garden, which we all know to be perfectly innocent, is a great pleasure."[25] But he disliked Pope's grotto, and when shown a grotto in Lincolnshire which a lady was making, he replied to her question, "Would it not be a pretty cool habitation in summer?" by snorting, "I think it would, Madam..., for a toad."[26] Despite these criticisms, when he went to Scotland in the autumn of 1773, he visited two more grottoes, so they must have held a certain fascination for him—the fascination he always found in people whose doings were only on the periphery of rational action.

The London visitors stayed for some days at Amwell, and both

Scott and Johnson apparently grew to have a genuine affection
for each other. On May 27 of the following year, 1774, Johnson
wrote to Scott:

Sir

I have excited in Mr Thrale and his Lady the curiosity to see your
Garden and Grotto. They purpose to visit your Dryads and Fairies on
Tuesday the thirty first of May, if it will not be inconvenient to You,
to receive them at that time. It was my purpose to have given you
more early notice, but it went out of my thoughts.

I am Sir Your most humble Servant

Sam: Johnson

May 27 1774
Please to favour me with an answer.

Six days later, Johnson was writing to Scott again, this time making arrangements to accompany some visitors to the grotto:

Dear Sir

On Tuesday the seventh of June, I hope to have the pleasure of
introducing some very judicious spectators to your Garden and subterraneous retirements. They will not be prevailed on to do more than
dine. If you can be at home be so kind as to let me know, that we may
have no uncertainty on either part.

I am, Sir, Your most humble servant

Sam: Johnson

Johnson's court Fleet street No. 7.
June 2. 1774[27]

As the reply to this letter is lost, we do not know whether Johnson paid a second visit to Amwell. However, the friendship between the two men, which had been strengthened by the 1773
visit, was a constant one through the rest of their lives, even
though they generally found themselves in disagreement on
political and critical questions. When Dr. Johnson later told
Boswell that he "liked individuals among the Quakers, but not
the sect,"[28] his toleration of individual "heretics" may have been
influenced by his friendship with Scott.

But he had taken a very comprehensive view of human life and manners, and, that he was well acquainted with the views and pursuits of all classes and characters of men, his writings abundantly shew. This kind of knowledge he was ever desirous of increasing, even as he advanced in years: to gratify it, he was accessible to all comers, and yielded to the invitations of such of his friends as had residences in the country, to vary his course of living, and pass the pleasanter months of the year in the shades of obscurity.[29]

III

In 1773, Scott spent a considerable amount of time on his non-literary endeavors in the field of economics and humanitarianism. The March issue of the *London Magazine* found the remarks "pertinent, just, and liberal" in his lengthy pamphlet *Observations on the Present State of the Parochial and Vagrant Poor,* which the following month was being reviewed with considerable approbation in the *Monthly Review;* the *Critical Review* echoed these praises in their August issue, though it disagreed with some of Scott's suggestions and said that he should have proposed a remedy of his own rather than merely have criticized the plans of others;[30] the same criticisms were voiced in the September issue of the *Town and Country Magazine.* By December, Scott's interest in highways had produced *A Digest of the Present Act for Amendment of the Highways,* and it was acclaimed that month in the *Monthly Review;* in January of 1774, the *Critical Review* gave brief but warm praise to the book.

When Scott came to write on the subject of poor relief, he had followed his humanitarian impulses and had come at last to a field which had always been tempting to class-conscious Englishmen.[31] That he too should speculate upon the position of the poor in society and their plight in the world does not in itself, however, mean that he had something original to say. Rather, the tracts on poor relief which appeared in the century before 1773 seem most interesting for their lack of anything *new* and for their restatement and regathering of older principles and ideas. With few exceptions, all the writers found that the same basic grievances existed, and there was divided opinion—but not multiplied thought—on the way these difficulties could be eliminated. The general interest in poor relief for the eighteenth-century reformers was due to varied reasons: the condition of the poor was deplorable and should be changed; there had been no system which, when tried, proved completely satisfactory; and there seemed to be no perceptible solution which all could accept. By being so defined, the subject of poor relief entered the scope of philosophical speculation, and it is in this aspect that Scott treated it.

In the facts which he stated and the practical solution which he had to offer, there was little that was original in Scott's pamphlet. In the attitude he took toward the poor as a people,[32] he may seem remarkable and a forerunner of late eighteenth- and early nineteenth-century thought which was distinguished for its humanitarianism, but even here he was not being unique. What he had done was to be one of the first of the eighteenth-century commentators on this subject to turn to seventeenth-century religious speculation for a stimulus. And his argument for the treatment of the poor was mainly an amplification of the position held a century earlier by Matthew Hale in *A Discourse Touching Provision for the Poor.*[33]

Observations on the Present State of the Parochial and Vagrant Poor appeared anonymously, and although Scott later acknowledged his authorship,[34] Eden in 1797 listed it as by an unknown author and does not seem to have considered it of great importance, perhaps because many of his own thoughts usually represented a humanitarian stream divergent from that seen in Scott.[35] Scott's original desire to remain unknown as the author was perhaps motivated by his membership in the Society of Friends: he did not want this work regarded as merely another Quaker tract. He was probably justified in his deception: the literary difficulties of being known as a Quaker were clearly demonstrated in 1782 when his *Poetical Works* was attacked on religious grounds. In 1782, however, one critic wrote of the poor-law tract:

> We much wish to see these Observations on the Poor enlarged, and published in one volume, as we are informed our author has sufficient materials in his hands to effect such a design. Pamphlets too often answer no other purpose than filling the garret of the Bookseller.[36]

This assertion may have been true (since Scott did not deny it when he commented on the article), yet nothing else was said about the project of enlarging this volume. However, since the subject was one in which he expressed extraordinary interest, he may well have intended expanding his original work, much in the fashion that he did when he republished his highway book in 1778 in a revised and enlarged form. In his last publication, the *Critical Essays,* he referred to his friend Potter's *Observations on the Poor Laws, on the Present State of the Poor, and on Houses of Industry* (1775) and revealed that none of his earlier interest in the subject had diminished.

Scott's 1773 pamphlet was 135 pages long and was one of his longest nonliterary productions. Unlike the political tracts which were hastened by the needs of the hour, this work was under no compulsion to appear at a certain moment. The gift of greater time, however, seems only to have extended the tract and not to have improved its organization, for the structure was digressive and tangential. This aspect bothered even Dr. Johnson, "who highly commended the good sense and benevolence of its principles; but rather objected to the stile, as being in a few instances somewhat inflated." Instead of being a closely reasoned argument, the pamphlet represented a gathering of observations, each of which was carefully explored and discussed, but between which there was not always a perceptible relationship. In its

structure and general prose style, therefore, it was similar to the
political tracts. And although the work concluded with a classical peroration in which Scott shifted to pseudo-Elizabethan diction to become an orator,[37] he did not feel compelled to be discussing the poor explicitly at the end of the tract, for there he
was condemning the luxury of the rich and their deplorable inclination to idle away hours reading bad novels. The pamphlet
also contained two appendixes, the first being a peroration on
the necessity of doing something about the poor—something
other than repealing all present laws—and the second was an
amplification of his argument about capital punishment.

Scott began his analysis of the difficulties of the existing parochial system of poor relief with a basic observation which had
been made by practically every commentator on the problem:

> For the management of a national concern like this of the poor, it is
> plain, that the whole system must be divided into a number of dis-
> tinct though similar divisions. The parochial division has been tried:
> but the inequality of expence in different parishes, arising from the
> disproportion of extent to population, sufficiently demonstrates its im-
> propriety for the purposes of taxation and maintenance.

Although he was willing to admit that a division larger than the
parish might not be suitable for administrative purposes and that
he wished, therefore, to have appointed a local servant somewhat
similar to an overseer in every parish and to have him serve
under a board of trustees, he still insisted that an economic clus-
ter larger than a parish was to be used for the financial adminis-
tration. Taxation for poor relief became then a general, standard
tax which was not arbitrary and local.[38] Such parochial clusters
should be administered, Scott recommended, by a trust composed of gentlemen, clergymen, and respectable tradesmen who,
when given by the government a sum of money large enough to
provide for the poor, would not succumb to "unrequired parsi-
mony, but prudent appropriation of the wealth committed to . . .
[their] management."

By the adoption of this plan of uniform taxation, all occasion for settlement, and all necessity of removal, must naturally cease. Settlement, that injury to parishes, that source of perpetual dispute and litigation, and removal, that injury to the poor, that wanton or malicious chase of the unhappy from one inhospitable region to another, will therefore, to the honour of our nation, be totally annihilated.

It is true that a critic like Jonas Hanway might find the workhouse unsatisfactory for his particular interests,[39] but by the end of the eighteenth century the workhouse theory had found general acceptance; though there would be a criticism often of the way in which a certain workhouse would be managed, the basic assumption that a workhouse was a good thing in itself was seldom challenged. Sir Matthew Hale had himself discussed workhouses as "The Remedy propounded," and in the mid-eighteenth century Henry Fielding lent his full support to the building of such institutions.[40] John Scott's attack on workhouses, therefore, as "mansions of putridity" at first glance appears unusual and seems reminiscent of Thomas Firmin or Daniel Defoe decades earlier. Because of his lengthy excoriation, one might suspect Scott of being opposed to the system; actually, he was opposed only to the abuses and defects of it. When he came to propose a remedy, he was inclined to follow Thomas Alcock's theory of hundred houses and to recommend the building of them and the placing of them under humanitarian management.[41] The basic difficulty, according to Scott's view, of the statute 9 George I was that it placed too much authority in the hands of one man, the overseer of the poor. Since the ostensible purpose of the law was to relieve the expense to the parish of caring for the poor, the position of overseer fell to a man who was noted usually for his ability to make the workhouse self-supporting. At once, therefore, the emphasis was shifted from a desire to do something for the poor, to a desire to extract enough labor from them to make them sufficient unto themselves.[42] Scott felt that human nature was not constitutionally inclined to be charitable under situations implicit with temptation: the only possible result of this system would be a disastrous treatment of the poor. If an overseer had the interest of the oppressed at heart, he would doubtless find the workhouse not paying for itself; as a result, the indulgent man would be replaced by one with a more stringent code. If the overseer, however, was determined—as he usually was— that he should not only make the workhouse self-supporting but that it should also provide him with a salary, then he had to drive the poor and exploit them. In such circumstances, the overseer, being totally practical, would not be interested in having on his hands the sick and impotent poor, and the mortality rate would rise alarmingly.

A further difficulty of the existing workhouse arrangement was that families were often separated, only the indigent members being carried away to the workhouse while the rest were left to their own resources. Should a man refuse to go to the workhouse, he was immediately denied any further aid from the parish, and he was thereby forced into being transported or starved. The system was made indefensible not only by its economic difficulty but also by its inattention to the emotional reactions of the poor, treating them not as human beings, percipient and sensitive, but as animals, dull and unfeeling.

There is often a secret wish, not easily accounted for, to resign the breath of life on the same spot where it was received; there is often as unaccountable an affection for some particular convenience of habitation. Such things, indeed, are of little importance in reality, but they are of much in idea; and in idea, exist many of our sublimest pains and pleasures.

One of the most unusual aspects of Scott's pamphlet was its concern for the foreigner in England who fell a victim to poverty and English poor relief. Highly influenced by Matthew Hale's utilitarian defense of the transplanted foreigner as a teacher of the woolen trade and a reviver of English commerce, Scott did not indulge in acrimonious statements about the foreigner abroad who, by working for cheaper wages than his English rival, was presumably the cause of increased English unemployment. By this abstinence, Scott's pamphlet was a deflection from the major trend of the time,[43] but it was consistent with his theory that the foreigner was basically a good man and a worthy type, especially when transplanted to English soil. It was not only the French immigrant or the Dutch weaver who faced the severities of English poor relief and the arbitrary and unindulgent law of settlement, however. Even the Irish and the Scots, when found in England without suitable provisions and without a proper settlement, were given no relief and were shifted from parish to parish until they arrived back in their native country, whose problem, presumably, they were.

Scott's theories about the status of the poor in society reflected almost all of the prevailing notions about the chain of being and class structure of eighteenth-century society. His initial observation about the state of the poor was that

vast as is the disparity in the external circumstances of beings placed by nature on an equality,...[the writer] is not by any means designed to inculcate the principles of the leveller, who would violate the subordination of society, by degrading the rich, and elevating the poor above their proper station; but merely to intimate, that the point of decency is a point beneath which none of the latter should ever be permitted to experience depression.

Scott's attitude was not consistently as stringent as his statement would appear, since it represented merely one aspect of his belief. In reality, he felt genuine compassion for the troubles of the poor, and the point of decency to which he wished the poor raised was really a high standard of living. More in keeping with his other theories, therefore, was his fundamental idea about the factor which distinguished the rich from the poor. God, believed

Scott, had placed everyone on an equal level in His sight, and all
the distinctions and gradations of men in this world represented
merely temporal and mundane evaluations. Mankind, he asserted, has placed great emphasis on the distinction between
honor and dishonor, but this is a differentiation which is meaningless to God

who beholds the high and the low with an eye of paternal regard,
which surveys at one comprehensive glance the whole of creation;
and who has vouchsafed to his rational creatures the revelation of one
grand criterion of morality, one standard of rectitude by which the
actions of every man should be measured, "Whatsoever ye would that
men should do to you, do ye even so to them; for this is the law and
the prophets."

The great difficulty with society was that it did not recognize
education as the only difference between men and it tended to
obscure the issue with notions about one financial standard having a higher intrinsic moral value than another. The result was
that everyone was bent on economic self-improvement.

The landlords, with consummate wisdom, are involving their estates,
by pursuing the fashionable town vices; and the tenants are raising
fortunes to purchase them: the rustic, of consequence, becomes the
independant gentleman; and the independant gentleman, when his
fortune is spent, is elevated to the envied dignity of wearing a court
livery."

In so considering the faults of his own age, Scott felt these
errors resulted from a deviation from an older standard, a falling
off from the nobility which had characterized English history.
(By implication here, he was close to Johnson's notion that severity toward the poor was an undoubted and constant attention
of Whiggism; yet Johnson himself believed that the ambition to
make money in business was a good one.) Thus, like so many
other writers of the period, Scott turned his eyes toward the past
to analyze the merits of a bygone age and to reassess the values of
his own.

The presumed successful charity of the past was predicated upon the existence of the "benevolent lord."[45] He was the man who distributed freely from his bounty to become the benefactor of the oppressed. The landed gentleman—the Mr. Allworthy— was assumed by some to be the eighteenth-century counterpart of the feudal lord of an earlier day. John Scott felt that the ancient noble patron was characterized mainly by a charitable spirit and a sense of responsibility for his fellow man. The "ferocious temper of the gothic age"[46] had been softened by a devout aspect which, although not unselfishly altruistic, had tended to mitigate the distresses of the poor; "... the national religion taught the doctrine of merit, derivable from works of charity and mercy: this influenced the conduct of both clergy and laiety; and the hope of reward, and the sense of duty, co-operated with the dictates of compassion in favour of the distressed."[47] Scott also sketched in a quatrain the contrast between the two types of men:

> The haughty lord, whom lust of gain inspires,
> From man and beast excessive toil requires:
> The generous master views with pitying eyes
> Their lot severe, and food and rest supplies.[48]

The fact that the benevolent lord had, by his prodigious wealth, been walled in from the ordinary people was not ignored by Scott. Economically successful persons found their walks of life leading through hitherto unopened doors in the social barrier, and with this penetration of a socioeconomic enclosure, there began on the part of most persons a frantic pursuit of wealth; advancement to a higher station became the goal. To counterbalance this tendency, which he felt was deplorable, Scott wished "the princes of the people, the lords of villages, the patrons and employers of the poor" to leave the cities and to return to their country estates, far from metropolitan orgies. The destruction of the older way of life and the nobility of the landed gentry was, according to Scott, caused solely by the breaking down of economic barriers, an act which introduced or stressed unfortunate qualities within the gentry, qualities which had previously lain dormant. Avarice and luxury now asserted themselves, perhaps in a vain attempt to maintain this older economic division, and the unfortunate result was a callous attitude taken toward the plight of the poor. Johnson snorted at such speculations: "I am always angry when I hear ancient times praised at the expense of modern times."[49] Yet even he once replied to the question of what had become of the gallantry and military spirit of the old English nobility, by saying, "... it is gone into the city to look for a fortune."[50]

More puritanical than writers like William Bell, Mandeville, and even Johnson who could see the virtues which could accompany luxury,[51] Scott felt that luxury was an inevitable corollary of avarice and covetousness. He felt that the possession of the latter two vices would destroy the last trace of sensibility in a people. If it did not do that, it would increase their irritation, for they would refuse charity to anyone who sought it. The hand of covetousness and avarice "has always been busy in constructing yokes for the neck of poverty," asserted Scott, and there had never been a rational inducement for it. Instead, he harped and harped again that it was a phenomenon peculiar to his own age; it was a result of the breaking down of the older economic classes and the allowing of every man who wished to rise socially to do so by rising financially. This explained why avarice was the ruling passion of those who were the wealthiest. Their old social position, now meaningless in terms of "station," came to have its security solely in the accumulation of money.

These men are on the ladder of ambition, exerting their utmost endeavours to attain a little eminence, whence they may overlook the level of their neighbours; and every thing that retards their ascent, excites their anger and detestation.

Because he was motivated by humanitarian sympathy for the poor, Scott deplored this tendency toward extravagance and luxury, a trend which was caused by a decaying social structure and a new idea of the position of wealth and the proper display of it. The emphasis of life had been shifted to amusement, and this caused him to attack inns, dances, horse races, and romances and novels.[52] None of these *divertissements* served any useful purpose, he felt, and they were products of the new social tendency which shifted concern from the altruistic to the egoistic. Man was no longer concerned with his neighbor but with himself, and charity had become a meaningless term.

In his attitude toward the poor, Scott differed from the majority by believing that the evil of alcohol was exaggerated, and it was in this attitude that he made one of his most surprising deflections from popular opinion. From John Cooke to John Arbuthnot everyone was sure that the poor were too frequently filled with the wrong sort of spirits.[53] Scott did not minimize the potential depravity of the alehouse, and he asserted that children should be kept from it or they would become deceitful and profane. He excoriated the taverns and their proprietors, saying that they had not been censored with sufficient severity; and he seemed to feel that the evil lay in the tavern and not in the individual who was misled into patronizing it. Yet he once told a relative that Goldsmith's kindly description of the alehouse in *The Deserted Village* might well have been written of the inn at Amwell,[54] and he could hardly have forgotten that his own fortune came from his father's malt mill. The drunken parent who refused to work, and the helpless children who were left to starve while the country supported taverns because of the rich taxes on them—these were vividly sketched by Scott. The remedy, he felt, was to have on the licensing board a minister who would decide whether or not a potential tavern keeper had character and merit sufficient to watch over the health and welfare of his patrons and not let them become charges of the community. The concept of the "benevolent lord" was once again to do service.

The common excuse that many people gave—that they refused to donate money to a beggar because he might spend it on drink—was really a rationalization of the problem, believed Scott, and a false exaggeration of the situation. Scott had implicit and, confessedly, unrealistic faith in man's judgment: he said that a man would not spend all of his money on drink when he knew that he must also supply himself with food. And even if a man should get drunk occasionally, that was no justification for cutting off all aid to the poor: alcohol was not necessarily the distillation of sin. In fact, Johnson had gone further and, in justifying such expenditure on tobacco or liquor by a beggar, had said, "Life is a pill which none of us can bear to swallow without gilding; yet for the poor we delight in stripping it still barer, and are not ashamed to shew even visible displeasure, if ever the bitter taste is taken from their mouths."[55] Nor was alcohol the only drink the poor were charged with. Tea was also condemned by Jonas Hanway and his supporters as being harmful and wasteful. Scott shared Johnson's conviction that tea eased more than one wearisome hour, and it was a blessing which should not be withheld from the poor; ". . . it cannot reasonably be thought, that the use of it has so universally obtained among so populous, so prudent, and intelligent a nation as the Chinese, without some knowledge or at least presumptive proofs of its utility." The eighteenth century's kindly attitude toward Cathay had started to color his thinking. Far better, he thought, to condemn gambling inns, state lotteries, "horse races, cock fightings, cricket matches, and the visits of those pests of society, itinerant mountebanks," fairs which were far more abundant than the need for trade would suggest, and holidays which were observed for reasons other than the encouragement of religion and virtue.

Scott similarly did not accept the assumption that the poor were inherently worthless, an assumption which earlier writers on poor laws certainly expressed.[56] His attitude rather was one which ever believed in the basic value of the poor, not in an economic but in a humanitarian and religious sense. His concern for the poor did not mislead him into believing that the worthless poor did not exist, however; and he showed his most uncompromising side when he prescribed the proper treatment for confirmed beggars and impostors. Much of the difficulty in discussing poor relief, believed Scott, was that too many writers were, like Defoe, "taking for granted what remains to be proved, that vagrancy and imposition are constantly united, and so precipitately arranging under one common predicament, and peremptorily consigning to one common punishment, the guilty and the innocent." He later was to attribute the fate of Chatterton to poverty and the indifference which such an economic plight commonly received. The death of the young poet was to Scott the best illustration of the folly of believing that economic and intellectual or any other value bore any correlation to each other and that poverty and lack of pride were concomitants.[57]

Scott felt that the poor wanted work and suffered because they were unable to find it. The blame for their poverty lay in an economic system and not in the moral character of the persons themselves. Most beggars were those who had been temporarily reduced to indigence and who, unable to receive adequate assistance from an antiquated parochial system of relief or from the scant charity of their neighbors, were forced to wander abroad: to begin, by seeking kindness; to end, by finding starvation. Even the worthless should be saved and helped, he insisted, for there was virtue even unto these last, and mankind should recognize it. There was no justification at all, he believed, in considering the poor with the idea of rewarding virtue and punishing error. If one examined the evidence, he would find that the only fault

lay in the plight of the poor and not in the people themselves. If
more than enough money were raised to take care of the
minimum requirements of the impoverished, then there could
be a rebate or one could "let the poor live better, the rich can
afford it."

By Scott's time, there had appeared a radically divided opinion
upon the proper uses of charity. Some reformers believed that
charity in the form of individual gifts should be entirely abol-
ished, with all relief coming in the form of state assistance. Most
followed Defoe's admonitions and felt that individual charity
should be encouraged, only so long as one made certain that the
recipients were worthy.[58] And finally, a few held the singular
belief that all charity, unhampered by any restrictions or hesita-
tions, was good—no matter what the nature of the recipient. It
was in the third rank that Scott took his stand. He felt that virtue
was in the truest sense its own reward and that any discussion
of other motivation tended to destroy that compensation. Since
there was still virtue in indiscriminate giving, the nature of the
person helped was not important, whether he was a virtuous
pauper or a fraudulent beggar. This attitude, which did not
neglect but, rather, knowingly reject the prevailing theories
about considered charity, was doubtless owing to his deep and
acknowledged admiration of William Law's *Serious Call to a
Devout and Holy Life,* the book which had first stimulated
Johnson's religious thoughts after he had become "capable of
rational inquiry."[59]

Impressed by this work, Scott emphasized that charity consists not in the receiving and in the proper employing of the
gift; it consists solely in the giving. Where there is deception,
the crime lies on the conscience of the beggar, but no ordinary
mortal can ever justify his penny-pinching and his penurious-
ness by playing Diogenes and looking for the honest man. Scott
saw too clearly that such a seeker of perfection would be too

stingy even to buy oil for the lamp he traveled by. If those we serve are ungrateful—and they probably will be—so much the better; it will make us realize our own animal state and the fact that as these people are ungrateful to us, so have we been and are we always ungrateful to our Creator.

One final humanitarian concern of Scott's deserves mention, and that is his attitude toward punishment, its purposes and abuses. Sir Matthew Hale had objected to penalties for the poor, apparently not from humanitarian convictions but from a feeling that such penalties were rather futile and impractical. Scott was motivated by both practical and humanitarian sentiments. He complained bitterly about false imprisonment and the abominable conditions of the prisons which needed investigation. And a few years later, he was to become one of Howard's outspoken supporters for investigations of the penal system.[60] He felt that the concept of justice implied mercy and that justice should be made to fit the offense; to consider it in any other light—such as a deterrent to crime—was foolish. For this reason, he opposed Johnson's defense of public executions.

It is not the fear of an ignominious death, of which examples are continually before the eyes of the transgressor, that will deter the sons of rapine from the pursuit of their unlawful occupation: it is not the fear of the horrors of an invisible world, more terrible to imagination as their nature is unknown, that will deter the sinner from the commission of wickedness.[61]

Therefore he attacked flagellation; it served only to obliterate the sense of shame in a person and to arouse his desire for revenge. A better means of subduing a bad disposition, Scott insisted, was fasting.[62] There was never a justification for capital punishment; the worst of men could be imprisoned where he might perform labor for the service of mankind.[63] Once again, the humanitarian and utilitarian purposes were blended, and the solution would better the condition of the world while attempt-

ing to improve the character of the condemned. And it is noteworthy that his idea of punishment held religious implications
with the notion that fasting brings one to a better life.

*Observations on the Present State of the Parochial and Vagrant
Poor,* therefore, is only a compendium of opinions on various
subjects which in their ramifications led far from the field of
poor relief, but which, nevertheless, had their origin in the same
ground. There was nothing truly *original* in Scott's pamphlet;
rather it represented a restatement of opinions on charity and
poor relief which had been formulated in the seventeenth century but which were applied by him to the problems of his own
day. The unusual aspect of his writing lies in the fact that he was
a forerunner of the humanitarian attitude regarding beggars
which was later popularized by the *Lyrical Ballads,* an attitude
which, while stressing that help should be given to the poor,
never minimized the fact that the donor of such aid was actually
giving himself an extreme pleasure and benefit in the gesture
of his giving.

The theory behind Scott's attitude was not only a revived one,
however, but one which had ever been advocated by the doctrines
of the Society of Friends. The one consistent theme running
through the annual minutes of the Society is that charity is
the greatest good and that the government should not be expected to take care of the poor, as that is the Christians' duty
and privilege by their ability to bestow beneficences.[61] Scott found
a justification for his position, therefore, not only in deductions
drawn from the writings of Sir Matthew Hale and William
Law but from the more doctrinal teachings of his faith. The
significance of this document lies not in the originality of the
proposals but in the emphasized and explicit humanitarianism
of its writer, who was among the first to express a change in
English sentiment—the revival and intensive application of an
attitude toward charity which the Age of Reason felt it had
outgrown.

Chapter IV

THE BENEVOLENT LORD

IN HIS FIRST political tract and in his poor-relief pamphlet, John Scott had mixed a romantic theory of benevolence with a Mandevillian notion of the nature of man. Idealism and practicality were the components of a new amalgam when he had taken his Quaker piety into the world of action, for Scott saw the world through religious eyes, a world where the poor were to be pitied and the rich to be condemned. It was only natural that such opposites should produce an unsatisfactory equilibrium, the product of Scott's inexperience with the subjects he treated. As a man of action, however, he soon moved beyond the theoretical, and he came to problems in which he had had experience: when he wrote of these issues, as apparently when he handled the situations themselves, he was no dreamer, no idealist. He was practical, resolute, and stubbornly independent. Having defined the character of the "benevolent lord," he was ready to assume the role. And in his assumption of the part, he was to demonstrate what he had never realized before: that the benevolent lord's effectiveness was due to his firmness in dealing with all situations and in assigning to men the duties they should fulfill. It also soon became obvious that to be such a ruler of affairs, one needed wealth and position: older notions of class equality were pleasant to consider but they were ineffective in handling a situation. To be successful, the Whig must parade himself in the garments of the Tory.

Scott's new attitude started appearing in 1773, the same year he published his poor-law tract, that eloquent testimonial to impractical benevolence. In the area of poor relief, he had had few suggestions to make. He could complain of man's iniquity, comment on man's fallen state, and plead for a humanitarian attitude toward the poor. But he had no new system. Within a matter of months, however, he had brought out his first book on highways, and here his new character was asserting itself. Writing from his personal experience, he had definite proposals, propositions, and suggestions to make. The new attitude began with a small work, consisting of a regrouping of the parliamentary codifications of highway laws made in 1766 and 1773.[1] This regathering of materials under headings more convenient and ingenious than those supplied by the original creators of the law, was followed by a collection of incidental remarks upon those sections of the law which Scott had found unclear, ineffectual, or unsatisfactory. The book was an experiment: it was an early attempt to present a scholarly edition of a parliamentary text in the pattern of Richard Burn's work with the poor laws in his *The History of the Poor Laws* and the parliamentary statutes in his *The Justice of the Peace and Parish Officer*. So encouraged was Scott with the results of this initial endeavor, that he began making plans for a larger volume—and five years later, he was to bring out his great work on the English road system, *Digests of the General Highway and Turnpike Laws*. The year 1773 was a transitional year; it did for his prose works what 1776 would do for his poetry.

In 1774, Scott was back at work again on *Amwell* and was at that time revising it with definite ideas about readying it for the press. By then, it had been much enlarged beyond its original conception; it had also been made more significant by the introduction of historical allusions and moral reflections and by the addition of explanatory notes which discussed the history and antiquities of the Ware-Amwell region. Whether Charles Frogley was at that time assisting in the revision is uncertain, but Scott later asserted that he had received invaluable assistance on

[1] For notes to chap. iv, see p. 211.

the poem, particularly from his old friend Frogley. Before the poem could be printed, however, Scott's thoughts were again directed toward political matters.

I

Johnson's *The Patriot* appeared in 1774, sometime after September 30, when George III called for a new parliament, and it went through two editions that year and a third (plus a Dublin edition) in the following year.[2] Scott, indignant at the doctor's sentiments, wrote his tract after the election of 1774. *Remarks on The Patriot. Including Some Hints Respecting the Americans: with an Address to the Electors of Great Britain* was published shortly after the first of the year in 1775, when it was reviewed in the January, 1775, issue of the *Critical Review*. Johnson's pamphlet turned upon the definition of the word "patriot" and showed how his opinions concerning the meaning of the word and its significance had changed since he had written his *Dictionary*. The argument, indeed, seems to suggest that the word had assumed symbolic significance to Johnson as a personification of opprobrium, and a reading of Boswell reveals how Johnson, in the years after this pamphlet, used the word with this especially Johnsonian connotation;[3] in fact, to the definitions of "patriot" which had appeared in the first three editions of the *Dictionary*,[4] Johnson in 1773 added a new one: "It is sometimes used for a factious disturber of the government." And though this peculiar usage of "patriot" seems not to have sprung from an immediate dislike of John Wilkes, Wilkes was the motivation for calling forth an indignation which had its origins early in Johnson's political experience when Walpole's control in the government was relinquished to Pulteney.[5]

The word "patriot" does not owe to Johnson its ironical use in the eighteenth century;[6] the Wilkes controversy merely revived the ironic meaning of the word when Wilkes himself became

known as the Patriot.[7] This dual meaning of the term "patriot"
had been mentioned by Scott in his first political tract, when he
complained that Johnson was wearing a pair of Court Spectacles.

These same Court Spectacles are supposed to possess a power somewhat analogous to that of the cylindrical mirror employed in a certain
optical experiment termed the Anamorphosis. This converts a monster into a man; those convert a man into a monster; a patriot into a
rebel; a respectful pensioner into a seditious incendiary; an honest
intelligent tradesman into a vile mechanic.—It were endless to expatiate on their virtues; yet, from the great regard I bear to Dr.
J——n, I most heartily wish, for his own reputation, he had *never
worn a pair.*[8]

Johnson's *The Patriot* had a simple structural organization:
after a brief introduction, which justified the existence of the
pamphlet in terms of the then forthcoming election, the pamphlet turned upon a definition of what was a patriot (with
numerous examples being given) and what was not a patriot
(with more examples being listed). But whereas this structure
seemed to call for a listing of positive examples of existing
patriots or patriotic actions, Johnson was able to give examples
solely in the negative—that is, what had occurred which was not
patriotic. As he apologetically confessed, Johnson, like an early-
day Carlyle, found it easier to give examples of evil than even
hypotheses of what was good, "for it is commonly easier to know
what is wrong than what is right; to find what we should avoid,
than what we should pursue." Scott's *Remarks on The Patriot,*
on the other hand, in having no organization but Johnson's own,
seemed to be only a glorified critical gloss on Johnson's text, with
the original ideas of the Quaker poet and philosopher being
restricted to his *Address to the Electors of Great Britain,* which
formed a separate section of his pamphlet.

Like most disagreements, Scott's and Johnson's stemmed from
a philosophical distinction—here, in the attitude toward change

and progress. Johnson believed progress existed only as a gradual ameliorating principle working through history. His scorn for new projects which would radically change the temper and form of government was not unlike Burke's belief in traditionalism, and there was throughout Johnson's writings the feeling that the excellences embodied in the British constitution and way of life were due to that elusive and indescribable natural force known only as the careful moulding and reshaping of centuries. Man, believed Johnson, could not look to an immediate delivery from those evils which have plagued all generations. (In fact, one wonders whether Johnson believed that man ever could find a Utopia.) Scott believed the opposite, for as Johnson had defied change and yet believed in progress, so Scott advocated change and yet belived that no progress would result. He had no use for Johnson's theory of traditionalism, saying instead, "If the mode of representation transmitted by our ancestors be imperfect, it ought to be altered, for antiquity cannot sanctify imperfection." The solution with Scott was a clear one: man must strive ever to change and improve his world; but he must labor not with the expectation of improvement but with the knowledge that the best he might hope to win would be a retention of the excellences of the moment. There was a quality of grimness in Scott's latent feeling which occasionally rose to the surface of this pamphlet, a feeling that man was fighting desperately to retain his present state which, even with all its imperfections, was preferable to the decay into which civilization might fall. Though he was still a liberal, he had become a conservative and pessimistic one—quite unlike the ordinary parliamentary variety. Man, according to Scott, labored not with the expectation of improving his world; he labored with the knowledge that if he did not struggle, things would inevitably get worse. It is against this Johnson-Scott philosophical dichotomy that the two pamphlets must be read; for where the two men disagreed, they believed it was owing to the example of the moment, whereas it was owing in reality to this basic difference of attitude toward man and change.

Johnson's basic definition—which his entire essay elaborated—was:

> A PATRIOT is he whose publick conduct is regulated by one single motive, the love of his country; who, as an agent in parliament, has for himself neither hope nor fear, neither kindness nor resentment, but refers every thing to the common interest.

Scott rejected this idea, saying it was based on the concept of "implicit love [which] is not invariably advantageous, but sometimes detrimental to its object." By an elaborate method of cataloguing and analysis, Scott showed that Johnson's idea was meaningful only in terms of a standard of normality, whereby the individual love felt by one man would be compatible with the love felt by all. As it was, that love felt by abnormal people would probably be in no way consonant with the love felt by normal ones.[10] Scott attributed these psychological differences to differences of education or instruction. He was here following Lockian philosophical thought concerning the nature of man's mind, and he was also seeing that the ramifications of such theories led to a basic understanding of the nature of man's psychological development. To be sure, Scott did not see how these psychological differences could stem from the unconscious influences which surround childhood; but in relating man's seemingly irrational conduct to a faulty education, he had progressed far along the lines of later psychological and speculative analysis, and he was certainly in the tradition of Rousseau. The conclusion of his criticism of Johnson's definition was that a generality is valid only in terms of its referent, for a "man must know what is the true interest of his country, and use his best endeavours to promote it, before he can have a just title to the honourable distinction of a Patriot."

Johnson's pamphlet reaffirmed his earlier notions about class structure and defensible class distinctions, whereas Scott's rebuttal showed him still believing in the equality of man and the brotherhood existing among human beings.

The doctrines of natural equality, &c. far from meriting derision, as the reveries of unsuccessful candidates for Court Favour, are the doctrines of reason, and of truth. Superiority of birth or fortune, of corporal, or even of intellectual abilities, though it may give power, never can give right to one to govern many without their own consent: consequently the people is the origin, and the Prince only the residence of authority.... It is the first principle of freedom, that Government should originate in the consent of the governed.

For a fitting conclusion to this argument, he quoted to the king's pamphleteer a sentence from the *Idea of a Patriot King,* the source from which George III seemed to have derived many of his ideas on the nature of kingship: *"Majesty is not an inherent, but a reflected light."* Therefore, the assumption that kings ruled by the grace only of God, an assumption which he felt lay behind the Johnsonian position,[11] was also analyzed and dismissed by Scott; he said this idea was typical only of the vulgar in former ages.

In a person such as Scott, with his romantic ideas about the nature of man, one might expect to find unquestioning adherence to moral principles, no matter what the result. But Scott, convinced as he was that the natural state of man could be improved by enlightened institutions, felt that expediency was justified as a principle of action. (Therefore, in his first political tract, he had defended Wilkes's virtuous actions by this principle.) In this respect, Scott differed from Johnson, who felt that man's intentions and means alone determined the moral nature of his success. Scott's argument, however, was that even a self-interested patriot could be used to advantage in the country.

He who assists to extinguish a fire in the house of his neighbour, may have solely in view the safety of his own property, yet his assistance is

not at all the less serviceable to the publick. . . . If the scale of power
too greatly preponderates, there is no occasion to be so very scrupulous
with what we replenish the scale of liberty. . . . Dignity of station, and
purity of morals, are not essential to Patriotism.

Such a statement seems surprising unless one remembers the
philosophical conviction which lay behind it: that the state of
man was going to become even more corrupt unless some form
of patriotic action—that is, action which was suited mainly to
the best interests of the majority of the community—was forthcoming. In fairness to Scott, it should be observed that even in
the extreme, his notion of expediency was not really a harmful
one: he did not justify a violent action to carry out his purposes,
for the purposes themselves would find such a solution contradictory. Instead, his theory of expediency was related to his idea
of character. The mind of a man might be evil and yet do good
works.[12] The works themselves would not be harmed, he felt, as
we always possess the right to withdraw our confidence from
such a man. Of evil *deeds,* Scott seems to have been curiously
unaware, although he did speculate and give a general premise
that "a temporary evil should ever be suffered for the security of
a lasting benefit." Throughout all of these discussions about
virtue in vice, Scott seems obviously under the influence of
Christian humanism.

On the question of religious toleration, Scott followed the
persuasion of Milton's *Areopagitica,* though he did not acknowledge his position as that only of a disciple. Scott readily admitted
that liberty of conscience is a natural right and that "No rational
person would wish to refuse toleration, even to those who refuse
it to others." Johnson, going beyond this position, had felt that
if liberty of conscience is a natural right, then man does not have
the power to withhold it. But Scott said that the idealistic principle was not adaptable practically; and, like a realistic Milton,
he said a theoretical course could have only calamitous results.

Therefore, on the question of religious tolerance in Canada, he felt that the Church of Rome should be controlled, since "the clergy of the Roman Church have been the constant and firm friends of tyranny." Milton had the same fears of tolerating Catholics that Scott had, and in late eighteenth-century England, opposition to the Catholics and alarm at their influence resulted in the Gordon riots of June, 1780. Scott's attitude toward the Catholics was clearly part of the intellectual current of his time. And it was ironic that he should have advocated toleration for all minor sects (especially the Quakers) and yet retained the traditional attitude toward the Roman faith.[18]

Although *The Patriot* ostensibly was concerned with the questions the average British citizen wanted answered in the parliamentary election, Johnson exercised all of his anti-American sentiments in the pamphlet, ideas which were expanded a year later into his last political pamphlet, *Taxation No Tyranny,* a pamphlet to which Scott is said to have prepared an answer, but it has never been discovered or identified. Johnson's apparently innate dislike for the Scots seems to have been exceeded only by his distaste for the Americans. They embodied everything he detested, including a leveling movement, and at that particular moment, they were opposing the Quebec Act. It was on the specific question of taxation without representation that Scott expressed his disagreement with Johnson and showed himself as an early supporter of the American colonists.

Scott realized—better than Johnson did or wanted to admit—that the English difficulties with the colonies constituted something other than the relationship between a rebellious child and its parents. Johnson had argued that the Americans shared with all Britons in "the general system of representation," but such a statement was, as Scott saw, really meaningless. The whole concept of taxation through representation was fundamental to Scott's political theory. Just as he had advocated town meetings to get the English Senators, as he called them,[14] together with their constituents; and payment of parliamentary representatives directly by the people to show the men in government where they really drew their support; so did he state that no man should be taxed except by his equals and his representatives. No man, felt Scott, should be able to institute a tax which would not fall equally upon himself as upon others, for without this check of self-taxation, the entire economic system could become oppressive. As it was, the intention of the system was being defeated, he felt, by the existence of rotten and pocket boroughs. Already, his political thought was leading toward the reform acts of the nineteenth century.

It is for all of these reasons, which stemmed basically from political convictions in maintaining the *status quo* through striving, progress through political institutions, and enlightenment through educating man, that Scott concluded his essay with his own theory of the true patriot:

> Patriotism has been generally understood to be a virtue; but that Patriotism seems to have little claim to the appellation, which is nothing more than a local attachment; a passion, which, for the advantage of one favourite nation, will not scruple to ravage and enslave all others.... Patriotism seems better defined, a rational and liberal sentiment, which, on conviction of what is the greatest good of a part, will wish to extend it to the whole of society. The lover of freedom would gladly establish it not only in one, but in every political system in the universe.

Scott never renounced this position, and in his *Critical Essays,* he expressed doubt that Cecil, Walsingham, Raleigh, or Drake could, by their actions, be entitled "to the high character of patriots, or assertors of freedom," presumably because of their nationalistic interests. In the application of the concept of freedom, the difference between Johnson's and Scott's opinions is most apparent: theoretically, the former is the aristocratic Tory's of England; the latter, the democratic Whig's of the world.

The second part of Scott's pamphlet consisted of *An Address to the Electors of Great Britain;* written in an oratorical tone, it was a plea for political action and an attack upon political apathy. For, consistent with his predominant theory that man must run to stand where he is, Scott said that the greatest evil in the English state was the attitude of indifference which dominated her citizens. Though the people might become actively aroused over the injustices done a Wilkes, they too readily forget the elected man, once he had been put into office. Therefore, he urged his fellow citizens to express themselves on all governmental issues and to tell their representatives what they thought. Scott felt that the English government was inevitably doomed to being a *"form without a spirit."* To prevent the gradual usurpation of power, which he insisted was inevitable if the people did not assert their interest and authority, he advocated a tripartite government, similar in theory to the American concept of checks and balances, where "the monarchical aristocratical and democratical parts of the constitution ... should be kept for ever separate as a check upon each other."[15] The conclusion of his address combined his belief in human virtue and political action, the union of a spirit and a form:

If from this state of deplorable abjection you ever are preserved, on your own virtue alone depends your preservation. You must unite, heart and mind, in exerting fortitude superior to all possible discouragement, in legal assertion of your rights and privileges: you must labour, without intermission, till you have recovered the lost ground which the constant attrition of the stream of power has imperceptibly deducted from the shores of Liberty....

Ironically, despite such an exhortation to action, Scott's *Remarks on The Patriot* seems to have gone unnoticed by all the world and to have had no influence upon its age.[16] The appeal of the second and best of Scott's political writings must lie therefore in what it reveals of the political theories of the Quaker poet

of Amwell. And these, to the modern man, cannot be uninteresting, when one sees how well Scott seems to mirror the political,
humanitarian, and psychological tradition of the enlightenment.
If our interest in history lies largely in the admiration we can
give to the significant speculations of minds in the past, then
Scott seems worthy of being accorded praise as a precursor of
American thought and a champion of personal liberty. He did
not change the stream, but he knew where the stream was going.

❖   ❖   ❖

On April 5, 1775, Scott dined at Dilly's with Boswell, Johnson,
Campbell, Miller, and Langton. This must have been an interesting occasion, for though no record remains of what Scott said
at that meeting, he heard what Johnson had to say about the
political tracts which were emerging in answer to his final
political pamphlet, *Taxation No Tyranny*. As Campbell recorded, Scott seemed

to be a very sensible plain man. The Doctor, when I came in, had an
answer titled *Taxation and Tyranny* to his last pamphlet, in his hand.
He laughed at it, and said he would read no more of it, for that it paid
him compliments, but gave him no information. He asked if there
were any more of them. I told him I had seen another, and that the
Monthly Review had handled it in what I believed he called the way
of information. "Well," says he, "I should be glad to see it."[17]

There was no reason that this meeting between Scott and Johnson should have caused discomfort on either side. Johnson frequently said that he would rather be attacked than unnoticed,
and he seemed to enjoy the controversies his writings stirred up.
Besides, Scott and Johnson would hardly have fallen out with
each other at this dinner, for there was in attendance a man
whom they both ridiculed far more than they ever did each
other. This was the future Sir John Miller, who, with his wife,
dominated a literary set at their villa at Batheaston near Bath and
who served as Campbell's target for criticism when the minister

recorded the dinner in his diary. Both Johnson and Scott detested the Batheaston set with its literary pretensions; every poetaster of the region wrote and dropped verses in that enormous and apparently ever-empty vase of Lady Miller, the weakest light in any gathering of sputtering luminaries.

The April 5 meeting with Scott may have caused Johnson to hunt among his books for Scott's poetry or, perhaps, at that meeting Scott gave Johnson a copy of his *Four Elegies,* which had been published fifteen years earlier. In any case, when Boswell visited Johnson on April 10, five days after the dinner, he found a copy of Scott's poems lying in the room.

Dr. Johnson observed, "They are very well; but such as twenty people might write." Upon this I [Boswell] took occasion to controvert Horace's maxim,

> "——*mediocribus esse poetis*
> *Non Di, non homines, non concessére columnae."*

for here (I observed,) was a very middle-rate poet, who pleased many readers, and therefore poetry of a middle sort was entitled to some esteem; nor could I see why poetry should not, like every thing else, have different gradations of excellence, and consequently of value. Johnson repeated the common remark, that "as there is no necessity for our having poetry at all, it being merely a luxury, an instrument of pleasure, it can have no value, unless when exquisite in its kind."[18]

By the middle of the summer, Scott was back in Amwell and ready to entertain guests. James Beattie and his wife, who had come to London for a visit and had left the metropolis July 10, 1775, stopped at Amwell on the way home, spending two days with the Scotts;[19] the friendship between the two families was a fast one, for the letters which later went from Amwell to Aberdeen reflected a close harmony of sympathy and critical understanding which existed between the two men. They had both published their first volumes of verse in 1760, and their critical thought had much in common. Indeed, one of the greatest influences on Scott's critical thinking was the writings of his Scottish friend.

II

Through the rest of 1775 and the early part of 1776, *Amwell: A Descriptive Poem* was given final preparation for the press. On April 5, 1776, Boswell met Scott at Dilly's and there received his copy of the poem which had been wrapped with Scott's card.[20] In the same month, the poem was accorded a short but cordial notice in the *Critical Review,* so it was probably published no earlier than March of 1776. In May, John Langhorne in the *Monthly Review* gave a warm review of the poem and, in giving a biographical hint about Scott, revealed himself as among Scott's most sincere admirers.

ABOUT sixteen years ago we reviewed some elegant little poems, characterised by a natural enthusiasm, harmony, and simplicity, under the title of *Elegies, descriptive and moral.* Not long afterwards we learnt that they were the production of the ingenious Author of the poem before us, a Gentleman of fortune, who lives in a beautiful retirement, embellished by his own taste and genius, at the place he describes. That, amidst the multiplicity of poetical publications which pass under our review, we retain a lively and distinct idea of those Elegies, is, at least, so far as our opinion may be reposed upon, an indubitable proof of their merit.

The July issue of the *Gentleman's Magazine* also praised the poem, saying, "EVERY poetical reader may here indulge such 'a feast of fancy and flow of soul,' as will in some degree compensate the loss of the bards of Auburn and the Leasowes." The poem was the only one of Scott's works to enjoy a genuine popularity in his lifetime, and it went through a second edition and also a Dublin edition in the same year.[21] There can be no question that *Amwell* represents Scott's major achievement of his first poetical period; it may easily constitute the finest of all his poems. Historically, *Amwell* was the "outstanding hill-poem of the decade,"[22] and as for its author, "In both poetry and critical theory he was the most progressive hill-singer of his time."[23]

Johnson was not so impressed with this genre of poetry, saying of Denham's introducing the local poem:

> To trace a new scheme of poetry has in itself a very high claim to praise, and its praise is yet more when it is apparently copied by Garth and Pope; after whose names little will be gained by an enumeration of smaller poets, that have left scarce a corner of the island not dignified either by rhyme or blank verse.[24]

Topographical poetry may not be as old as the hills, mountains, streams, and plains which it began by commemorating, but its origins lie far back in antiquity, and from seeds planted as early as the sixth century B.C. it has overgrown the world, concealing nature in rhetoric and stifling it with poetry. Professor Aubin has carefully traced the origins of this poetic ivy, and there has appeared no offshoot which he has not been able to relate to the family vine.[25] Among the most important sources for this eighteenth-century landscape and garden verse would be the *Aetna* (55–44 B.C.), with its invocation to the muses and Apollo, and its moralizing observations; the *Mosella* of Decimus Magnus Ausonious, with its "mock-modest climax, the falsetto of which reappears with great frequency in the eighteenth century," and its use of a river mirroring a town; and Drayton's *Poly-Olbion,* in which there has never been "a fuller collection of motifs belonging to topographical verse."

Besides these general influences which doubtless affected Scott indirectly, there was a famous sixteenth-century landscape poem which well may have caught his attention; it was William Vallans' *A Tale of Two Swannes, Wherein Is Comprehended the Original and Increase of the River Lee, Commonly Called Ware-River: Together with the Antiquities of Sundrie Places and Townes Seated upon the Same* (1590). This blank verse allegorical poem was included in *The Itinerary of John Leland the Antiquary,* which was edited by Thomas Hearne and went through at least three editions in the eighteenth century before

Scott published his poem. Dealing with the procession of the
king and queen of the swans and their entourage of forty swans
down the Lee to London, the poem devotes lines to their arrival
at Ware, which apparently was much the same as it was two
centuries later in Scott's time:

> Then by the Crowne, and all the *Innes* of Ware:
> And so approching to the late built bridge,
> They see the barges lading malt apace.

From there they progressed downstream

> To *Amwell,* when they easilie did 'spie
> The spring and rill that comes out of the hill,
> And is suppos'd to rise at *Chadwell* head.

This poem concluded with notes on the localities mentioned in
it, and it also contained an appendix on the history of Alfred's
wars against the Danes. The use Scott made of footnotes and
historical material on Alfred, as well as the verse pattern itself,
may easily have come from Vallans' poem, though to be sure
these were common devices by the time Scott began to write.

It is ironic that late in his life Scott should have devoted so
much energy to destroying the reputation of Denham's *Cooper's
Hill*—which he felt was the most over-valued of all poems—
because Denham's poem more than any other helped to crystal-
lize a form for the topographical poem and, ultimately, *Amwell*
itself. All of the devices which Denham used (topical allusions,
references to earlier literature, the "retreat" theme, panegyrics,
invective, the modesty theme, the rural sports motif, the selective
narrative, and "most important of all, history with exegesis and
abundant moralizing") were liberally employed by Scott in what
he took to be his greatest poem. Scott would doubtless have pre-
ferred tracing his indebtedness to Dyer's *Grongar Hill,* which,
as Professor Aubin pointed out, "encouraged the picturesque
vision along with such devices as the Miltonic 'come' invocation,

the genre sketch, ruin sentiment, retreat, and a lyric, more personal approach." But the form of Denham stood large in the
background and Scott's choler was deepened by the shadow of
the seventeenth-century predecessor which fell upon him. Scott's
struggle later to destroy the colossus of Denham and to level
Cooper's Hill was motivated by a long suppressed desire to
let the light fall upon *Amwell* and heighten its own pleasant
prospects.

The repetitive quality of landscape poetry should not be explained away as only too heavy a formal influence, however.
Each poet seems to have attempted to describe a unique scene—
though admittedly both Bath and Bristol were worked over so
many times one wonders if a single tree was uncommemorated
there—but while nature is everywhere unique, she is perhaps in-
describably so. Poets fell back upon traditional imagery as much
as devices, and this was the cause of many a defeat. It became
recognized that it was impossible to pay nature her due devotion
with words, and nature poetized became covered with a fine
critical frost. Painters were considered far more satisfactory as
portrayers of nature, and almost everyone thought the landscape
poet their inferior. Scott was unique in deflecting from this attitude. He never apologized for *Amwell,* other than in his conventional conclusion to it. His *Critical Essays* were concerned
entirely with an analysis of the landscape piece, and he never
mentioned the genre as inferior. The attack on *Cooper's Hill* was
to show the defects of one famous poem and to emphasize that
it had been surpassed by a number of eighteenth-century poems
which had audiences far smaller than their merits deserved.

Amwell, therefore, is a poem which is appreciated more easily
when considered by itself or in the context of Scott's other poems,
than it is when plunged into its historical milieu. Professor
Havens long ago contrasted "the admirably simple, natural
blank verse of John Scott's descriptive poem, *Amwell,* with the

couplets of his Moral and of his Amoebaean 'Eclogues,' in which
close observation is concealed by the stilted poetic diction, the
frigid conventionality, and the monotonous cadences that went
with the rimed pastoral."[26] *Amwell* is Scott's most successfully
sustained long poem; it has an organization, skillful transitions,
and material for which the poet had a genuine enthusiasm: he
was able to transmit somewhat effectively to his readers his unquestionably sincere reactions to Amwell and its region. Unfortunately, the stature which the poem gains in the context of
Scott's poetry is not gained in the context of a century's poems.
It was the finest hill-poem of a decade, but literary remembrance
does not settle upon poems by this award alone. Both before and
after Scott wrote *Amwell,* other poets created far more successful
poems. Goldsmith's *Deserted Village* and Thomson's *Seasons*
have retained a critical reputation, and even Denham's *Cooper's
Hill,* which is perhaps as feeble as Scott thought it was and
partly at least inferior to *Amwell,* has an attention drawn from
a historical significance which cannot be questioned.

The sort of competition Scott faced in his most ambitious
poem can be determined by examining the lists of such poems
published in the eighteenth century. Of hill-poems (in which
category Professor Aubin places *Amwell*), there were three in
the seventeenth century, and sixty-six in the eighteenth century
before Scott published *Amwell.* In the decade of Scott's poem,
thirty-six hill-poems, or poems with sections devoted to hills,
emerged; and in 1776, the year of Scott's poem, three others
came out. Not all of these enjoyed publication under their own
covers, of course; many were in magazines or letters and other
collections of verse, but they constituted a threat to that poet
who always feared having his material anticipated by others.
About the only thing in Scott's favor historically was that none
of these other poems celebrated Hertfordshire. But the historical
context does not reveal the importance to Scott of his *Amwell*

and its enormous significance in a consideration of the achievements of his life.

Amwell was the author's magnum opus; after having spent twenty-one years upon it, he regarded it fitting evidence of his poetical ability: when he published it, therefore, it was the first of his poetical works to bear his name on the title page. And it appears finally so to have met the approval of the author, that when he republished it six years later in his *Poetical Works,* only one of the poem's 446 lines was changed.[27] Lacking Scott's manuscripts we are unable to know anything about the genesis of the poem, other than that it was to deal with the towns of Amwell and Ware. As time went on, the poem increased and took on more learned pretensions by including historical information about the region, drawn from town or county histories; it was perhaps among the first poems to do this, since this revision was made in 1774, and in 1775 appeared Hippesley's *Bath and It's Environs* which used a similar device, presumably for the first time.[28] Metrically, the poem marked something unusual for Scott: it was written in blank verse. Though we know he admired Milton enthusiastically, liked Thomson's *Seasons,* and was intensely fond of Dyer's *Ruins of Rome,* this is the only evidence we possess that he himself ever worked with blank verse; yet, he showed uncommon skill at it. Doubtless he thought of himself as the eighteenth-century son of Milton, with his use of enjambment and carefully effective repetition; but he never approached Milton's imaginative conceptions, his sublimity and rapturous heights. Instead, Scott, with his emphasis upon a description of the particular, the immediate, and the tangible was in the tradition of Thomson and the eighteenth-century landscape poets who had preceded him. It was, nevertheless, a personalized style. It had acknowledged affinities with others, but it was finally the Amwell poet's own and represents a happy adaptation of an older tradition to his newer conception of what local poetry could and ought to do:

Scott is much more simple, direct, and natural than his predecessors.
As compared with theirs, his style is neither pompous nor involved,
and his diction, though conventional, is not learned or Latinic. In
these respects, as in his genuine love for the milder, more familiar
aspects of nature and in his charming expression of that love, he takes
a distinct step forward.[29]

> There dwells a fond desire in human minds,
> When pleas'd, their pleasure to extend to those
> Of kindred tastes; and thence th' inchanting arts
> Of Picture and of Song, the semblance fair
> Of Nature's forms produce. This fond desire
> Prompts me to sing the lonely sylvan scenes
> Of AMWELL; which, so oft in early youth,
> While novelty enhanc'd their native charms,
> Gave rapture to my soul; and often, still,
> On life's calm moments shed serener joy.

With these lines, which broadly define the subject and his motive
for treating it, Scott began *Amwell*. Although these lines do not
put before the reader a purpose as explicitly defined as that
offered by both Virgil and Milton, they do strongly imply a
purpose of glorifying Amwell and extending to others vicari-
ously the pleasure which the village held for the poet. Such a
beginning for a landscape poem was perfectly conventional, but
one should not overlook Scott's viewing his poem somewhat in
the tradition of the epic. Like an epic, *Amwell* represented for
Scott a major achievement, both in magnitude and in time spent
on it. It was also to deal with the important: the profound and
not the trivial. Like his predecessors, Scott was fascinated by
legends of battle and the past, and he included them in his poem.
But he was also like Cowper, and he found enormous significance in the quieter side of life, the seemingly uneventful things
which yet comprise the totality of man's existence; and by
putting these things in his landscape-epic, he was to emphasize
their importance.[30] Always before, he had done this in a rather
obvious and didactic fashion. Here, he was to be subtler and, he

hoped, more effective. *Amwell,* therefore, marked a notable moment in that development which let the early poet write about God, His worth and power, but which let the older poet write not about God Himself but about the Godly existence as displayed by man in the true life. Scott would not describe heaven; let others aspire to that. He would describe Amwell, which was all he knew and all he wished to know.

After the opening lines, the poet included an invocation to the descriptive muse and a dedication of this poem to his friends, who had visited the scenes it depicted, and to his wife, Maria De Horne Scott. When he came to describe the historical nature of the prospect and to paint a vivid scene, he wrote some of his most felicitous lines. He had endeavored for a long time to find the proper images, the right adjectives for the correct nouns. There was to be too much here, of course, that was conventional and rather pointless. But in his happier moments, he was to capture the sensation of the Danish wars and the meaning that Alfred had for his people as a restorer of liberty and for Scott himself as a symbol of the strength which lies behind peace.

> Far tow'rds the west, close under sheltering hills,
> In verdant meads, by Lee's cerulean stream,
> Hertford's grey towers ascend; the rude remains
> Of high antiquity, from waste escap'd
> Of envious Time, and violence of War.
> For War there once, so tells th' historic page,
> Led Desolation's steps: the hardy Dane,
> By Avarice lur'd, o'er Ocean's stormy wave,
> To ravage Albion's plains, his favorite seat,
> There fix'd awhile; and there his castles rear'd
> Among the trees; and there, beneath yon ridge
> Of piny rocks, his conquering navy moor'd,
> With idle sails furl'd on the yard, and oars
> Recumbent on the flood, and streamers gay
> Triumphant fluttering on the passing winds.
> In fear, the shepherd on the lonely heath

Tended his scanty flock; the ploughman turn'd,
In fear, his hasty furrow: oft the din
Of hostile arms alarm'd the ear, and flames
Of plunder'd towns thro' night's thick gloom from far
Gleam'd dismal on the sight: till ALFRED came,
Till ALFRED, father of his people, came,
Lee's rapid tide into new channels turn'd,
And left a-ground the Danian fleet, and forc'd
The foe to speedy flight. Then Freedom's voice
Reviv'd the drooping swain; then Plenty's hand
Recloth'd the desert fields, and Peace and Love
Sat smiling by; as now they smiling sit.

This prospect led the poet to remember the seventeenth-century Sir Richard Fanshawe, the translator of Guarini's *Il Pastor Fido* and Camoëns' *Lusiad,* a man who had lived at Ware-Park and lay buried at Ware.[31] The death of this man turned Scott's thoughts toward that change which all men know and find either in themselves or the world about them. Such a topic naturally gave Scott opportunity to speak about something which was close to his heart: the state of the London water supply and the creation of the New River! Later Scott wrote:

The common sewers of a city might seem a subject of no great dignity; the common sewers of Rome, however, derived importance from their extensive plan, and enormous magnitude; and in our Poet's [Dyer's] description [in the *Ruins of Rome*], that importance has suffered no diminution. In the hands of a common writer, they would have been made ridiculous, either with bombast or meanness.[32]

Scott does not appear to have thought of himself as a common writer who would suffer defeat if he attempted such a subject; and though he did manage fairly well to keep the topic above the bathetic, he slipped into poetic diction near the end, and it is to be feared that he did not realize how these lines—when read by a person unfamiliar with the economic severity of the situation—could seem only humorous. One could almost see traces

here of metaphysical imagery in Scott; and how he would have
shuddered at such a suggestion!

> Our mercenary stream,
> No grandeur boasting, here obscurely glides
> O'er grassy lawns or under willow shades.
> As, thro' the human form, arterial tubes
> Branch'd every way, minute and more minute,
> The circulating sanguine fluid extend;
> So, pipes innumerable to peopled streets
> Transmit the purchas'd wave.

Some of the images were certainly farfetched, but Scott's accusa-
tion was apparently defensible. London drew its water supply
from this one river, and the consumption was so considerable as
to be alarming. City life being regarded by him as detestable,
Scott saw that even in his own Amwell there was to be ever
before him a symbol of the city's parasitic hold upon the
country.[33] After this economic brooding, Scott began his description of early tournament life in Ware. He deplored those bar-
barous customs and that excessive amount of pride which had
called for jousts and dangerous games of skill when war itself
was not present. Turning again then to the countryside, he—by
a repetition of the phrase, "Elysian scene"—drew together the
elements of rural life and made of them a unified scene.[34] This
rural prospect then brought him to a moral mood:

> Beneath thy branchy bowers of thickest gloom,
> Much on the imperfect state of Man I have mus'd:
> How Pain o'er half his hours her iron reign
> Ruthless extends; how Pleasure from the path
> Of Innocence allures his steps; how Hope
> Directs his eye to distant Joy, that flies
> His fond pursuit; how Fear his shuddering heart
> Alarms with fancy'd ill; how Doubt and Care
> Perplex his thought; how soon the tender rose
> Of Beauty fades, the sturdy oak of Strength
> Declines to earth, and over all our pride
> Stern Time triumphant stands.

This view led the poet to reflect on John De Horne, his brother-in-law, and on Turner, his old friend, both of whom had died.[35] After examining and describing the scenery around Amwell, where the three of them had wandered together, Scott turned his thoughts toward home.

> As one long travell'd on Italia's plains,
> The land of pomp and beauty, still his feet
> On his own Albion joys to fix again;
> So my pleas'd eye, which o'er the prospect wide
> Has wander'd round, and various objects mark'd,
> On AMWELL rests at last, its favourite scene!

When Scott came to describe Amwell and the joys which he had known in this particular community, his poem attained its highest degree of excellence. Because of the nature of landscape poetry, it was difficult to say anything about the general, for prolonged stretches, and still retain the reader's interest. With the particular and specific, however, a poet could show the unique and, presumably, the interesting. In *Amwell,* Scott tried mixing the two types so that neither would bore the reader. Although he had liked the entire Ware-Amwell region, he felt his greatest love for the village and hills of Amwell itself; this genuine enthusiasm permeates his verse, and his joy is transmitted to the reader.

> Here rests
> The empty wain; there idle lies the plough:
> By Summer's hand unharness'd, here the steed,
> Short ease enjoying, crops the daisied lawn;
> Here bleats the nursling lamb, the heifer there
> Waits at the yard-gate lowing....
> . . . .
> Such rural life! so calm, it little yields
> Of interesting act, to swell the page
> Of history or song; yet much the soul
> Its sweet simplicity delights, and oft

> From noise of busy towns, to fields and groves,
> The Muse's sons have fled to find repose.

It was to Amwell particularly, felt Scott, that many an illustrious name had come. There were Izaak Walton, William Warner (author of *Albion's England*), and John Hoole. There was also Thomas Hassal, the seventeenth-century vicar of Amwell, who nursed his people through the plagues of 1603 and 1625; as Scott later said of Goldsmith's *The Deserted Village,* it is only proper to introduce the clergyman as a principal inhabitant. And since Hassal was a man so distinguished by service and charity, he received Scott's highest praise.[36] By wandering down to the churchyard and looking at the graves of those who had gone before, Scott had come to the heart of Amwell and to the end of his poem. There was left only the recapitulation. There remained time to speak only about Emma's well—Emma, the legendary wife of Alfred, who was said to have given the village its name—and then the poet bade farewell, in lines which well may be the finest in the poem:

> Thou, sweet Vill,
> Farewell! and ye, sweet fields, where Plenty's horn
> Pours liberal boons, and Health propitious deigns
> Her chearing smile! you not the parching air
> Of arid sands, you not the vapours chill
> Of humid fens, annoy; Favonius' wing,
> From off your thyme-banks and your trefoil meads,
> Wafts balmy redolence; robust and gay
> Your swains industrious issue to their toil,
> Till your rich glebe, or in your granaries store
> Its generous produce: annual ye resound
> The ploughman's song, as he thro' reeking soil
> Guides slow his shining share; ye annual hear
> The shouts of harvest, and the prattling train
> Of chearful gleaners:—and th' alternate strokes
> Of loud flails echoing from your loaded barns,
> The pallid Morn in dark November wake.

But, happy as ye are, in marks of wealth
And population; not for these, or aught
Beside, wish I, in hyperbolic strains
Of vain applause, to elevate your fame
Above all other scenes; for scenes as fair
Have charm'd my sight, but transient was the view:
You, thro' all seasons, in each varied hour
For observation happiest, oft my steps
Have travers'd o'er; oft Fancy's eye has seen
Gay Spring trip lightly on your lovely lawns,
To wake fresh flowers at morn; and Summer spread
His listless limbs, at noon-tide, on the marge
Of smooth translucent pools, where willows green
Gave shade, and breezes from the wild mint's bloom
Brought odour exquisite; oft Fancy's ear,
Deep in the gloom of evening woods, has heard
The last sad sigh of Autumn, when his throne
To Winter he resign'd;[37] oft Fancy's thought,
In extasy, where from the golden east,
Or dazzling south, or crimson west, the Sun
A different lustre o'er the landscape threw,
Some Paradise has form'd, the blissful seat
Of Innocence and Beauty! while I wish'd
The skill of CLAUDE, or RUBENS, or of Him
Whom now on Lavant's banks, in groves that breathe
Enthusiasm sublime, the Sister Nymphs
Inspire; that, to the idea fair, my hand
Might permanence have lent!—Attachment strong
Springs from delight bestow'd; to me delight
Long ye have given, and I have given you praise!

In *Amwell,* therefore, Scott presented the last poem of the
first period in his poetic development, a period in which he had
begun in the accepted traditions of Augustan poetry but had
ended in something which, although still traditional, was
peculiarly personalized. Though there were many faults in
Amwell—the diction was always conventional and sometimes
inflated, and the images occasionally seemed stereotyped—Scott,

in this poem, had presented not only a transitional work but a work which had an artistic unity and validity within itself. The ease with which he used blank verse, the effortless simplicity with which his poetic abstractions and personifications entered the scene—all these were indications of a genuine poetic ability shackled to the system and confined to the limits of eighteenth-century descriptive verse. But there was a paradox even at the end of the poem: there he emphasized his poetic inability and wished that he had the power of Claude or George Smith, painters of the most conventional, and glorifiers of the norm. Even *Amwell* was, ultimately, to be but a specific demonstration of the universal with a conventional conclusion. And all of his emphasis on specific images (which would have carried him in the direction of Wordsworth) was cast aside at the last when he said that his ideal was something quite the opposite. Like Boswell and Johnson, he had difficulty in deciding whether minute details and the particular were as important as a more universal and unspecified view. He kept bobbing uncertainly in this critical sea all of his life. Such inconsistencies implicit in *Amwell* did not annoy his readers, however; indeed, the popular success which the poem received may well have been the cause of Scott's turning his thoughts to a still more ambitious project: the compilation of his *Poetical Works*.

◇ ◇ ◇

During the same year, 1776, Scott visited Bath and wrote his "Ode on Leaving Bath," a poem which he later acknowledged as perhaps the weakest of his published odes, though he confessed he was "not ashamed of it."[38] By the first of October he was back in Amwell after having paid a visit to a relation's house in Essex.[39] This was probably the home of his brother-in-law, George De Horne, who, with his wife and children, often came from Stanway Hall in Essex to visit the Amwell branch of the family. For his sixth wedding anniversary, Scott also composed

"The Author to His Wife. 1776," in which he reaffirmed his love
for Maria De Horne Scott. This same poem may also reflect
Scott's discovery of his wife's pregnancy, as it is believed their
only child, Maria, was born the following year.

III

In 1777, Scott turned his thoughts to the exotic but hardly the
unusual in poetry when he began to follow Johnson, Hawkesworth, Langhorne, and Collins into the area of Oriental culture
for English literary themes. In that year, he wrote "Zerad; or,
The Absent Lover," the first of his "Oriental Eclogues." In the
same period, he also engaged in the Rowley controversy and
wrote from London, on June 19, to the *Gentleman's Magazine*
a lengthy letter in which he described himself in his signature
as "A Detester of Literary Imposition, but a Lover of good
Poetry." Hoole states that Scott wrote two letters to the same
journal, one appearing in the July number and one in the August
number, both dealing with the Chatterton forgeries. And though
there do exist letters in both of these issues, it is obvious that they
were not written by the same person and that Scott clearly wrote
the one for August. Apparently Scott frequently wrote letters to
journals and signed them with pseudonyms, but this is the only
one which can be identified, and it is an interesting document as
revealing his critical theory and technique of close critical
analysis at work six years before he printed his *Critical Essays*.

The tone of Scott's letter was judicious, and the approach to
the problem was eminently logical and well-considered. The
poems were objected to primarily by considering the historical
development of poetry; Scott proved that Chatterton (or the
author of the poems) had used stanzaic and metrical forms
which had been unknown in the time of Rowley but were quite
popular in the eighteenth century. There were comments on the
historical and factual knowledge and the linguistics of "Rowley,"

but the emphasis of the article was upon the poetics of the writer. The letter also contained brief thrusts at the folly of modern society, its propensity to admire anything ancient (whether or not it contained any merit), and the deplorable situation which would let the young genius of Chatterton be starved into destruction. Scott later wrote an ode in praise of Chatterton's genius, though he spoke of the poet's "headstrong rage"; so here he praised Chatterton's ability but deplored his deception, "that, with such uncommon powers, he should posses a disposition untractable and disingenuous." (Intractability and disingenuity were always considered major flaws by Scott. When he dealt with farmers and the highway problem, he was plagued by the first of these two mental "diseases"—and all of his political controversy with Johnson he doubtless attributed solely to the doctor's having succumbed to both of these vices.) Only in one degree did Scott later modify his original opinions about Chatterton. In this letter, he did not insist that Chatterton was the sole author of the Rowley poems but allowed that the Bristol youth may have found an old manuscript and adapted it; in his later writings, Scott attributed the authorship solely to Chatterton. In so changing his mind, he was probably being influenced by the extensive body of literature which appeared on the controversy and which he read avidly and discussed in his correspondence with Beattie. What was most perceptive in Scott's analysis of Chatterton's poetry was his discovering the probable sources of many of Chatterton's thoughts and ideas in Cibber's *Lives of the Poets of Great Britain and Ireland.* This was the sort of historical detective work he reveled in, and in his *Critical Essays* he occasionally entered a footnote to give more of this type of information. In the Chatterton letter, he also discussed the *"furor entheus"* which would be the subject of some poems in his own *Poetical Works,* and he made a basic distinction between a man and his work, a distinction which underlay all of his philosophy:

...whatever may be thought of the *author,* I cannot see any reason to depreciate the work. "If the pieces are modern," it has been hinted, "they are of little value." I must own, I am of a contrary opinion. Whether a poem was written three centuries ago, by a Romish priest, in real old English, or seven years ago, in fictitious old English, by a lawyer's clerk, surely, cannot either enhance or diminish its merit, considered merely as a poem. The *furor entheus* is common to all ages, and wherever it exists it produces poetry. The constituents of a poem are, bold images, pathetic sentiment, natural description, and musical language; and with that *furor entheus,* and these constituents, the work in question abounds in an unusual proportion.

This attitude would be summoned by Scott some five years later to defend his own poetry against attacks motivated by his being a Quaker.

One humorous touch about the Chatterton letter is Scott's postscript in which he insisted that his own remarks were original and that he was not being influenced by others. He was ever to be obsessed with the notion that other people considered him a plagiarist, and this accounted for a most unusual appendix to his *Poetical Works* in which he traced his own literary echoes and, in many cases, stated that these were coincidences, he not having read the work in question until his own poem had been written! This was not a unique fear, although it almost became psychotic with Scott. Beattie, too, was terrified by accusations of plagiarism, and to eliminate such charges, he carefully dated all his works. This defense of originality seems to be one of the most amusing aspects of Scott's life, but it was related to his basic concern with ingenuity, which he considered to be one of the greatest virtues in art.

In January, 1778, Beattie was attacked by "Crito" in the *Gentleman's Magazine* for having failed to fulfill his promise and publish his long-awaited continuation of *An Essay on the Nature and Immutability of Truth.* This attack upon Beattie angered Scott, and he dispatched an indignant letter to the

Gentleman's Magazine on March 18, 1778, protesting against this injustice done his friend. In his note, Scott did not presume upon private and personal information as to the Aberdeen philosopher's literary plans; instead he quoted from Beattie's works all those passages which should have explained the delay of *An Essay on the Nature and Immutability of Truth*. Beattie had stated that he had been ill, and Scott referred to page and edition to point out the philosopher's excuses, saying only that

illness I should think a circumstance of sufficient force to absolve any author from a promise which in time of health he might have made to the public. Those who know what writing is, know that some kinds of composition require an application fatiguing to the strongest constitution.[40]

In this letter, Scott asserted that he was Beattie's friend and knew "him to be a truly modest and amiable man," but he did not on the basis of personality alone refute the charge made against Beattie's character. This was probably done because Scott was ever one to look for the facts before he wrote anything, and he was inclined less than were many of his contemporaries to reduce all arguments to the basis of personality where reason was veiled by puffs of emotion. He concluded his letter with the statement, "Who *Crito* really is, notwithstanding he dates from *Hertford-shire,* I do not know, nor even so much as guess." But he obviously cared a great deal, since he was baiting Beattie's accuser to reveal himself; Scott disliked dueling with a shadow.

In the April issue of the same magazine, "Crito"—still retaining his anonymity—replied, saying that he had not seen the quoted passages, otherwise he would not have aroused Scott. Though "Crito" seemed to praise Beattie here, saying that the publication of the work would aid the cause of virtue in a sceptical age, Scott was not sufficiently pleased with the apology and he replied again to "Crito" in the following issue of the magazine, berating him for his rudeness and defending his own affection for the Aberdeen philosopher. He concluded with his major resentment:

I repeat what I before declared, that I know not who Crito is; my proceeding, therefore, cannot possibly be the effect of resentment. I am not angry; but if I was, it could not be at the man, but his conduct. I do not *wish* to know who he is; but as I have now done justice to my friend, I do not think myself obliged to hold altercation with a person who conceals himself under a fictitious name.

This closed the incident, and Beattie later wrote to Scott his gratitude for this defense in his behalf. Some time later, Scott seemed to feel that the author of the attacks on Beattie was also the book reviewer of the *Gentleman's Magazine*. He therefore attributed his own bad critical reception in that periodical to his defense of Beattie; and since he wrote Beattie of these feelings, it seems clear that he also felt Beattie should come to his defense as he had come to Beattie's.[41]

IV

In the May, 1778, issue of the *Monthly Review,* John Langhorne reviewed Scott's revised work on highways, *Digests of the General Highway and Turnpike Laws; with the Schedule of Forms, as Directed by Act of Parliament; and Remarks. Also, an Appendix, on the Construction and Preservation of Roads.* Reviewed also in the September issue of the *Critical Review,* the volume probably appeared in April or May of 1778. The state of English highways had long been a matter of concern to Scott. A conscientious member of the local turnpike and navigation trusts (at the time of writing the 1778 book, he was a trustee of the Cheshunt, Wadesmill, and Watton[42] turnpikes, and he dedicated this volume to his brother trustees), he had been responsible for improving the roads of Hertfordshire: presumably in 1768 he had begun supervising the building of a spacious road between Ware and Hertford, and to this day he is credited with having improved immeasurably the principal streets of Ware.[43] This practical experience had led him in 1773 to write the first of two volumes on highways—the laws relating to them and the methods suggested for their improvement: *A Digest of the Present Act for Amendment of the Highways: With a Calculation of the Duty, Composition, and Contribution for Every Rent from £1 to £400 Per Annum. For the Use of Surveyors, &c. Also a List of Forfeitures and Penalties, with a Schedule of Forms and Remarks.* Evidently this volume consisted of Scott's codification of the highway law and of his remarks on the various sections of the law which he thought needed clarification or improvement.

By 1778, Scott had expanded this into his longest nonliterary work, and it dealt also with the laws relating to turnpikes, which he codified and criticized as to their effectiveness. He also followed a suggestion made in the *Monthly Review* after the publication of the 1773 volume and gave references throughout to the appropriate section of the statute being quoted, so that the reader could refer to the original act if he desired. The principal addition to this volume, however, lay in the appended essay on the construction and preservation of roads. This 1778 volume was widely praised (it was in Langhorne's account of this work that the *Monthly Review* first referred to Scott as a latter-day Man of Ross), and though the *Critical Review* made some thrusts at Scott's taste and character, there was no attempt made to disparage the work. One road commissioner, who claimed that he did not know Scott, was indignant that the volume had not been mentioned in the *Gentleman's Magazine,* and he wrote to the editor of that journal, criticizing him for his inexcusable negligence.[44] Perhaps it was partly this forgetfulness that caused the *Gentleman's Magazine* to devote half of Scott's obituary to a discussion of this one work.

Scott justified his book by the chaotic organization of the

parliamentary acts regarding highways and turnpikes, a confusion which he ordered by placing together all parts of the acts which were treating the same matters. He emphasized throughout the book that when he suggested reforms he was writing from experience and not from unapplied theory; yet Scott in the act itself of compiling a volume of all the extant laws governing highways and turnpikes was doubtless emulating the example of Langhorne's friend, the much-admired Richard Burn. It has been seen how Scott relied upon and praised Burn's *The History of the Poor Laws* and used it as a basic source in his *Observations on the Present State of the Parochial and Vagrant Poor*. Burn had also published *The Justice of the Peace and Parish Officer,* the handbook of every county official, and Scott not only read it but he carefully noted the differences between editions.[45] Being so influenced by Burn's codifications, Scott easily found an inspiration for his work not only in his labors but in his library as well. Although modern scholarship has not always agreed on the value of Scott's highway book,[46] the general reputation of his advocates speaks up strongly for him. Of these, the Webbs have been the most famous, and any revival of interest in Scott's economic tract may well be owing to their writings about him. Ranked by them with Sir Henry Hawkins, Richard Burn, and Arthur Young as one of the four "most eminent observers of, and participators in, the local government of the latter half of the [eighteenth] century,"[47] Scott was also called "the ablest Turnpike Trustee of his time,"[48] "the ablest contemporary road administrator,"[49] and, finally, the "ablest of eighteenth-century writers on Local Government."[50]

By stating that he "did not chuse to incumber ... [his] Text with any thing not clearly and positively *Law,*" and that his volume represented "every Thing that *is now Law* respecting Highways and Turnpikes in general," Scott hoped to establish the definitive edition of a parliamentary statute. His procedure was to divide the book into two main sections: one dealing with the laws governing highways, and one dealing with the laws governing turnpikes. He also appended an essay which gave his own proposals for the correct way to build roads and the necessary legislation to preserve them. Within each of the two main parts, separate chapters were given to such general topics as the method of appointing a surveyor, the jurisdiction to be given to a surveyor, directions for the provision of materials, rules governing statute duty, the punishment of offenders, and the schedules of forms for those taking office or paying assessments or serving their statute duty. Following each of the two sections on legal provisions, however, was an appendix of remarks and observations on parts of the law which to Scott seemed either perplexing or which he felt deserved greater explanation. In this gloss on his text, he pointed out inconsistencies in the law, suggested improvements, and was never reluctant to give his own opinion and to relate his own experience in these matters.

Scott's work, viewed in this light, assumes significance greater than that ordinarily given to a legal codification. It represents a detailed essay on the faults and virtues of a statute that had been produced not without a considerable amount of trouble by a government which was becoming increasingly aware of the problem of bad roads. Scott was not content, however, to let his work exist only for his own time or the needs of the late eighteenth century. Aware as he was of the frequent changes of statutes, the slightest alteration of which would make his volume unreliable and obsolete, he desired for his work a lasting value. This was to be obtained from the permanent significance of his remarks—not on a particular statute but on the follies and foibles of mankind which, presumably, would not be amended so easily as would a parliamentary decision. It is clear that in his tract Scott was always attempting to give his words wit and color and to diffuse through the entire production the cast of his own personality. The *Critical Review* attacked this aspect of the book, saying, "We would only observe that Mr. Scott's performance deserves more praises than what are due to the *pleasantry* of his remarks."[51]

Scott had many criticisms of the 1773 codification—a codification, incidentally, which he felt was not justified, since the old act was frequently superior to the new one—but the one most frequently voiced was a complaint about the obscurity of the statute. That law's vagueness, which often left the most important points in perplexity, seems to have driven Scott frantic with exasperation, and he began by chiding and ended by excoriating the legislators for the obscurity which they wove with apparent delight into their statutes. The writing of every member of parliament was characterized mainly by "an over-scrupulous Adherence to old Forms of Expression," and Scott later in his treatise made a sly thrust at this vice, when he wrote about the proper soil for building roads:

As on all naturally soft or loose Soils the adventitious Materials derive their Power of resisting Pressure from that Compaction which enables them to act like an Arch, and as the Strength of an Arch depends upon the superior Strength of its Abutments, those adventitious Materials should always be extended to such a Width, that, when they are completely cemented, the lateral Parts may be sufficient to enable the central Part to sustain not only its own Weight but whatever incumbent Weight may be superadded. Or, to speak in Words intelligible to every Capacity, the Road should be made wider on wet or loose Soils, than on dry or solid ones.

There were dozens of things in the law which Scott disliked: the law was concerned too frequently with trivialities, and it was often inhuman, as it limited the number of animals which could pull a vehicle. Instead of enforcing too many things, however, the statute of 1773 was more often guilty of letting actual faults go unremedied; there seemed to be a legislative reluctance to change radically any practice which had the sanction of antiquity. As for Scott, his opinion of his forebearers varied, depending upon which of their practices he was discussing. He felt the traditional treatment of Quakers reflected only "the illiberal Principles and Practices of our narrow-spirited Ancestors,"[52] and our ancestors were content to endure roads, no matter how bad they might be, rather than to effect a sound policy of improvement: but he was not consistently opposed to ancestral customs and attitudes. He said that watering roads had never been an Elizabethan practice—despite contemporary opinion which believed that it was—and he was determined to show, in this case at least, that the sixteenth-century Englishman was wiser than the eighteenth-century one. His most temperate criticism of ancestral practices was reflected in his observation, "The Antiquity of an Expedient, which, on Trial, is found not to answer the End it was designed for, cannot be a good Reason for persisting in the Practice of it." Though he had once been willing to attribute to ancestral character a benevolence lacking in that of his contemporaries, he was seldom willing to accept unquestioningly older engineering practices. What is most curious in this light is that when he proposed his own system for establishing roads, he seems unaware that he was only restoring what was the most ancestral of road-building practices—that of the Romans.

The statute also failed to prohibit narrow wheels and to provide authority for cutting down trees which overhung the road, trees which provided shelter for highwaymen and kept the roads damp and narrow. Scott opposed farming out roads in the same way he had opposed farming out the poor, calling it "that most pernicious Practice."

The Trustees, when once a Road is *farmed,* have nothing to do, but meet once a Year to eat Venison, and pay the *Farmer* his Annuity: the *Farmer* has nothing to do, but to do as little Work, and pocket as much Money as he possibly can; he has other *Fish to fry,* other Mat-

ters to mind, than *Road-mending:* Incroachment after Incroachment
takes place, the Hedges and the Trees grow till they meet overhead,
the Landholders are excused from their Statute-duty, and the Water
and the narrow-wheeled Waggons complete the Business. At length,
perhaps, the universal Complaint of Travellers, or Menaces of In-
dictment, rouse the Trustees for a Moment; a Meeting is called, the
Farmer sent for and reprimanded, and a few Loads of Gravel buried
among the Mud, serve to keep the Way barely passable.

The surveyor, who was the most important man in the eighteenth-century road program, was given certain specified powers
which, Scott felt, were too limited by the 1773 codification: after
all, Scott said, if the man was of good character, all of those
legally imposed restrictions were unnecessary; and if he was
not of good character, he should not have been appointed a surveyor in the first place. In the same way he had urged a universal
poor tax which would eliminate the local financial problems,
Scott urged that there be instituted a general and universal
assessment on occupation. Parliament should levy a tax of so
much on the pound for roads, in the same manner the land tax
was raised. One of the biggest problems in the construction of
new roads or the widening of old ones was getting land away
from farmers who refused to part with it. To deal with reluctant
landowners, Scott wanted the power of public domain; the land
would then be appraised in value by an impartial source and then
condemned.[53] Only this could straighten out the roads in England, which, in their existing labyrinthine state, wound around
so many farms and trees and barns that distances were often
twice as great as they needed to be. It was not without bitterness
that Scott attacked selfish landowners who, by refusing to sell
some of their land, prevented the roads from being widened. It
was from his experience with this difficulty that Scott coined his
traveler's maxim: if you wish to know where there are people of
importance, find a narrow stretch of road, as people of influence
must hold the land on both sides! Because there was no law

impowering the trustees to take over land, only gentle persuasion could possibly win what the law could not.

It was in his appendix, however, that Scott presented his theory of the proper way to build roads. On his lengthy journey through Scotland, England, and Wales, Matt Bramble had found the ideal streets to be in Glasgow where they "are straight, open, airy, and well paved."[54] Scott's definition of the perfect thoroughfare called for a generous width, freedom from water, and a slightly convex surface as well; such a road would also be well marked with signposts and fences. The most common plan for a road was to give it a regular horizontal surface, terminated on each side by a ditch or embankment. Scott objected to such a plan, saying that there was great danger of falling into the ditch; such roads in the wintertime, particularly, were treacherous with ice, since there was no way for the water to drain off. A rarer type of road—but a type equally objectionable—was the angular one, which had one side of the road lower than the other, and at the low side a ditch for the water to drain into. Such a road was particularly bad because there was always a danger of the carriage's overturning. The concave-surface road was also objectionable, because rushing water turned the pavement into a ditch and made the road a watercourse. To be sure, where there was considerable fall, this road was not muddy, but it was always sandy and disagreeable to the traveler, since farmers were inclined to use it for a drainage ditch. A fourth kind of road had a waved surface and steep sides, and was usually built about four or five feet above the level of the ground. It waved longitudinally on the notion that such a design would make the moisture evaporate quickly; Scott called this type of road absurd and nonsensical, and he was advocating the changing of such a surface in the south end of Watton Town and on that part of the Watton turnpike between Ware and Westmill in Hertfordshire. As Scott pointed out, such a waved surface really did not disperse the water more quickly but only gathered it in the valleys of the road.

The fifth kind of surface, the convex one, was that kind particularly advocated by Scott. This, though he did not discuss it as such, was the Roman pattern of road. The universal recommendation was to have the center of such a road two feet higher than the edges. Scott urged that small aqueducts be built under the road to drain off the water in the ditches, and where the road ran down hill, he would have the degree of convexity increased so that the water would drain off to the side immediately, instead of running down the hill and creating a waved or hollow road. Water was the greatest menace to the road, and when it was not immediately drained off, it created bogs and impassable ruts. One intrepid traveler, Arthur Young, tells of meeting with ruts four feet deep in one road which floated with mud during the summer. It was not without some small degree of concern that he puzzled how the natives got through in the wintertime. On a jaunt of eighteen summer-swept miles, he met with three carts which had been given up to the terrors of the road.[55] Scott also insisted on wide roads and smooth thoroughfares, and he considered the best available materials for building roads were ballast, chalk, and burnt clay.

For Scott, the corrupt state of the roads was but a reflection of the basic corruption of the legislature. Human nature, whether conditioned by environment or created by God, was the villain, and humanity was the victim; mankind was obviously lazy. "Everybody's business is nobody's business"—this, the most frequently quoted expression in Scott's writing, is found here in the highway tract.[56] There was a "general Aversion to improving Roads," and more than one commentator had become alarmed at the indolence of the public. It was not by accident that Scott listed spirit as being as necessary as judgment in a person if he were going to build successful roads. In making the distinction between the spirited gentleman and the rest of mankind, Scott was refining his notions of class supremacy, made some years earlier. He was not prepared to say that all gentlemen were completely virtuous—he still found some of them wasteful in their pursuits—but he did feel that the lower classes were generally uninterested in helping anyone except themselves, and he strongly opposed a law which could make the gentleman the assistant surveyor when the surveyor could be a member of the lower classes. He looked to the gentry for improvements in the conditions of roads.[57] And although the surveyor was to be made independent of the vestry, he would still remain under the supervision of the trustees, who were also his social superiors.

Although Scott intensely disliked wagoners and hackney coachmen—he found them insolent, arrogant, and peculiarly addicted to maltreating the animals they drove—his main enemy among the middle or lower classes was the farmer, whom he invariably regarded as grasping, penurious, and avaricious. To prevent a tavern keeper from being a trustee, was, to him, ridiculous; it would have been far better to have disqualified the farmer, a person of confined ideas, who viewed "with the same unfeeling Eye, the sufferings of unhappy Paupers and unhappy Animals." Scott's assailing the farmers would have been supported by his friend Johnson, who agreed that they were often worthless.[58] These changes in class attitude reaffirm that as Scott grew older, he took on many of the aristocratic assumptions that as a youth he had despised. Jane Austen would have soon squashed Scott's new notions, as she attacked Charles Bingley's sisters: "They were of a respectable family in the north of England; a circumstance more deeply impressed on their memories than that their brother's fortune and their own had been acquired by trade."[59]

When Scott traveled through England, he always directed a scientific inquisitiveness toward the state and condition of the

local roads; and like many another traveler, he had listed in his
work those roads which he had found deplorable. Scott said he
had "travelled several Hundred Miles in distant Parts of this
Nation," but his travels were never as extensive as Arthur
Young's. The roughly rectangular area enclosed by boundary
lines drawn from Harwich to Bedford to Bath to Brighton,
would represent the major region of his explorations. Wherever
he went, however, the minds of the road builder and traveler
were merged into one, and the experiences obtained abroad were
to produce in the study suggestions for a change at home.

In his 1773 work on poor relief, Scott had briefly mentioned
the condition of the roads and had suggested that roads between
the country and city served to the disadvantage and draining of
the country. This idea was later consciously ignored by him (except in his poetry), for when he wrote his book on highways he
wrote under the assumption that a good road was of necessity
a blessing to the nation. Seeing the print of a wagon wheel in the
road made him think of the finer side of English life, and he
could easily have sympathized with the feelings which Johnson
had had on seeing again this sign of civilization after his journey
to the Hebrides.[60] That his recommended pattern of the convex-
surface road, with its smoothness, permanence, and arrow-
straight length, should also have been the Roman ideal, may not
have occurred to Scott. For though he praised the Romans for
their aqueducts and canals, he did not mention them as being the
first great road builders of Britain. Yet, possessing the same assumptions as did the antique Roman, he was to evolve basically
the same program. The style of carriages might change, but the
road which supported them best had existed in Britain for hun-
dreds of years; and in the end, Scott was to give his society a
foundation of permanence by imitating that first ancestral plan
which remained the best of all proposed systems.

CHAPTER V

THE CONFIDENT POET

I

SOMETIME EARLY in 1778, Scott apparently began making plans to have his collected poems published in one volume, and he started getting his various works together with a view toward revising them. Feeling that "Detached Pamphlets be their Merit ever so Great are too often Neglected and forgotten after the first Attention to them is over,"[1] he was determined that his works should appear within boards. Though he had been writing poems since his late teens, he was reluctant to publish everything that he had written; yet, there was scarcely enough already composed to make a very large volume. In 1778, therefore, he began working again on some eclogues—presumably these were the poems of 1755 which had been criticized by Cockfield in 1767—which he hoped would constitute a major contribution to his volume. Believing, however, that the critics of both the *Critical Review* and the *Gentleman's Magazine* would "pick any hole they can in any Piece they know to be written by me,"[2] he wished to elude their scorn by a trick of publication. He would publish the eclogues under the title of *Moral Eclogues* ("I like short titles, I think them most modest or unassuming"),[3] and they would appear anonymously. The merit of them would be noticed, he hoped, and then after the reviewers had committed themselves to a good opinion of this production, he would reprint them the following spring (1779) in his *Poetical Works,* and they would be acknowledged as his. By having, therefore, poems in the volume which would have met with the praise of the critics, Scott hoped to ensure a kinder

[1] For notes to chap. v, see p. 215.

reception for the entire production. But if his plan was to be successful, he must first gain a satisfactory reception for *Moral Eclogues*.

To receive a critical appraisal of these poems before he sent them to the press, Scott, early in September, 1778, sent the third eclogue to Beattie and asked him for a criticism of it. There was some delay in receiving an answer, and Scott, anxious to get the eclogues out in the fall, wrote again to Beattie on October 24, 1778. In this letter, we learn that Scott had written five eclogues but had resolved on publishing only four. (We never know what happened to the other one, since it did not appear in the *Poetical Works*.) Like Johnson, Scott liked a Latin motto for the title page, and he was having some difficulty in finding one which was not "too common or at least too obvious." Beattie evidently replied with haste, sending a Latin motto (perhaps he sent two, because there are two on the title page of the quarto),* and the poems were quickly published and appeared in time to be reviewed in the December, 1778, issue of the *Critical Review*. Beattie highly approved of the eclogue "Armyn," which he had seen in manuscript, and he wrote to Scott:

> I am astonished, my dear Sir, at the activity of your mind, and the versatility of your genius. It is truly amazing that one and the same person should, in one and the same year, publish the most elegant poems, and, A DIGEST OF THE LAWS RELATING TO HIGH-WAYS. Go on, Sir, in your laudable resolution of delighting and instructing mankind; of patronising the poor; and promoting the publick weal.

Beattie's genuine interest in Scott and Scott's productions, however, was not uncoupled with a continual amazement at, and delight in, the rather curious aspects of Scott's manner of living. This was at a time when being "one of the people called Quakers" was enough to attract attention in polite society, and Scott was even more perplexing by being an eccentric among eccentrics and not being the true embodiment of Quaker thought, strictness, and solemnity. As Beattie wrote to the Duchess of Gordon on July 5, 1779:

BY the first convenient opportunity I hope to send your Grace a sort of curiosity,—four elegant Pastorals, by a Quaker;—not one of our Quakers of Scotland, but a true English Quaker, who says *thee* and *thou,* and comes into a room, and sits down in company, without taking off his hat. For all this, he is a very worthy man, an elegant scholar, a cheerful companion, and a particular friend of mine. His name is John Scott, of Amwell, near Ware, Hertfordshire, where he lives in an elegant retirement (for his fortune is very good); and has dug, in a chalkhill near his house, one of the most curious grottos I have ever seen. As it is only twenty miles from London, I would recommend it to your Grace, when you are there, as worth going to visit. Your Grace will be pleased with his Pastorals, not only on account of their morality and sweet versification, but also for their images and descriptions, which are a very exact picture of the groves, woods, waters, and windmills, of that part of England where he resides.[5]

Beattie, too, must have suffered from eye trouble: "very exact picture"? "Very idealized picture" would have been more accurate a description of these typically middle eighteenth-century notions of rural beauty. Shortly afterward, Beattie wrote to a friend that he had sent the Duchess of Gordon a copy of *Moral Eclogues,* and she had liked them very much.[6] The *Critical Review* stated that the poems were not filled with original sentiments but were, nevertheless, agreeable, tender, and pathetic. George Colman, in the *Monthly Review,* pointed out some slight faults of the poems—an occasional jumbling of accents and harmony—but praised the style and imagery. The *Gentleman's Magazine* merely announced that the poems had been printed, gave the individual titles of them, and quoted sixteen lines from the third eclogue. Such reviews would hardly ensure a favorable critical reception for a volume of poems, and the *Poetical Works* was postponed for three more years.

When Scott reprinted his *Moral Eclogues* in the *Poetical Works,* he prefaced them with the following statement:

The most rational definition of Pastoral Poetry seems to be that of the learned and ingenious Dr. JOHNSON, in the 37th Number of his RAMBLER. "Pastoral," says he, "being the representation of an Action or Passion, by its effects on a Country Life, has nothing peculiar, but its confinement to Rural Imagery, without which it ceases to be Pastoral." This Theory the Author of the following Eclogues has endeavoured to exemplify.

Johnson's essay had specifically attacked the pastoral notion of the Golden Age, and Scott seems to have neglected this criticism, since his shepherds are golden and ageless and quite improbable. Reading Warton, too, should have warned him of this error, since that writer had also emphasized "THAT the design of pastoral poesy is, to represent the undisturbed felicity of the golden age, is an empty notion."[7] Scott's poems, written in heroic couplets, were, in subject matter and language, quite similar to the *Four Elegies* of 1760. There was not the expected cycle here of one poem for each season in the year (since the second and third eclogues dealt with summer, and there was no eclogue for winter); still there was an over-all unity in the temporal plan. The first eclogue, "Theron; or, the Praise of Rural Life," occurred in the morning; the second, "Palemon; or, Benevolence," took place at forenoon; the third, "Armyn; or, the Discontented," occupied the afternoon; and the fourth, "Lycoron; or, the Unhappy," drew out the evening. Beattie's favorite was the third of these, and a brief investigation of it will reveal the typical qualities of these poems.

> Summer o'er heav'n diffus'd serenest blue,
> And painted earth with many a pleasing hue;
> When ARMYN mus'd the vacant hour away,
> Where willows o'er him wav'd their pendent spray.
> Cool was the shade, and cool the passing gale,
> And sweet the prospect of the adjacent vale:

> The fertile soil, profuse of plants, bestow'd
> The crowfoot's gold, the trefoil's purple show'd,
> And spiky mint rich fragrance breathing round,
> And meadsweet tall with tufts of flowrets crown'd,
> And comfry white, and hoary silver-weed,
> The bending osier, and the rustling reed.

After an opening description, there was a soliloquy in which Armyn lamented his unhappy state. Albino, however, was nearby, and he counseled the distressed with the shopworn theory that man should draw joy from past pleasures and from the knowledge that thousands of others also share his present discomfort and misfortune, which was caused merely by his having seen and done everything in life and having little left to do— a precursor of Scott Fitzgerald's notions of emotional bankruptcy.

> The soft reproach touch'd ARMYN's gentle breast;
> His alter'd brow a placid smile exprest.
> "Calm as clear ev'nings after vernal rains,
> When all the air a rich perfume retains,
> My mind," said he, "its murmurs driv'n away,
> Feels Truth's full force, and bows to Reason's sway!"
> He ceas'd: the sun, with horizontal beams,
> Gilt the green mountains, and the glittering streams,
> Slow down the tide before the sinking breeze,
> ALBINO's white sail gleam'd among the trees;
> Slow down the tide his winding course he bore
> To watry Talgar's aspin-shaded shore.
> Slow cross the valley, to the southern hill,
> The steps of ARMYN sought the distant vill,
> Where thro' tall elms the moss-grown turret rose;
> And his fair mansion offer'd sweet repose.

Although this resolution and conclusion seems in the vein of those of the *Four Elegies*—certainly, there was no profundity of thought in any of them—these poems differed from their earlier counterparts. In *Moral Eclogues,* Scott was moving toward some

particular notions about natural description. Scenes themselves
would seem to be vaguely defined, but the constituent elements
of those scenes would be related with a new particularity. The
catalogue of flowers in these poems was an indication of a poetical trend which was given its clearest demonstration in the
"Amoebaean Eclogues" of the *Poetical Works*. Although the
catalogue of flowers doubtless was influenced by *Lycidas,* it was
a product of Scott's attempt to create new images and to introduce into poetry those natural phenomena which had never
before been put into verse. A new image would give a new sensation of pleasure, and it was in the creation of that sensation that
poetry was largely justified. He did not ignore the other part of
the classical theory, however, and his *Moral Eclogues* was, as
indicated by its title, to inculcate certain virtues. Of all of Scott's
poetry, that written for *Moral Eclogues* is perhaps most obviously
a musing with a message.

II

Between the appearance of *Moral Eclogues,* late in 1778, and
Beattie's visit to Amwell on April 20, 1781, nothing is known of
Scott's activities. Designed to appear in 1779, the *Poetical Works*
was delayed three years for reasons never explained. A log of
visitors to Scott's grotto exists for this period of time,[8] however,
the first entry being made May 17, 1779 and the last, August 8,
1786, and there is no suggestion in it that Scott's life had changed
its pattern in any appreciable manner. He was still playing the
benevolent lord with enthusiasm. During this period, nearly
three thousand people signed the register. On September 10,
1779, George De Horne and his family from Stanway Hall,
Essex, toured the grotto; Charles Dilly, Scott's London publisher, went through the chambers on May 7, 1780. Samuel Scott
signed the book for the first time on July 16, 1781, but thereafter
he made frequent visits to the grotto, sometimes in the company

of his wife, Mary, but more frequently alone. He signed the log eleven times before his brother died, and fourteen times after. His final visit was paid July 19, 1786, when he added a brief note to the ordinary listing of his name: "Samuel Scott of Hertford visited these Plantations of his late celebrated Brother J. Scott on the 19th of the Seventh Month in the Year 1786—Perhaps the last Time—His wife M. Scott & his Neice Maria De Horne Scott were also here the Same Afternoon—He had been previously entertained & edified in the Perusal of some just & noble Sentiments contain'd in the Poems of William Cowper of Lincolns Inn Esq." How like Samuel unto the last: full of conscious piety and sentiments, and even a mute log for visitors became a place for pious thoughts and pedantry. Scott's grotto had become a favorite visiting spot for Londoners in this period, and one anonymous poet (later revealed as Ald. E. Ind of Cambridge)[9] about the first of April, 1780, wrote in the log ("...an album, in which the visiting moralist was requested to deposit his sentiment, and the poet his couplet"):[10]

> Great Bard! delighted as I oft have been
>   With Amwel's beauties and thy Themes of love,
> Unknown to fame, by every eye unseen,
>   I come to pay thee honour in thy grove.
> And, oh! wherein I turn my raptur'd eye,
>   Whate'er of nature & of art I see,
> I pause, & lost in admiration cry—
>   Worthy the muse and elegance & thee!

Outside of that curiously ambiguous third verse, the poem must have been regarded without suspicion.

Nothing is known of the events of Beattie's brief visit with Scott at Amwell on April 20, 1781, except that Beattie and his son Jamie arrived there on that day and departed the next, reaching London about two o'clock in the afternoon.[11] On this visit, Beattie pleased Scott by announcing that the Duchess of Gordon planned to visit him, his gardens, and the grotto on her next visit to London.[12] But as for Beattie and his son, they either did not tour the grotto or else they failed to sign the register.

About Christmas of 1781, Hoole introduced Scott to the Wartons, whose critical and poetical abilities the Amwell poet had long admired. He had looked forward with anticipation to the second volume of Joseph Warton's *Essay on the Genius and Writings of Pope,* since he had "always thought [the first volume] a judicious and elegant Piece of Criticism."[13] Both Scott and the Wartons were apparently pleased with their first meeting, but they never happened to see each other again. (Joseph especially was struck with "the unaffected frankness and amiable simplicity that appeared in the conversation" of Scott.) Although Scott may not have seen the Wartons personally again, he certainly studied Joseph Warton's thoughts on Pope which were a major influence on his own *Critical Essays* two years later.

III

On January 25, 1782, Scott wrote from Amwell to Beattie and reported on the progress he had been making in the *Poetical Works* which, although announced some years earlier as being in an advanced state of preparation, had still failed to appear. What had happened was that Scott would write a few poems, would have them printed, and then would write a few more. His odes particularly were done in this manner: "As my Friend seemed to like my *Odes* and I thought that species of Writing had fewer Pieces of Merit to boast than most others; it encouragd me to proceed, and I have done much more than I expected or indeed proposed to do."[14] Thus, the *Poetical Works* does not constitute the work of a short period or even a collection of work done earlier; it represents the slow and rather constant printing of things over a period of years, the collected sheets finally being bound together and published when the author was satisfied

with the total compilation. It was a slow process, but Scott felt
no compulsion to publish before he was ready. He did most of
his writing late at night, after the family had retired, "and it was
frequently his custom to sit in a dark room, and when he had
composed a number of lines, he would go into another room
where a candle was burning, in order to commit them to paper.
Though in general very regular in his hour of retiring to rest, he
would sometimes be up great part of the night, when he was
engaged in any literary work." "Summer is a Season in which
I cannot write nor indeed hardly revise and correct," Scott said
of himself. "With Inspiring *Autumn* (as Thomson if I recollect
right calls it) the Muse returned and I resumed my task of preparing for Publication."[15] Dr. Johnson would have been incensed
had he seen this statement in Scott's letter to Beattie, for he held
no brief with the climatic theory.[16] Only a person of independent
means, of course, could write when the weather suited his poetic
fancy, and Johnson was never given this leisure. Scott was
Milton's disciple, and not Johnson's, and he was being independent like his master when he said that summer was no time to
compose poetry.

As fast as Scott printed some poems, he sent them in sheets to
Beattie for criticism and approval, and in this January letter, he
included his ode on Chatterton, which had just been printed and
evidently was one of Scott's most recent compositions. He had
no sooner finished the poem than Bryant's book on the controversy was published, and, startled that Chatterton's claim to
fame might be disproved, Scott hastily sent for the volume;
"...but when I had read it I was very Easy as many of the
Arguments Adduced to prove that Chatterton *did not write* the
Poems only tended to convince me that he *did*."[17] On March 30,
1782, Scott wrote from London to Beattie that the entire
volume—with the exception of one sheet—had been printed, and
he hoped to have the book put out sometime in April. "We have

had few Publications this Season Especially in the Poetical
Way—perhaps it may be the better for me I shall stand more
alone."

On May 10, 1782, news came from Scott to Beattie that at last
the work was completed, and now Scott was entering into a
second state of anticipation: the work having been done to the
best of his poetic ability, he was now ready to receive critical
reaction to his project and to defend his labors. He was particularly apprehensive about the "Essay on Painting," on which,
together with his "Oriental Eclogues" and his "Mexican Prophecy," he felt his reputation and rank as a poet would depend.
This letter is interesting as it deals with Scott's intention in his
poems, and it needs to be discussed with the works themselves.
The letter is also important for containing the genesis of Scott's
last literary endeavor, the *Critical Essays* which appeared after
his death.

Did I ever mention Dr. Johnson's prefaces? My friend has doubtless seen that fund of entertainment and information; of striking observations, and useful reflections; of good sense, and of illiberal prejudices; of just and of unjust criticism. That a mind, so enlarged as
Johnson's, in some respects, should be so confined in others, is amazing. The titled scribblers of the last century; the prosaic Denham, the
inane and quaint Yalden, and even the Grub-street Pomfret, meet
with all possible favour.... Dyer, Shenstone, Collins, Akenside, and
Gray, are the authors whom I most regret as sufferers by Johnson's
unjust censure.[18]

But despite this criticism of Johnson's *Lives of the Poets,* Scott
still had a deep affection and respect for the man. Eight days
after writing this letter, we find him presenting a copy of the
Poetical Works to his old acquaintance, who inscribed it: "This
book I received from the Authour. May 18. 1782 Sam: Johnson."[19]
One cannot help wondering if Johnson ever read these poems,
however. People frequently presented him with books, and his
library numbered nearly five thousand volumes. And Johnson's

own comment on the matter cannot be ignored: "People seldom read a book which is given to them; and few are given."[20]

Another source of concern to Scott was the choice and use of engravings in his *Poetical Works*. With the exception of *Moral Eclogues,* each of his earlier poetical productions had contained an appropriate engraving on the title page, and in the reprinting of these poems in the *Poetical Works,* many of these engravings were also reproduced. However, the *Poetical Works* was to be a lavish volume, and fourteen engravings were included throughout its pages, including four made by the twenty-four-year-old William Blake.

With regard to the Decorations, judging by myself for I am always pleased with the Pictures of Persons and Places and of ideal Scenes. I was easily perswaded by my Friend and my Bookseller to procure a number of Elegant Engravings which I thought in conjunction with the Poetry would effect my Design of giving to the Publick a Rational and Inoffensive Amusement, in which (what can be said of the works of too few Poets) *Taste* might be gratified without the Contamination of Morals. Some of the Engravings are not quite what I could wish; My own Portrait in particular though executed by the Most Eminent Artist in that Line, might have been better, it conveys the idea of a lustier heavier person.[21]

Well might Scott think with alarm about the engravings. Although the *London Chronicle,* in its highly complimentary review of the volume,[22] singled out the "beautiful copper-plates" for praise, within a matter of weeks Scott's position as a poet was being challenged, his volume of poems was being derided, and his choice of engravings in particular was being ridiculed in the pages of the *Critical Review.*

THESE poems are written by a *quaker;* a circumstance rather extraordinary in the world of letters, rhyming being a sin which gentlemen of that fraternity are seldom guilty of: Mr. Scott is, notwithstanding, strongly attached to it; and having received some flattering applause on his former productions, that were not unsuccessful, has made some considerable additions to them, which, he hopes, "are not of inferior merit." With the author's opinion, in this respect, we cannot entirely coincide, as we do not think the greater part of the additional pieces now before us equal to what he before published. Amwell, a descriptive poem, the Elegy written in 1768, with some others, had their share of poetical merit: the Amoebaean, and Oriental Eclogues, Odes, Epistles, &c. now added, are of a much weaker feature, and many of them incorrect; but they were necessary, we suppose, towards making up a volume, that trophied pillar consecrated to vanity, which every author erects with so much pleasure, and contemplates, when raised, with so much satisfaction: this noble structure our poet has adorned with a variety of head and tail-pieces, executed in a good style, by some of our most ingenious engravers. Mr. Scott has at least, we must acknowledge, spared no pains to decorate his work with all that can allure the eye, or gratify the taste of a dilettante reader, who loves to see the sister arts uniting to render a neat page truly delectable, as our author sings.

"Nor less than books th' engravers works invite,
    Where past and distant comes before the sight."

To say the truth, there is a profusion of ornament and finery about this book, not quite suitable to the plainness and simplicity of the *Barclean system;* but Mr. Scott is fond of the Muses, and wishes, we suppose, like captain Macheath, to see his ladies well dressed.[23]

When these remarks were coupled with others which suggested that, since an essay on painting had already been done in verse by Hayley, Scott might have spared himself the trouble of making a duplicate which was only inferior to the original, Scott had been attacked where he most feared an assault. The review concluded, "This volume of poems is, upon the whole, an amusing and agreeable collection," but Scott was outraged at what he felt was the injustice done him. Unlike Johnson, who suppressed his rage at what the critics said of him and pronounced on one occasion, "...depend upon it, no man was ever written down but by himself,"[24] Scott felt compelled to answer this attack. He called it a "curious portrait of me and my Performance, a picture obviously designed by Malevolence, and executed by Absurdity."[25] He was particularly indignant because he had sent the *Critical Review* a copy of the volume, "to try the effect of civility," and he was convinced that their early unfavorable review would kill off any prospective readers of his poetry. He had never recovered from his anger at the initial injury done him when *Amwell* appeared: "Of this Amwell, on its first publication, you gave but a superficial account in your Monthly Catalogue; that rear post of your Journal, which is often occupied by no very creditable productions."[26] Against the wishes of his friends, he fired off a lengthy letter on August 6, 1782, to the *British Magazine and Review,* in which he discussed the attack of the *Critical Review*. On November 26, 1782, he wrote a still longer letter to the *European Magazine,* discussing their review of his poems and defending himself against their accusations; in that letter he also announced the publication of his lengthy answer to the *Critical Review: A Letter to the Critical Reviewers: Occasioned by Their Account of Scott's Poetical Works, in Their Review for July 1782.* Whereas Churchill, who also had been criticized on religious grounds, had answered the *Critical Review*'s attacks on him with his satirical *Apology,* written in heroic couplets, Scott relied on an essay with a reasoned argument where logic, he hoped, would carry the day for him.

It has been the fashion among Scott's biographers to deplore this tract, because its critical nature and defense of his own poetry make the author appear egotistical and hardly the benevolent man of feeling he was supposed to have been. Actually we are fortunate that Scott had enough conviction in himself to defend his own writings. For quite aside from the unfortunate light it may throw on Scott's personality (and this is rather a minor quibble, because if a poet regards his craft seriously—and Scott did—how is he to defend himself unless he speaks in his own behalf?), the document is especially significant in revealing Scott's theories of poetic composition and his purpose in constructing his poetical works. Viewed in this light, this pamphlet becomes not the most unfortunate of Scott's productions: it may well be one of the most significant.

An analysis of the critical principles discussed in this pamphlet must await treatment in a consideration of Scott's critical works, but something should be said here of the biographical interest of the pamphlet, as it shows Scott embroiled in the war of the literary reviews. The *Gentleman's Magazine* and the *European Magazine* were to have important meaning for different phases of Scott's career; his principal critical concern, however, was with the *Monthly Review* and the *Critical Review.*[27] The *Monthly Review* took notice of Scott's first publication, the *Four Elegies* of 1760, and, without exception, reviewed every subsequent production of his, whether acknowledged or anonymous; they even reviewed the elegy of 1768 which was printed privately and never published for sale. Invariably these reviews were favorable—often they were filled with magnificent praise— though on occasion the reviewer did not hesitate to point out minor flaws in Scott's productions, and Scott often accepted these suggestions in his revisions of the poems. The tenor of the reviews was always kind—doubtless because frequently the reviewers were friends of the poet—and Scott seems to have appreciated the attention he received from this journal which, being Whig, was naturally sympathetic to his own philosophical position.[28]

The *Critical Review,* however, was never so temperate. Although it conceded praise for many of Scott's efforts, it emphasized the faults and always phrased its remarks so as to suggest that the fault of the writing reflected a fault in Scott's own character. Since the journal reviewed all of Scott's works, with the exception of the *Four Elegies* of 1760 and the elegy of 1768, this criticism could not but affect the poet's audience. And since the critical attacks never revealed a political motivation, it was possible that many should mistake Tory vituperation for critical sagacity. When the review of his *Poetical Works* appeared, Scott realized this critical procedure, and he berated it.

I do not recollect it usual with you, in your account of Books, to mention whether they are written by a Churchman, or a Presbyterian, or an Independent: why then this officious information, that mine is written by a Quaker? But you doubtless supposed the appellation (though perhaps erroneously) a stigma or disgrace, and of course you must affix it. To mention any man's religion with a sneer, is inconsistent with the character of gentlemen; and it is certainly extrajudicial; a man's religion can have no business with the merit or demerit of his literary compositions.... Your scurrilous allusion to the hero of the Beggar's Opera, if shame has not totally deserted your bosoms, you will, on reflection, be ashamed of. Whatever resemblance my character may bear to that of a highwayman, your attempts to deprive a Writer of his justly-acquired reputation, must place you more on a parallel with one of that *respectable* profession.[29]

After Scott's death, Isaac Disraeli wrote an account of this review and the man who had made it;[30] it appears that Scott had been the victim of a dull hack reviewer who really had meant little harm by his observations. His comparing Scott with Captain Macheath was supposed to have been the only humorous sally he made in his lifetime, and long after this poetical controversy had been forgotten, he would still allude to his remarks with pleasure, "as an evidence of the felicity of his fancy, and the keenness of his satire." His main interest in criticizing poetry was to detect false rhymes; his main critical device, "to employ indefinite terms, which, as they had no precise meaning, were applicable to all things." He appeared to have no critical sagacity at all, and his usual fortune was to single out those lines as bad or awkward which invariably proved to be the favorite of the poet and his audience. Scott's refutation of this criticism, which took the form of a detailed analysis of the critical remarks and a demonstration of the contradictions in them, seems to have had no effect merely because all readers agreed with Johnson that "every man is of importance to himself, and therefore, in his own opinion, to others, and, supposing the world already acquainted with all his pleasures and all his pains, is perhaps the first to publish injuries or misfortunes which had never been known unless related by himself, and at which those that hear them will only laugh; for no man sympathises with the sorrows of vanity."[31] The tireless defense of his own name and reputation became tiresome to many: Scott replied in a newspaper article to the short notice in the January, 1783, *Critical Review* which his own pamphlet answer to the original review had evoked, but a journal as favorable as the *British Magazine and Review* dismissed his pamphlet answer with the observation, "This subject has been sufficiently discussed...."[32] After Scott's death, the *Critical Review* reviewed the posthumously published *Critical Essays,* in which it spoke with high praise of Scott's character and regretted its past difficulties with him, though it carefully pointed out that it had not changed its opinion of his poetry as poetry: "The limae labor & mora seem to have destroyed each characteristic relief, the glowing thought, and the ardent language of the heart."[33]

In August, 1782, the *British Magazine and Review* and, in September, both the *Monthly Review* and the *European Magazine* reviewed Scott's *Poetical Works.* The *British Magazine and Review* acclaimed Scott's volume, finding no fault in it at all: "... it is impossible to read a single piece contained in it, without receiving amusement, instruction, or edification." This journal doubtless won Scott's favor most by their suggestion that he write a lengthy didactic poem on painting, as he seemed to possess all the requirements necessary to do so; as it was, the "Essay on Painting" was, in some respects, compared with Dryden's melodious versification and bold and striking thoughts; it was regarded as having little in common with Hayley's work and was an original contribution to the subject. As usual, the

Monthly Review (Edmund Cartwright, who was Langhorne's old protégé, wrote the account) was favorable to Scott's production, although it did admit that Scott in the "Oriental Eclogues" "has not wholly escaped the impropriety of sometimes blending European with Asiatic ideas, [but] he has, however, other beauties that will more than atone for what, perhaps, in an Englishman might be unavoidable." This particular review also paid Scott what many must have thought the most flattering of all compliments by complaining that the translation of the eighth Psalm, which had been appended to Scott's first production, the *Four Elegies* of 1760, had been omitted from the collected poems. Such enthusiastic appreciation of his poetry was to be a rare thing; in the reviewer of this journal, he for once had gotten the devoted reader he had sought unsuccessfully for so long. And since the reviewer did not know of Scott's attitudes toward religious poetry (attitudes which made him suppress the psalm), the poet could hardly have been upset by a request which he still would not grant.

The review which appeared in the *European Magazine* was more generalized, and though it did not say much about the poetry, it is significant for giving the only account of Scott's life which Scott himself later approved of as accurate. The review itself consisted of generalized observations, the sort which Scott particularly detested in criticism.

To a great majority of readers his poetical works will afford a liberal, and even an elegant entertainment. They breathe a spirit of tenderness and philanthropy, and display an amiable and virtuous mind. With regard to poetical enthusiasm, they are imperfect; and the author does not rank in the higher classes of our Poets. He is more ingenious than animated, and more diffuse than correct.

Scott admitted that the memoirs were "expressed in a liberal and courteous manner,"[34] but there was little else in the review that was; in his rebuttal to this criticism, he tried to define the critical terms that had been used against him and then to defend himself by showing how inaccurate and unwarranted he felt the attack was.[35]

IV

Besides containing the poems which have already been discussed in this study, Scott's *Poetical Works* included two "Amoebaean Eclogues," three "Oriental Eclogues," two epistles, an "Essay on Painting" and twenty-eight odes, plus a handful of miscellaneous shorter works. Of the two "Amoebaean Eclogues," "Rural Scenery; or, The Describers," and "Rural Business; or, The Agriculturists," Scott wrote:

> Much of the Rural Imagery which our Country affords, has already been introduced in Poetry; but many obvious and pleasing appearances seem to have totally escaped notice. To describe these, is the business of the following Eclogues. The plan of the CARMEN AMOEBAEUM, or Responsive Verse of the Antients, inconsistent as it may be deemed with modern manners, was preferred on this occasion, as admitting an arbitrary and desultory disposition of ideas, where it was found difficult to preserve a regular connection.[36]

Both of these eclogues were also written in heroic couplets, usually in stanzas of four lines, although some extended to six and eight lines. In the first poem, there were two speakers; in the second, three. When these poems were attacked by the *Critical Review,* Scott stated that although the style of these eclogues was less elevated than that of his former poems, the eclogues were deficient neither in the strength nor the melody of their versification. "They were designed to be like Virgil's, descriptive of nature, simple and correct."[37] Langhorne had described the Amoebaean eclogue as one "whose only purport is a trial of skill between contending shepherds,"[38] but for Scott it was a manner with a message. The great claim Scott made for these poems was "that in these Eclogues I had drawn, from the great prototype Nature, much imagery that had escaped the notice of all my predecessors. You might also have remarked, that when I introduced images that had been already introduced by others, still the arrangement or combination of those images was my own. This praise of originality, you might at least have allowed me."[39] And the fact that Philips in *Cyder* had omitted a description of apple-gathering justified, Scott felt, his including a sketch of it in his second eclogue.[40]

The subject matter of the poems, therefore, was, according to the poet, the chief basis of their claim to superiority, and the treatment of that subject matter was to emphasize their unusual worth. Scott was going here to use original material, and he was going to draw it from his own observations of nature. "Rural Scenery; or, The Describers" seems the more acceptable of the two poems, being a particularized description of the rural countryside. Both of these poems abound in copious technical footnotes as to the proper names and habits of plants and animals, and it is clear that Scott regarded them as being, in reality, a poetic-scientific treatise; it was these poems which were to earn him the appelation of "the poet of the botanists."[41] The second of the two poems, however, "Rural Business; or, The Agriculturists," was more pretentious in its intention. This was to be a didactic poem on the ways of planting crops and performing the chores on the farm. In its subject matter, therefore, it came perilously close to the uninteresting. As Scott himself commented, ". . . it is no trivial difficulty to describe such subjects without swelling into bombast, or sinking into doggrel."[42] A few lines will show that Scott was not always successful in escaping these two evils.

FIRST.
In vacant corners, on the hamlet waste,
The ample dunghill's steaming heap be plac'd;
There many a month fermenting to remain,
Ere thy slow team disperse it o'er the plain.

SECOND.
The prudent farmer all manure provides,
The mire of roads, the mould of hedge-row sides;
For him their mud the stagnant ponds supply;
For him their soil, the stable and the sty.

THIRD.
For this the swain, on Kennet's winding shore,
Digs sulphurous peat along the sable moor;
For this, where Ocean bounds the stormy strand,
They fetch dank sea-weed to the neighb'ring land.

In concluding the second of these poems. Scott referred to
Virgil as the source for this poetic genre and, presumably, hoped
thereby to ensure a favorable reception for his verses. He could
have turned as easily to poets of his own time, however, and
pointed out the long tradition which had included Dyer's *The
Fleece* (which he thought the "noblest of didactick poems"[43] but
which Johnson had criticized because he felt such a subject could
not be made poetical)[44] and Mason's *The English Garden*. Poetry
such as this, being so specialized—in reality, it is only a versified
handbook to gardening—must draw an audience first by its
ideas. And the same difficulty which James Grainger had had in
interesting readers in his lengthy *The Sugar Cane* (1763), with
its notes and commentary, was felt twenty years later by Scott.
For an age fascinated by the new farming programs of Jethro
Tull and Robert Bakewell, such verses would not seem totally
uninteresting; as Cockfield had written in 1766, ". . . the man of
fashion and erudition begins to instruct the unlettered farmer."[45]
Even George III, priding himself upon being the "Farmer
King," might have liked them. But for following generations,
there was little about this poetry which could seem appealing.
On the other hand, the poems are important in a study of Scott's
theories, for they reflected an increasing emphasis upon nature,
the natural and the particularized. The subject matter of these

poems would prevent their ever being more than literary curiosities, but the techniques developed through them would have implications for Scott's other creations.

Besides *Moral Eclogues,* which was reprinted, and "Amoebaean Eclogues," which was first published in the *Poetical Works,* a third group of eclogues, "Oriental Eclogues," was included in that volume. These three eclogues were also written in heroic couplets, with a setting, a conversation about a moral problem, a resolution of the problem, and a final brief natural description, being the ordered parts. It has been pointed out that "Scott's use of oriental material forms an interesting link between the simple Johnsonian manner of orientalizing by a few phrases—a manner exemplified in the eclogues of Collins—and the elaborate orientalization in the verses of Southey and Moore."[46] Long intrigued by Oriental material (he particularly liked Hawkesworth's *Almoran and Hamet* and Johnson's *Rasselas* and was doubtless familiar with Langhorne's *Solyman and Almena*), Scott was here following a tradition created by eighteenth-century poets like Eyles Irwin, Chatterton, Collins, Roberts, Wolcot, and Percy.

It is clear that Scott himself saw his particular model to be Collins' *Oriental Eclogues* (commented upon in 1765 by Langhorne in his edition of Collins), whose excellence he admired but whose scenes and sentiments were different from his own, so his poems were not merely pale imitations.[47] There was one disadvantage to this sort of subject, Scott felt: "He, who describes what he has seen, may describe correctly: he, who describes what he has not seen, must depend for much on the accounts of others, and supply the rest from his own imagination."[48] Quite obviously Scott felt at a disadvantage when he described not what he had seen but what he imagined as being possible; and to a very real degree, this type of writing violated his philosophy of what poetry ought to be and how it should be written. Unlike Wordsworth, who could recall specific, precise, and sharply delineated images from nature even though he might be far from them at the time, Scott had only the haziest recollection of a landscape once it had vanished from his sight. At times one is persuaded to believe that his most conventional eighteenth-century descriptions, with their stylized pictures, may represent not so much his preference for the general rather than the particular, as his congenital inability to be precise when he conjured up pictures in his imagination. The first eclogue, "Zerad; or, The Absent Lover: an Arabian Eclogue," was based on a passage from Sir William Jones's essay *On the Poetry of the Eastern Nations.* Scott quoted from that work the passage which stated how the nomadic tribes came briefly together and how young lovers from different tribes met and were separated by the vagaries of tribal migration. The second eclogue, "Serim; or, The Artificial Famine: an East-Indian Eclogue," was based on *A Short History of English Transactions in the East-Indies,* in which it was stated that in Bengal and the adjacent provinces the British had produced artificial famines by cornering the food supply, so that the helpless natives had to give up all of their possessions or starve. Hoole complained about the subject matter of this poem, wishing

that the philanthropy of the author had not led him to make choice of a story so apparently disgraceful to the British name in India, the circumstances of which have been, doubtless, greatly exaggerated, while the enormities of a few individuals have been swelled, by designing men, into a general and universal spirit of rapine, avarice, and cruelty.

In this poem, Serim was an Indian who deplored his country's fate at the hands of the British. After lamenting his country's plight and having cursed the British, there was a sudden period to his speech and to his existence—as well as to the poem:

> Enrapt he spoke—then ceas'd the lofty strain,
> And Orel's rocks return'd the sound again.—

A British ruffian, near in ambush laid,
Rush'd sudden from the cane-isle's secret shade;
"Go to thy Gods!" with rage infernal cried,
And headlong plung'd the hapless Sage into the foaming tide.

Scott's orientalizing showed an unfortunate influence of Gray's "The Bard."

The third of the eclogues, "Li-Po: or, The Good Governor: a Chinese Eclogue," is unquestionably the best of the group; in places, it has some of Scott's better writing. In Oriental poetry, such as these poems were intended to be, the reader could legitimately expect a portrayal of Oriental life—not English life and manners—otherwise, why were they called "Oriental"? Scott attempted to evade this difficulty by apologizing for his lapses, but it is clear that in the first two eclogues he lacked a successful comprehension of either Arabian or Indian life and customs. Curiously enough, when he came to write his Chinese eclogue, which was based on Jean Du Halde's *The General History of China* (selections from which had been made by Johnson in 1738 for the *Gentleman's Magazine*) and other unspecified accounts, he had an idea of Chinese political philosophy, upon which he based this poem; he had a sympathetic feeling for the customs and traditions of the Chinese people, even though Du Halde's book was not the most reliable account, since it was based on secondary sources and Du Halde had never been to China. The stylized quality of Scott's verse seemed ideally suited to what was believed to have been the excessively mannered culture of China.

Where Honan's hills Kiansi's vale inclose,
And Xifa's lake its glassy level shows;
LI-PO's fair island lay—delightful scene!—
With swelling slopes, and groves of every green:
On azure rocks his rich pavilion plac'd,
Rear'd its light front with golden columns grac'd;

High o'er the roof a weeping willow hung,
And jasmine boughs the lattice twin'd among;
In porcelain vases crested amaranth grew,
And starry aster, crimson, white, and blue;
Lien-hoa flowers upon the water spread;
Bright shells and corals varied lustre shed;
From sparry grottos chrystal drops distill'd
On sounding brass, and air with music fill'd;
Soft thro' the bending canes the breezes play'd,
The rustling leaves continual murmur made;
Gay shoals of gold-fish glitter'd in the tide,
And gaudy birds flew sportive by its side.

. . . .

He spoke, and rose; but now along the way
That from the city-gate fair-winding lay,
Stretch'd thro' green meads where lowing cattle graz'd,
Amid the lake's wide silver level rais'd,
Led up steep rocks by painted bridges join'd,
Or near thin trees that o'er the tide inclin'd,
Slow towards his palace came a suppliant train;—
Who'er his presence sought ne'er sought in vain—
The ready vessel, waiting at his call,
Receiv'd, and bore him to the audience-hall.

For the *Poetical Works* Scott also rewrote his 1756 "Winter
Prospects in the Country. An Epistle to a Friend in London" and
made it the second of two verse epistles, both written in heroic
couplets. The first of these, "The Garden. To a friend," treated
the problems of the grotto, whose history Scott traced from its
conception to his ultimate displeasure with it. The second epistle,
"Winter Amusements in the Country. To a Friend in London,"
dealt merely with the poet's life at Amwell and gave a brief tour
of the village and the countryside. The style here was quite different from that of *Amwell,* however, as there was that concern
with particular plants and minute details which characterized
the "Amoebaean Eclogues." The epistles are pleasant autobiographical sketches, but seem to have had no basic structural plan

or meaning for anyone other than the person addressed; too clearly they reveal their hasty birth, when they were written after most of the other poems in the volume had already been printed.[49] Factually, they are of considerable significance in showing what Scott thought about his life. Considered objectively as poems, however, they seem rather pointless; as Johnson said, "... occasional poetry must often content itself with occasional praise."[50] Scott himself seems to have realized that the verse epistle was not the best of forms; he thought the most that could be said of it was that it was easy and familiar and flowed from a good and benevolent heart.[51] (This was one of the curious instances when he felt that the value of poetry lay not in itself but in what it revealed of the author's true character.[52] If that character were admirable, presumably the verses were.) But in writing verse epistles, he was following the tradition of his age. There is hardly a poet in the eighteenth century who did not include a few such epistles in his collected works, and when John Gilbert Cooper had published his *Epistles to His Friends in Town, from Aristippus in Retirement,* he had observed, "The unconfined return of the rhymes, and easiness of the diction, seem peculiarly adapted to epistolary compositions."

Scott called his longest poetical work an "essay," but it seems clear that he considered the "Essay on Painting. To a Young Artist" really as another epistle. It differed from the epistles only in that it did not deal with Scott's personal life and it was not directed to a particular person. As both of the epistles had been concerned with presenting rather didactic material—the proper way to landscape a garden, the proper way to spend idle time profitably—so was this poem to be a presentation in heroic couplets of Scott's artistic theories, derived from a lifelong interest in painting (for many years he never missed an annual exhibition). Not only the longest of his poems (it runs to 458 lines), it was, apparently, the last poem he ever wrote, having been begun only after the earlier part of the *Poetical Works* had been completed. It was written in five weeks and took its origin from a few lines of poetry which Scott had written earlier and had tried unsuccessfully to work into another of his compositions. He had conceived the notion of such a poem long before Hayley's *Essay on Painting* appeared in 1781, but the fact that he had been anticipated in print made him limit his subject considerably: "On Landscape he [Hayley] had said little; I had therefore room to expatiate. On Portrait he had said much; and I was necessitated to say something; but even there I wished not to imitate, but rather to rival, my predecessor. Hayley's piece has great merit, but is tedious from its length and inequality."[53] Hayley's was not the first of such poems, however. Du Fresnoy's was the most famous (Warton had called it "a cold, uninteresting, unpoetical, performance"),[54] and Walter Harte had published "An Essay on Painting" in 1727; Samuel Pratt, *The Progress of Painting,* 1775; and George Keate, his *An Epistle to Angelica Kauffmann,* 1781.

The theory of composition which Scott's lengthy poem illustrated was best expressed in the following verses:

> 'Tis General Nature, in thy art and mine,
> Must give our fame in future times to shine:
> Sublime and pathos, like the Sun's fix'd flame,
> Remain, and please thro' every age the same;
> Humour's light shapes, like vapours in the sky,
> Rise, pass, and vary, and for ever fly:
> HOGARTH and SWIFT, if living, might deplore
> Half their keen jokes, that now are jokes no more.

In this theory of general nature, Scott emphasized the normal as being synonymous with the important. The abnormal, therefore, would not be considered appropriate. In his theory here, Scott seems to have regressed to earlier neoclassical conceptions about the proper subject of art. His own poems never revealed a tendency to display the unusual, but he seldom gave such emphasis to the importance of the norm. These general conceptions, coupled with the didactic nature of the subject matter itself, made the "Essay on Painting" one of his less fortunate works. The images were generalized, rather than particularized, and though there was a catalogue of those painters Scott especially admired (Kauffmann, Romney, West, and Copley), the peculiar abilities of each were not satisfactorily analyzed. Much of the poem consisted merely of a description of subjects which would have made suitable paintings.

Though it is fashionable in literary criticism to show how an author's final work is the most impressive of his achievements or indicates a new direction in which his energies could have carried him, had he lived, in the case of Scott no such observation can, with justice, be made. The "Essay on Painting," by its subject matter and its structure, its images and its language, was one of the most conventional of poems. The careful theories about particularity and the unique in art which Scott had been evolving seemed here completely discarded for older concepts of the general and the abstract. The final lines of the poem will reveal the rather disjointed and didactic aspects of this work. Only the final couplet demonstrated a poetic power which was greater than the rest of the poem suggested, and though this one couplet recalls Pope's brilliant imagery, nothing else in the poem does.

> One caution further must the Muse impart;
> Shun Naked Form, that scandal of thy art:
> Even DRYDEN blames them who refuse to spare
> The painful blushes of the modest Fair.
> Let Decency her veil of drapery throw,
> And Grace diffuse its folds in easy flow.

> And now, my Friend, for Thee may Fortune find
> Employ congenial to thy liberal mind;

Not tasks impos'd by power, or chosen for gain,
Begun reluctant, and pursued with pain.
What warms the heart, the hand with force reveals,
And all that force the charm'd spectator feels:
For Genius, piercing as the electric flame,
When wak'd in one, in others wakes the same.

V

The largest collection of poems under a single title in the *Poetical
Works* was the odes, which numbered twenty-eight: twenty-
seven being placed together in series, and "The Mexican Prophecy," the longest of the group, being set apart to emphasize its
importance. It is not known when Scott wrote his first ode, but
by 1758, he had written the "Ode: Occasioned by Reading Dr.
Akenside's Odes." From that time on, he seems to have been
especially fond of the genre, and he developed a skill in it which
was unequaled by his ability in anything except blank verse. He
thought of his odes as "pleasing Lyrical Compositions, spirited,
correct, and musical";[55] and his *Letter to the Critical Reviewers*
was primarily a detailed defense of them and an explanation of
his purpose. Indeed, in that critical essay, he said, ". . . it will be
necessary to observe the nature of my design, before we proceed
to the merits of my performance." Scott conceived of the ode as
being divided into two kinds: the greater and the lesser, Pindar
being the exemplar of the former, and Horace the latter. Scott
said he was modeling his odes after the odes of Horace as translated by Philip Francis; this strongly suggests that he was unable
to read Horace in the original Latin. "Above the style of this
work, in several of my Odes, I did not attempt to rise; and below
it, I may safely assert, I have not fallen. This Ode, indeed, seems
to require no great elevation of diction, provided it is not debased
with colloquial vulgarities. Between this lesser Ode and the
Song, there seems but a slight distinction. Both may be vehicles
of description: the Ode seems most properly the vehicle of rea-

son, of political or moral sentiment; the Song seems most properly the vehicle of passion, or of wit and humour."[56] With his conception of the ode, Scott believed that the poet was justified in devising for his stanzas any metrical pattern that was effective. But once the basic stanzaic pattern had been chosen, it was to be retained throughout; he pointed with pleasure to the fact that though the basic stanzaic patterns he employed were sometimes unusual, he never deviated from them within the poems themselves.[57] Warton had dismissed the ode form as being unsuited to English, "Owing to the harshness and untuneableness of modern languages, abounding in monosyllables, and crowded with consonants."[58] This objection Scott ignored by saying rather cavalierly that it was not his business to discuss whether or not the ode form was successful in English; others had used it with public acclaim and this was sufficient proof of its merit, he felt.[59]

The most ambitious of the odes was "The Mexican Prophecy," which, though perhaps influenced by Edward Jerningham's poem, *The Fall of Mexico* (1775), was based primarily on a legend recorded in De Solis' *History of the Conquest of Mexico:*

...on the approach of Cortez to the neighbourhood of that city, the Emperor Motezuma sent a number of magicians to attempt the destruction of the Spanish army. As the sorcerers were practising their incantations, a daemon appeared to them in the form of their idol Tlcatlepuca, and foretold the fall of the Mexican empire.[60]

Written in trochaic tetrameter couplets with a consistent use of catalexis, the poem was, because of its subject matter, closely related to the "Oriental Eclogues." Indeed, the only difference between them seems to lie in the metrics and in the impersonality of the ode's subject matter. Though there was a narrative structure for this poem, the emphasis of the work was directed toward the prophecy of the demon of Tlcatlepuca. In having called this an "ode," therefore, Scott seems to have desired emphasis on the invocatory and supernatural aspects of the poem. In this respect,

the poem was another one of Scott's to show the influence of
Gray's "The Bard."

Scott considered "The Mexican Prophecy" to be one of his
most successful works, but the poem is so generalized and conventional, and the diction is so inverted, that the ode does not
evoke the emotional response which obviously was intended.
The poet appears to have aimed at dignity and solemnity. Only
in the image of the last couplet was there that vivid verbal quality which Scott, in his best work, could impart to a scene. The
demon concluded his speech:

> "Cease your boast, O stranger band,
> Conquerers of my fallen land!
> Avarice strides your van before,
> Phantom meagre, pale, and hoar!
> Discord follows, breathing flame,
> Still opposing claim to claim;
> Kindred Daemons haste along!
> Haste, avenge my country's wrong!"

> Cease'd the voice with dreadful sounds,
> Loud as tides that burst their bounds;
> Roll'd the form in smoke away,
> Amaz'd on earth th' exorcists lay;
> Pondering on the dreadful lore,
> Their course the Iberians downward bore;
> Their helmets glittering o'er the vale,
> And wide their ensigns fluttering in the gale.

In the twenty-seven odes he published as a group in his *Poetical Works,* Scott gave evidence of his poetic ability at its highest
point of development. Some of the poems were dull, insipid, flat,
and completely conventional. Others were the equal of the best
writing he was ever able to do and constitute his closest approach
to memorable eighteenth-century poetry. Although each poem
contained a mixture of ideas, the primary themes make the

odes fall into four categories: descriptive poems,[61] personal lyrics,[62] moral reflections,[63] and poetic expressions of critical theory.[64] There were separate odes written to Lettsom, Cockfield, Frogley, De Horne, and Payne, and there were odes on war and disease, the latter being one of the most conventional in its subject. Armstrong's *The Art of Preserving Health* (1774) was the most famous work in this tradition, and Scott was especially fond of it, though Shenstone, Parnell, Blacklock, Garth, Cooper, Thompson, and innumerable other poets had all proclaimed that they were not in favor of disease either. But Scott's poem had its own message: he disliked the practice of burying people in churches, because he was certain that the vapors rising from decaying corpses could not but contaminate the worshippers. Nor was this the most bizarre of the poems. Another ode chided pirates for their evil deeds. All of the odes united, however, in being the best demonstration of the theory of "classical simplicity."

> "PASTORAL, and Elegy, and Ode!
> Who hopes, by these, applause to gain,
> Believe me, Friend, may hope in vain—
> These classic things are not the mode;
> Our taste polite, so much refin'd,
> Demands a strain of different kind.
>
> "Go, court the Muse of Chevy Chace,
> To tell in STERNHOLD's simple rhymes
> Some tale of ancient English times;
> Or try to win rude Satire's grace,
> That Scold, who dirt around her throws,
> And many a random stain bestows." ...
>
> The plan that VIRGIL's choice could claim,
> The plan that HORACE design'd to chuse,
> Trust me, I wish not to refuse:—
> To AKENSIDE's or SHENSTONE's name
> The praise that future days shall pay,
> Methinks may well content my lay.[65]

The theory could be demonstrated effectively in personal verse,
he felt. In one ode, written at his brother-in-law's (George De
Horne's) home at Stanway Hall, Essex, where he advised a
young man to prepare himself for the life of a country squire, he
said:

> Domestic Life must soon be thine—
> 'Tis various as an April day;
> 'Tis pleasure now, and now 'tis pain:
> Thro' storms of soul and gleams of fine
> Contented hold thy steady way,
> And these enjoy, and those sustain.
>
> From London's streets to solitude,
> From brilliant shops to dirty fields,
> From beaux and belles to rugged hinds—
> The change I own is strange and rude:
> Yet scarce a place so little yields,
> But he who seeks amusement finds.
>
> Perchance thou'lt not disdain to hear
> The ploughman's history of the plain;
> Thy sight the prospect's scenes may charm:
> And sure fastidious is the ear,
> That slights the milkmaid's simple strain,
> At evening echoing from the farm.
>
> The market lore of artful swains;
> The price of cattle and of corn,
> The sportsman's feats of dogs and guns;—
> To practice that will cost thee pains;
> And these with patience must be born,
> For he will be dislik'd who shuns.

In these simple lines, with their stylized and yet vivid con-
trasts and careful selection of detail, one saw more of Scott the
country squire than he did in so many of those works which pur-
ported to be autobiographical. These lines eminently illustrated,

too, the effectiveness of this theory of composition. To be sure, the words occasionally came in an unnatural order. But with the exception of a few words ("swains" was both Beattie's and Scott's favorite word for the rural workers, despite Scott's praising Goldsmith's *The Deserted Village* in which there are "no poetical swains, but the men who actually drive the plough, or wield the scythe, the sickle, the hammer, or the hedging bill"),[66] the vocabulary was common and not prosaic. In the music of the verse, the alliterative quality of the lines, he had emphasized the gentle humor that he found in and the understanding that he had for rural life. When he moved from the particular to the general, however, he was not always so fortunate in his description. Perhaps the most prosaic lines he ever wrote were in the following stanza:

> On the eastern hill's steep side
> Spreads the rural hamlet wide;
> 'Cross the vale, where willows rise,
> Further still another lies;
> And, beneath a steeper hill,
> Lies another further still:
> Near them many a field and grove—
> Scenes where Health and Labour rove![67]

And yet, who can deny that prosaic as these lines are, they are superficially close to an early Wordsworth? Unlike a Wordsworthian poem, however, this ode was merely a pleasant piece of observation; no attempt to delineate the indwelling law of our nature was being made by Scott, who was too often gratified by morals expressed rather than implied.

Before he had finished writing odes, however, Scott demonstrated a developed ability at the landscape piece. The tour de force of the series was a set of three odes, "The Tempestuous Evening," "The Melancholy Evening," and "The Pleasant Evening." Each was written in a different stanzaic form, but each dealt with the same natural elements, and the opening stanza set

the tone for the piece. To be sure, each ode concluded with a
moral thought which arose from an observation of natural phenomena—Scott, after all, would not have been Scott without his
moral sentiments—but the especial effect of each ode seems to
have been derived from the natural description of the setting.
Had he not mastered the opening, the effect of the poem in each
case would have been destroyed. The opening stanzas, with the
moon, the sky, and the earth, as consistent elements, set the tone.

> THERE'S grandeur in this sounding storm,
> That drives the hurrying clouds along
> That on each other seem to throng,
> And mix in many a varied form;
> While, bursting now and then between,
> The Moon's dim misty orb is seen,
> And casts faint glimpses on the green.[68]

> O HASTE, ye hovering clouds, away,
>   Ye clouds so fleecy, dim, and pale,
> Thro' which the Moon's obstructed ray
>   Sheds this sad whiteness o'er the vale!
> Forbear, ye bells, that languid strain!
> The sight, the sound, are fraught with pain;
> The words of dying friends I hear,
> The open grave I linger near,
> Take the last look, and drop the parting tear![69]

> DELIGHTFUL looks this clear, calm sky,
> With CYNTHIA's silver orb on high;
> Delightful looks this smooth green ground,
> With shadows cast from cots around:
> Quick-twinkling lustre decks the tide;
> And chearful radiance gently falls
> On that white town, and castle walls,
> That crown the spacious river's further side.[70]

The finest of all of Scott's odes, however, was his shortest.
Only sixteen lines long, it was the most effective illustration of

his theory. The poem fell in the category of the antiwar poem—
a genre which increased in popularity as the eighteenth century
drew to its close—but to dismiss it as only a poem with a common theme is to ignore the "classical simplicity" of its structure
and beauty. Scott, who was ever fond of an elongated last line in
a poem, was here able to use this device most effectively, the
length and dying fall of the line emphasizing the condemnation
he was making. Here, for one of the few times in his poetry, he
was able to suppress an obvious moral and to use it for the motivation but not the matter of the piece. The language was simple
and plain. The use of repetition was especially effective, whereas
the logical order of details all listed additively—a manner which
allowed the poet to suppress his own wrath and to let the topic
itself impress the point—gave a cumulative effect which made
this the most unified and moving of all of Scott's poetical
creations.

> I HATE that drum's discordant sound,
> Parading round, and round, and round:
> To thoughtless youth it pleasure yields,
> And lures from cities and from fields,
> To sell their liberty for charms
> Of tawdry lace, and glittering arms;
> And when Ambition's voice commands,
> To march, and fight, and fall, in foreign lands.
>
> I hate that drum's discordant sound,
> Parading round, and round, and round:
> To me it talks of ravag'd plains,
> And burning towns, and ruin'd swains,
> And mangled limbs, and dying groans,
> And widows tears, and orphans moans;
> And all that Misery's hand bestows,
> To fill the catalogue of human woes.[71]

This was the most popular of Scott's poems and was widely reprinted after its initial appearance[72] and was even translated into

Latin by a friend of the author's and published in both versions
in December, 1782.[73] With its appropriate topic and its careful
execution, it was a poem which could not but appeal to that
rising generation of Romantics who considered themselves in
revolt against older ideas and conventions, both political and
poetic. Southey reprinted this ode and described Scott as "A very
amiable man, whose opinions were seldom wrong, and whose
feelings were always right."[74] In this poem, Scott had made his
most effective illustration of his critical theories of "classical simplicity." For an age in which these theories would have notice-
able importance, this mirror of them inevitably received attention: the poem and the theory reflected each other.

   In the poetry of a lifetime, therefore, Scott began and ended
in convention. His first poem, "Epidemic Mortality, from Eccl.
xii," and his last, "Essay on Painting," were of the same school
in theory and in attitude. But before Scott's poetic wheel had
come full circle, he had swung through areas where he had never
been before, and in those newer fields he had produced work of
merit. Most of his life, he wrote in heroic couplets; and when he
wrote like an Augustan, he tried to think like one; but he was
temperamentally unsuited to the rigid classifications and strictures of early eighteenth-century poetic style. He lacked a keenness of wit and sharpness of insight which gave the heroic
couplet a unique brilliance, and he was generally profuse and
unprecise. When he attempted to ignore convention, however,
and to develop a form which would best express his own convictions, he wrote his finest work. *Amwell* and the best of the
odes are not the result of a man's adapting his own nature to a
form. In these two genres of blank verse and the ode, he had
devised a manner which would best express his matter, a style
which would best express his thought. It was his implicit assumption that this was the purpose of poetry: good writing
should reflect the mind of man, his ideas, his convictions, and

his personality. In *Amwell* and the odes, we see Scott at his best. In these poems, which stress the love of man, of England, and of the simple life, there is ample assurance that from the first until the last "The patriot's fire yet sparkled in the friend."[75]

VI

By the time the controversy over the *Poetical Works* had subsided, Scott was ready to bring out another of his literary productions; after complaining so vehemently about the improper criticism which his own works had received, he was to demonstrate the proper critical method by a minute investigation of nine poems, eight of which had been discussed by Johnson but which, Scott felt, had been given improper praise or censure by that critic. By May 23, 1783, *Critical Essays on Some of the Poems, of Several English Poets* was in the hands of James Phillips, the printer, and Scott was asking for an idea of the format, the page proof, and the choice of type.[76] He had no hesitation in delaying the printing of the book for two weeks, in order to accommodate Phillips, and he admitted that he himself would be rather busy attending the annual meeting in London of the Society of Friends. On June 6, 1783, he wrote to Beattie that the volume would be printed immediately but would probably not be published until winter.[77] The old troubles were still bothering him, however, and he was again having his subject matter anticipated by others. He had finished his examination of Gray's churchyard elegy by the end of May, and by the sixth of June, an anonymous pamphlet was being advertised as a criticism on this same poem. "This I have not seen, but be it what it may I shall Neither Suppress nor alter Mine on Account of it." Scott need not have concerned himself with this essay, presumably written by John Young, professor of Greek at Glasgow University.[78] It was a satire on Johnson's style in the *Lives of the Poets* and it was not intended as a critical examination of Gray's poem.

But Scott never saw the joke, and when his own essay appeared,
there was included a final mention of this pamphlet "in which
that Poem seems to have been examined on principles very dissimilar to mine."[79] One sees here most evident a Scott who was
desirous of that fame which would stem from the acceptance of
his presumably wise and original ideas, and who, it must be confessed, only rarely exhibited even the faintest sign of having a
sense of humor. Always to have been anticipated was his unfortunate fate, and he wistfully suggested to Beattie:

I forget whether my friend ever gave me his Opinion of my Essay on
Painting, Some Artists who are Men of Taste have spoke well of it.
The Publick in general I apprehend never read it. The Critical Review said it was superseded by Hayley's and Consequently such as do
not judge for themselves thought mine not worth reading.[80]

By August 29, 1783, the *Critical Essays* was in the press, and the
author of them was writing from Amwell to Beattie, that since
criticism was now supposed to be fashionable, he hoped for once
to be in step with the time.[81] "I might often have been in fashion,
but for a restive kind of disposition, that liked to write and print
what pleased my own fancy, rather than what I had reason to
think would please the readers of the day." Scott said he was
temperamentally unsuited to join either the Batheaston set or
the Hayleyian school, for "I love good poetry, but I cannot admire bad, how much soever it may be the *ton* to admire it." The
death of the poet delayed the production, however, and Scott
never became the popular man of letters which it was quite obviously his secret ambition to be.

On the twenty-fifth of October, after she had been suffering
for some time from an unidentified illness, Scott's wife was taken
by the poet from Amwell to London to be examined. They were
still in the metropolis on the first of December when the poet
was suddenly struck with a putrid fever which, from the beginning, was considered to be very dangerous. Always apprehensive

of this particular disease, Scott from the first seems to have felt that he could not recover from it, and his mental state and early resignation to his fate were said by some to have been the deciding factors in the illness. Because of this mental dejection, he turned his thoughts toward death and, in making preparation for it, began to reproach himself for sins which he imagined himself to have committed. During 1783, he had been more attentive at functions of the Society of Friends than had been his usual custom, and he had been in attendance at the London annual meeting. His thoughts, therefore, were concentrated on the religious aspect of his life in his last days, but it gave little comfort to him and caused him on the ninth of December to send for his brother, Samuel, who was at Hertford, to have him come and minister to him.[82]

For reasons which are not clear, Samuel did not respond immediately to his brother's request, and only when a letter was received on the tenth, saying that John entreated him to come, did he leave Hertford and arrive at his brother's bedside by four in the afternoon of the same day. When Samuel appeared and asked John how he felt, John replied, "Very bad; I wanted to see thee, and if thee had come sooner, I had a great deal to say to thee, but I fear now I cannot." John then discussed his great sins of disbelieving, which means that he did not have as great a faith in God as he felt he should have had. "Oh! said he, the SAVIOUR, He is the Way, and there is no other; I now see there is no other; Oh the SAVIOUR! I have done too much against him; and if I live I hope I shall be able to let the world know it, and that in many respects my mind is altered. But I dare not make resolutions." This was a painful scene, as Scott continually charged himself with responsibility for what he felt had been his unrighteous actions. When Samuel, who disliked visiting deathbeds because he felt this was a hypocritical gesture, referred to this visit as unprofitable, John replied with an asperity which struck the fire of

his earlier days: "Oh! it is not a time to be solicitous about forms!"
Samuel's account of this visit is mixed with his own religious
speculations and exhortations for universal repentance, but still
he did seem to be visibly shaken by the death of his brother. But
he was also impressed with the religious opportunity afforded;
the day before John's funeral, he had written up the memoirs of
the deathbed scene and had shown them to Scott's widow in
preparation for their publication. It would be unjust to attribute
this pamphlet only to Samuel's self-praise of his own life. He
felt it his religious duty to publish the account, though he delayed doing it until August 26, 1785. In his diary he recorded his
reluctance to set his brother's testimony before the world, but
he felt that to suppress it would be contrary to his religious command to publish testimony to God, and this certainly was one of
the most remarkable of all such documents.[83]

The deathbed scene of Scott is, without question, a fearful
thing, and the poet, who was the most humane of men in his lifetime, appears to have died in the presence of friends who, by
altruistic standards, would be called the most unfeeling of men.
In this deathbed repentance, however, there is little really that
Scott said which in any way contradicted the actions of his life.
He reaffirmed his faith in Christ, but his life had been a testimonial to that devotion. His only sin was that he occasionally
received religious impulses which he apparently denied, and this
was a major heresy in the Society of Friends: ". . . he frequently
experienced the convictions of the Spirit of Truth for not faith-
fully following the Lord, and adhering to the Cross of Christ,
by which true believers are crucified to the world, and the world
to them." He charged himself with the basic sin of pride, but
even Samuel said this was not a valid criticism, as he was the
most humble of men and always available to the lower classes.
The most dreadful part of his death was his dominant prayer
that "he should not be a companion of accursed and wrathful
spirits."

Despite his continued rational state, his speech soon began to falter, and on the twelfth of the month, he was dead. Six days later, he was buried in the Friends' burial ground at Ratcliff in London, where among the few mourners at his funeral was his old friend and future biographer John Hoole. By the end of the month, his obituary had appeared in the *Gentleman's Magazine* and the *British Magazine and Review* with the statement that he had died at Amwell, and the first two of many inaccurate biographies about Scott had been written.

CHAPTER VI

THE DETERMINED CRITIC

I

THE ROLE of a literary critic was one which Scott seldom publicly assumed,[1] but throughout his life he had been fascinated by criticism and the determination of those principles which lie at the basis of art. In letters to his friends, he had freely given his views on various literary works (one of the main functions of his letters to Beattie was to report on the latest literary publications and his opinion of them); and his earliest training had instilled in him the ability to analyze a text, to determine its structural pattern, and then to devise a similar pattern for his own creations. But it is incorrect to think of him as a master of critical theory; he seldom moved beyond the analysis of a specific work to come to general notions on the meaning of any of the army of critical terms which laid waste more than one mind in the century. Despite these limitations, he worked rather successfully in his last public role. The general literary public did not see the range of Scott's critical activity until two years after his death, although they, from a reading of his prose writings and his critical poems, had been prepared to expect such an interest. It was only in 1785, when Scott's 386-page critical volume appeared, that the public realized how concerned he had always been with the creations of other writers.

Critical Essays on Some of the Poems, of Several English Poets consisted of nine essays, each on a separate poem; although he originally said it would "make a small Octavo,"[2] it emerged as the longest of his writings and the major demonstration of his applied criteria. The volume grew from Scott's dissatisfaction

---

[1] For notes to chap. vi, see p. 219.

with Johnson's *Lives of the Poets;*[2] and like the second volume of Warton's *Essay on the Genius and Writings of Pope,*[4] it was regarded largely as a direct answer to charges made by Johnson. Shortly before the *Critical Essays* was sent to the press, it had been described by Scott in a letter to James Beattie:

It will consist of a series of essays on several celebrated poems, by an investigation of whose beauties and defects I have exemplified the difference between good and bad composition. My criterion of merit is classical simplicity; that is to say, the manner of Homer, the Greek tragic poets, Virgil, Milton, Pope, in contradistinction to every species of false ornament. There never was a time when it was more necessary to counteract the public taste, which is now running wild after this fashionable *clinquant,* as I think it is termed by Addison. The poems I have criticised are, Denham's Cooper's-Hill, of which I have nothing to praise, and all to censure;[5] Milton's Lycidas, and Dyer's Ruins of Rome, which I have vindicated from the censure of Dr. Johnson, and given the praise they merit; Pope's Windsor Forest, Collin's Oriental Eclogues, Gray's Elegy, Goldsmith's Deserted Village, and Thomson's Seasons; in all which I have much to applaud, and something to blame.[6]

Sometime after writing this letter, Scott decided to expand the work further to include an essay on Dyer's *Grongar Hill,* which, although the shortest in the volume, was designed to call attention to one of Scott's favorite poets.

There was reason for Scott's choosing each of these poems for a critical examination in his volume: the briefest consideration of their subject matter shows to what extent his interest was restricted to descriptive and landscape poetry. Dr. Johnson generally disliked such verse, desiring moral poetry instead, and Pope himself in his later years had disapproved of descriptive poetry;[7] yet Scott insisted that the Twickenham poet could have done as well in that genre as in "fiction" or satire. Warton had defended descriptive poetry, however, saying that Virgil's *Georgics* and Lucretius' *On the Nature of Things* were fine examples of the type.[8] Warton and Johnson both had praised Denham's *Cooper's Hill,* though Johnson did admit that "if it be maliciously inspected [it] will not be found without its faults."[9] Scott's diatribe against this poem was unusual for its time and he was among the earliest of Denham's late eighteenth-century detractors. His excoriation was directed primarily at the famous Thames passage, where Denham compared the flow of the river to the flow of his verse, a passage which was becoming the cliché of eighteenth-century criticism on the poem; Scott carefully analyzed these lines to show them as repetitious and nonsensical. *Lycidas,* which was Johnson's famous target for scorn, received Scott's critical support, and he had several *aperçus* to offer on the poem: he showed that the poem had a three-part structure (morning, noon, and evening), shown, respectively, by the appearance of the lawns, the hum of the "grey fly," and the appearance and descent of the evening star. And he also pointed out that the famous "fame is the spur" passage is ambiguous because fame is regarded both as a motive and as a reward. This essay has considerable historical significance, as it was the first lengthy detailed criticism of *Lycidas,* and Scott's commentary is especially significant in any study of Milton's reputation.[10] As for Pope, Warton had stated that Pope's reputation would be based principally on *Windsor Forest, The Rape of the Lock,* and *Eloisa to Abelard,* but he criticized the first of these for being so generalized;[11] Scott in his affection for Pope wished to show how that poet had stressed the basic assumptions of "classical simplicity." Warton had praised Dyer's *Grongar Hill,* and Scott, who thought of Dyer as "that sublime, but strangely neglected poet,"[12] regarded his critical discussion of *The Ruins of Rome* as a proselytizing one. (That two essays should be devoted to Dyer shows Scott's considerable concern about what he felt to be that poet's undeserved obscurity.) Beattie had been a close friend of Gray and probably passed his personal enthusiasm for the poet on to Scott. Beattie, however, did not regard the churchyard elegy as Gray's finest poem, but it was a favorite of Scott's, and he defended the poem against the charges of Vicesimus Knox that the poem had no plan.[13] Goldsmith had been omitted from Johnson's monumental work on the British poets, and Scott was indignant at this omission. To be sure, Johnson, in his life of Parnell, had praised Goldsmith highly, but Scott seems to have felt that Goldsmith was denied treatment in the series, perhaps for some personal reasons. (He was, therefore, unaware, or acted as though he were, that Johnson had not selected the poets for inclusion in the collection, and that Goldsmith could not have been discussed, since the bookseller who owned the copyright to *She Stoops to Conquer* refused to give permission for the reprinting of that work.) Collins had long been one of Scott's enthusiasms, and though the merits of the poet had been rather well established by Langhorne in 1765,[14] Scott felt that Collins needed to be newly defended from the criticisms made against him by Johnson.[15] Scott's discussion of Thomson defended the poet's figures of speech against criticisms made by Lord Kames, and it reëmphasized that Thomson was peculiarly distinguished for his description and delineation, being famous, as Warton had shown earlier,[16] for having drawn his images from direct observation of nature and not from other poets. For these reasons, the essay on Thomson's *Seasons* stood last in the volume and it was the longest of the nine discussions: his poetry was the epitome of the virtues of landscape verse.

Scott's letter was apparently an explicit statement of his intention and fundamental theory, but it was unfortunately characteristic that his lengthy volume itself did not use the term of "classical simplicity" as the ever-apparent critical calipers or as even the basis of his critical argument. Rather, these works are all discussed in terms of sublimity, consistency, pathos, imagery, correctness, and that vast army of critical terms which marched through the writings of the century. If they are difficult to understand in earlier writers, who at least made some attempt at definition of them, one can imagine the difficulty with Scott's approach: he never defined any of his critical terms, and he employed most of them so vaguely that it is impossible to see much meaning in any of them. His literary allusions do not suggest he was familiar with even the most famous critical documents, and one has the distinct impression that Scott was unfortunately influenced by the tossing about of these terms in the magazines which he seldom missed reading. It cannot be too much emphasized that Scott's theories, although almost completely conventional, were derived not from the great historical figures of English criticism, but only from the writings of his contemporaries who remouthed them. Although he read the newest works of his friends, he appears never to have turned to Hobbes or Dennis, unquestionably the main sources of much of his critical thought. Scott's failure to establish a detailed critical apparatus emphasizes his expressed belief that his notions were not new. He thought of himself as a defender of older critical positions, and his purpose in writing the book was to apply traditional points of view to these poems, since he felt they had not been examined with justified thoroughness before.

But despite his vagueness, Scott had always directed his attention, if not his pen, toward "classical simplicity," and his assumption was that art is effective, only so far as it attains this; for convenience of discussion, he would point out, works may be considered in terms of special attributes, the summation of which represents "classical simplicity." Such criticism as he intended in this volume was important, Scott felt, for more than the final judgment it produced on a work of art; it had a fundamental contribution to make to the realization of the aesthetic experience:

When Genius, ranging Nature o'er,
Collects his tributary store,
What Matter's tract immense supplies,
Or wide in Mind's vast region lies,
And every thought with skill combines,
And all transmits in tuneful lines;
Then rapture sparkling in thine [Criticism's] eye,
Then rais'd thy solemn voice on high;
Thy comment still his work pursues,
The plan explains, the style reviews,
And marks its strength, and marks its ease;
And tells us why and how they please.
And when, perhaps, disdaining care,
He blends with faults his products fair;
Whate'er of such thy sight surveys,
Thy tongue in triumph ne'er displays,
But hints, as spots that dim the sun,
Or rocks that future sails should shun.[17]

The Society of Friends distrusted work in the world and all literary labors except those dedicated to piety, but Scott himself seems to have found no conflict between his religious beliefs and his literary career. Because of his evangelical disposition, which made him wish to change the world to his own pattern of moral thought, he wrote of fundamental things, all dealing with man's basic nature and his relationship to the universe and his fellow man.[18] Scott believed in simple faith and all those virtues which had been espoused by Christ. On the simplest level, therefore, the works of the world—and, especially, works of art—could be judged on their moral worth. In having this conviction, Scott was actually following the theory that the purpose of all art is to please; but art which pleases must instruct, or it fails to please—a theory which found one proponent in Beattie, who probable passed it on to Scott. Instruction was not to be regarded in the narrow ritualistic light of inculcating the tenets of one religious dogma. But instruction was to be moral, in the general broad definition of Christian morality, and in advocating such a cause of virtue, Beattie and Scott were certainly in the camp of Johnson. In their basic assumptions, the Anglican, the Presbyterian, and the Quaker had the same notion about the fundamental purpose and virtue of art. But they were not isolated in this contention, since it was one of the most widely held critical beliefs and was in no way unusual. By these moral judgments Scott could condemn almost all novels. Having spoken of them with moral disapprobation, he never found need to discuss them again as works worthy of critical attention or emulation; the genre itself was disreputable:

> ...you have your monthly chronicles of scandal and debauchery; your romances and novels, those "thieves of time," where one insipid tale is again and again repeated in language a little diversified; while curiosity, excited by the gradual developement of improbable events, lures the infatuated reader through a perplexing wilderness of uninteresting characters and unnatural incidents, where no fruit of useful knowledge or fountain of unpolluted instruction is met with to repay his labour; or worse, far worse, through a region of deleterious enchantment, where the hand of the Genius of seduction withdraws the veil of modesty from the eyes of youthful Innocency, and permits her to gaze on the painted scene of delusive happiness that conceals the gulph of ruin.[19]

From this excoriation, Scott exempted only a few novels: Richardson's *The History of Sir Charles Grandison,* Johnson's *Rasselas,* Hawkesworth's *Almoran and Hamet,* Brooke's *The Fool of Quality,*[20] "and perhaps one or two more." Beattie would not have unconditionally approved even these few: he found Hawkesworth's novel contaminated with some of Hobbes's notions on pity, and the whole narrative was so confused it left the reader with disagreeable impressions as to the ways of Providence.[21]

Such a general condemnation was to be the unusual, rather than the usual, action by Scott. For he held, as a basic principle, a notion of "particular criticism," and of this theory, the *Critical Essays* is an excellent illustration. He had once objected because his own poems had not been given this particular scrutiny; when reviewers discussed them, the remarks made were always so general that it was difficult to understand the criticism and to defend himself from the attack.[22] One of his favorite battle cries was *Qui bene distinguit bene docet,* which he had originally heard in the pages of the *Critical Review;* when he made his pamphlet reply to that journal's review of his poems, he shouted this same motto three times at his enemy. Scott hated ipse dixit criticism, as he called it; and in the *Critical Essays* he was not guilty of this error. In discussing Milton's *Lycidas,* for example, he quoted 174 of the poem's 193 lines, and in every instance he quoted that part of the text which was the subject of his commentary. Though he said that in long works where so much was praised it was not necessary to quote everything, he was always favorably disposed to the minute examination of poems, even if they had received the approval of the ages: so he was able to attack Denham's *Cooper's Hill* with the assumption that its reputation was due solely to generations who had acclaimed it without examining it. "Criticism descends to her lowest task, when she objects to single works; but that task is often useful."[23] He felt that no matter how small the fault examined, it was important; only attention to trifles could bring a poem near perfection. In this critical approach, he was following Warton's suggestion that "general and unexemplified criticism is always useless and absurd."[24] Even Johnson had stated that "CRITICAL REMARKS are not easily understood without examples,"[25] but in his *Lives of the Poets,* Johnson had examined "not so much with attention to slight faults or petty beauties, as to the general character and effect of each performance."[26]

Scott shared Gray's opinions that such intensive criticism cannot be expected of the masses of people who distinguish merit

only in a generalized way.[27] Close critical analysis was a skill
which was useful for the intellectual who read poetry with in-
tensity, and it was a skill which must be developed by the
potential poet. For Scott did not conceive of his book as a philosophical treatise on the value and benefit of poetry, as Beattie,
Harris, Wordsworth, and so many other commentators did
when they wrote on art. Rather, proceeding on the assumption
that poetry had a recognized value, he was interested in showing
how it could be brought closer to that standard of perfection
which he called "classical simplicity." The *Critical Essays* became, when viewed under this light, a handbook on the writing
of poetry, with implicit advice for the poet intent on self-
improvement. Its importance as such a document can be easily
exaggerated, but no one should forget that in his first separately
published poem, Wordsworth referred the reader to this book as
an influence on his own writing.[28]

Because he did not establish a philosophical system which
would explain the merit and demerit of certain ideas, poems,
and philosophies, Scott had to resort mainly in his criticism to
arbitrary statements that certain practices were good and others
were bad. It is clear that he relied heavily on the assumptions
about the nature and end of poetry popularized especially by
Beattie, and his work seems to have proceeded from Beattie's
attitude. Therefore, though Scott cared nothing about the personal character of a writer and was willing to judge the merits
of a work without reference to its author,[29] he did feel that any
work of merit must be based on ideas and sentiments which were
in themselves valid and acceptable: "... whether the sentiment
is fashionable or unfashionable, just or unjust, it certainly de-
tracts nothing from the merit of the poetry."[30] Truth was always
better than fiction, he maintained; yet he liked the creations of
the mind which were not too preposterous to be believed.[31] Then,
reversing his field, he became irritated when poets agreed with

popular prejudices, and he was secretly alarmed when poets possessed ideas about human nature which contradicted his own. When Gray described his peasants as keeping the noiseless tenor of their way along the cool sequestered vale of life, Scott complained that the idea was poetically pleasing but not just, for peasants were justifiably discontented with their status in life. Obviously, the concern for the poor, which had produced the poor-relief tract, never left him.

It was apparent that a poem could please and not be just, but the best poem would do both. This was not a new idea. Dennis, Warton, and Johnson were champions of truth and probability. Of all right ideas which could be, with justification, treated as subjects of poetic composition, morality was one of the most proper and also, paradoxically, the most dangerous to the unskilled writer. In Scott's time, Warton, Johnson, and Beattie all agreed that a moral sentiment introduced with ease and elegance constituted a high form of poetic pleasure. But a moral sentiment was also "the cheapest product of the human mind,"[32] and only a genius could handle it with the conciseness required and end with the felicity desired. Scott felt that Collins was an admirable example of one who handled his moral sentiments with discretion, and he seems to have thought himself not completely lacking in the same ability.

II

Underlying Scott's critical theory, and presumably essential to an understanding of it, is a rather inexact notion of what is poetry. He never came to a clear definition of it in all its complexity, preferring instead, like Johnson, to say what it is not rather than what it is. His most important observation on this subject was made in his discussion of Denham where he said that Pope had best defined poetry when he "misnamed" it wit in the famous couplet:

> True Wit is Nature to advantage dress'd,
> What oft was thought, but ne'er so well express'd.

This definition, presumably intended as clarification of Scott's attitude, tells more about his concept of wit than of poetry. By Scott's time, wit, as a critical term, had been tossed about for so long by so many that its meaning became worn away through too much handling.[33] Professor Hooker has shown how by John Oldmixon's time (1727) the term was confused with humor, good sense, wisdom, reason, craft, and even philosophy; but in general the term was used for two main kinds of wit: broadly, it meant the combination of fancy and judgment, or imagination and judgment; in a restricted sense, it was identical with fancy or imagination and, therefore, separated from the judgment or reason. As the century progressed, wit was becoming the expression of mirth or ridicule in which fancy was involved. Scott's criticism of Pope's "misnaming" poetry as wit was derived from an assumption that "wit" earlier in the century had the same meaning it had in the Amwell poet's own time.

Pope's critical couplet held slightly different meanings for everyone who studied it, but Scott's basic reading of it seems to have been close to Johnson's own. Admittedly, Scott's analysis was less sophisticated than Johnson's quite complicated attitude, and he could never have made such penetrating discoveries as Johnson demonstrated in his commentary on the *Rape of the Lock,* which has been shown to reflect Johnson's concept of wit.[34] Scott asserted, "The great merit of a poet is not, like Cowley, Donne, and Denham, to say what no man but himself has thought, but what every man but himself has thought, but no man expressed, or at least expressed so well."[35] Like Johnson, he would insist that genius is shown only by invention. Johnson had complained about Pope's couplet, saying it reduced wit "from strength of thought to happiness of language,"[36] but Scott did not see these two views as antithetical. Indeed, he thought that one was the result of the other, the strength of the thought causing the happiness of the language. Johnson felt that "the two most engaging powers of an author [are]: new things are made familiar, and familiar things are made new,"[87] and a modern critic of Johnson has asserted that this "demand that literature express both the familiar and the unfamiliar is perhaps his [Johnson's] most basic aesthetic requirement."[88] Scott also reëmphasized the old critical assumption that poetry could universally interest only "when it 'brings back the memory of the past,' when it recalls the objects we have seen, and the emotions we have felt."[89] Johnson's emphasis lay upon the value of art as leading us back to life; the source in reality alone made the work meaningful and valuable. Scott, too, held a strong moral position about the purpose and origin of art, but he was also drifting toward notions about the validity of emotional experiences considered by themselves, the creation of which were the effect of poetry. He never explored fully the implications of his arguments, but if he had, he would have found himself being carried toward Wordsworth's concept of the origin of poetry as emotion recollected in tranquillity, or being swept back to Dennis' original position of the essential relationship between passion and poetry.[40]

In his concern with literary expression, Scott was not rejecting the older concept that Pope popularized in the distinction between the poet and the man of rhymes, the poet being the one who makes the reader "feel each passion that he feigns ... And snatch[es him] o'er the earth or through the air, / To Thebes, to Athens, when he will, and where."[41] Accepting this assumption, Scott was concerned with doing this most effectively; such motivation turned his thoughts to language and expression. One would have thought he would have been more interested in the psychological state of the poet, since it was the imaginative and not the rational power which most impressed him in a work.

But it was reason which received his attention, and this shifting of subject doubtless reduced for many the importance of his work. To Scott, a poet was

a person who combines picturesque imagery, and interesting sentiment, and conveys them in melodious and regularly measured language. This is a definition, which will exclude the writer of Romances, and Prose Dramas, however sublime or pathetick, on the
one hand; and the meer maker of Verses, however humorous or
witty, on the other; were indeed the claim of either to be allowed, it
must be that of the former; inasmuch as poetry must be nearer allied
to the dignified and elegant, then to the mean and indelicate.[42]

For this reason, he once flatly asserted:

Camden, Speed, and the Author of the Tour through Great-Britain,
have as much right to the title of descriptive poets, as Denham and
Pope, unless the latter paint nature with more precision and elegance,
relate transactions with more dignity and ease, and convey their
thoughts in a musical and correct versification.[43]

Johnson had said: "To circumscribe poetry by a definition will only shew the narrowness of the definer,"[44] but Scott's final definition is significant for the broadness of approach he brought to the problem. Whereas Beattie was inclined to say, ". . . it is the *form* chiefly that distinguishes poetry from other writings,"[45] and then to admit that a work of prose could certainly be a poem, "though perhaps not a perfect one,"[46] Scott concluded by feeling that verse was essential to the perfection of all poetry "that admits of it." Beattie had his difficulty because he failed to distinguish between poetry as subject matter and a poem as embodiment of that subject matter; he was continually getting trapped in his own linguistic difficulties. Scott was successful in avoiding this snare, probably by following Warton, who had emphasized, "A minute and particular enumeration of circumstances judiciously selected, is what chiefly discriminates poetry from history, and renders the former, for that reason, a more close and faithful representation of nature than the latter."[47]

Warton urged that the poet, therefore, keep his eye close to nature, the result being the introduction of new images; Scott followed this concept and championed this idea. Warton had said further, "The judicious addition of circumstances and adjuncts is what renders poesy a more lively imitation of nature than prose."[48] Scott felt that it was in its language that poetry differs from prose. To be sure, he retained conventional notions about rhyme, meter, and versification, but he took the general concepts of Warton, and many of those of Beattie, and by being concerned with an almost scientific eye for nature, attempted to see the implications of these theories better than they had been seen before. He was not successful in clarifying the problem, but he was clearly in the stream of critical thought which was already rising into the Romantic movement.

By Scott's definition of poetry, which was largely a concern with expressing old ideas in new language, the thoughts of the reader were turned toward originality and, inevitably, plagiarism, a subject which Johnson had touched on when he mentioned Langbaine's *Account of the English Dramatic Poets* in his own *Lives of the Poets*. This obsession with being original had caused Scott in his *Poetical Works* to include an appendix which traced his own poetic allusions and echoes and to stress which were unconscious borrowings and which were acknowledged ones. Like Warton, whom he quoted, he felt "THE use, the force, and the excellence of language, certainly consists in raising, *clear, complete,* and *circumstantial* images, and in turning *readers,* into *spectators.*"[49] To do this, man must copy nature directly or he will end as Johnson said Cowley did, by giving "inferences instead of images."[50] But if the same scene is to be described by a multitude of poets, will their language be the same? Warton insisted: "Descriptions therefore that are faithful and just, MUST BE UNIFORM AND ALIKE; the first copier may be perhaps entitled to the praise of priority, but a succeeding one ought not certainly to be condemned for plagiarism."[51] Scott, however, felt plagiarism as plagiarism could exist, too; but he agreed with Warton that if a poet improved on his source, it was a virtue rather than a fault.[52] Finally, in a discussion of plagiarism, Scott admitted that one of the pleasures of poetry results from the recognition of poetic echoes; such echoes did not detract from a poet's stature. Scott, therefore, never really settled satisfactorily the question of plagiarism; but then neither has any age. The one avenue out afforded him led toward the realm of figurative language; by following the road toward "classical simplicity," where there was an embargo on figures of speech, Scott left himself no possibility of escape.

III

To be a poet, Scott felt, one must possess imagination; to be a good poet, he must possess both imagination and judgment. And with this division of powers into these two categories, he was following the most traditional critical theory which, though expressed or implied by nearly every critic, was doubtless reemphasized for him by the writings both of Beattie and Langhorne, two of his oldest literary friends.

> Without the Entheus Nature's self bestows,
> The world no Painter nor no Poet knows:
> But think not Mind in its own depth contains
> A source of wealth that no disbursement drains:
> Quick Observation, ever on the wing,
> Home, like the bee, its useful stores must bring;
> From hills, and vales, and rocks, and streams, and trees,
> And towns, and all that people those and these;
> From meanest objects that may hints inspire,
> Discolour'd walls, or heaps of glowing fire.
> Care too beside thee still must take her place,
> Retouch each stroke, and polish every grace;
> For when we join not dignity with ease,
> Nor thou canst paint, nor I can write, to please.[53]

Under the category of the imagination were listed those powers which appealed to one's emotions. Scott attacked poetry which had no soul and which appealed only to the head and not the heart. "Whatever I have wrote I have felt, and I believe others have felt it also."[54] He was like his contemporaries in making no distinction between imagination and fancy. Nor did he define the pathetic or the sublime; he used these terms in a loose and general manner, apparently operating on the assumption that he meant by them precisely what everyone else meant—without, of course, distinguishing between the nuances of meaning which these words had for their users. Although he did not express it as clearly as such a minor critic even as Langhorne did, he felt that the imaginative powers were closely related to his notion of observing nature: "... the closest pursuit of nature is the surest way to excellence in general, and to sublimity in particular."[55] But it was not primarily with the category of the imaginative powers that Scott was to deal in his essays. He would occasionally comment on the "sublimity" or the "pathos" of a passage, but he was more concerned with showing how the passage conformed to his notions of "classical simplicity." Since the components of this constituted the powers of judgment, it was to that function he turned most of his attention.

The cult of simplicity had become a well-established faith by the time Scott joined its persuasion. Professor Havens has demonstrated that this attitude received an enormous impetus from the new science which stressed the economy and simplicity of nature and frequently said nothing new but delighted in expressing observations about phenomena more simply than they had been put before.[56] Pomfret's *The Choice* became one of the basic documents of the new faith, but as is too frequently the case with documents designed to quiet a minor confusion, it split the sect in two, one part believing in the simplicity of art; the other, in the simple life. Soon, "simplicity" began to take on as many meanings as "wit" and, indeed, to be contrasted with it. Early in the eighteenth century, simplicity of style in poetry was thought "best achieved through using the end-stopped heroic couplet, or, for certain purposes, the octosyllabic or short stanza. Even the triplet and alexandrine favored by Dryden were given up when Swift ridiculed them. Like the sonnet and Spenserian stanza, they seemed tainted with 'wit' and too involved to be attractive."[57]

The simplicity which was so much in vogue by the time Scott wrote was, as Professor Havens has shown, not neoclassic simplicity, which "had been largely intellectual, critical, restrictive, and Latinic, concerned with literature, with propriety and regularity, tending to be elegant and sophisticated." Instead, it "was enthusiastic and emotional; it was inspired by the Greeks and looked back, not so much to literature as (through sculpture, architecture, vase-painting, and gems) to life, to the ideal beauty and vitality of joyous Athenian youth."[58] Under the influence of this new simplicity, Scott called his "classical simplicity," and although he seems to have thought of Pope as the model for it, he was fond of referring to the classics and especially Virgil as his ultimate inspiration.

Scott's "classical simplicity," unlike so much which was to be positive and emotionally enthusiastic, was coldly and analytically negative. It was distinguished not by the presence but by the absence of things. It was to be the style of Virgil; it was to have few figures of speech, and only those were acceptable which seemed to arise naturally from the circumstances. There was to be nothing of the flowery or the metaphorical and no violation of diction with strained conceits, such as the flowers in *Lycidas* wearing a gay *wardrobe,* or a citron grove in Collins' *Oriental Eclogues* "drooping its fair honours." Things would be clearly understood; there would be no inexactness of detail and no awkward attempts at profundity and a false tugging at the beard of tragedy. It was pure in its origin, Scott thought, and it came from the classics. Yet Langhorne questioned the claim of the Greek tragedians to simplicity. "Their language, at least, was infinitely metaphorical; yet it must be owned that they justly copied nature and the passions, and so far, certainly, they were entitled to the palm of true simplicity."[59] It is possible to see this concern in the youthful Pope's *Discourse on Pastoral Poetry,* where Scott's later notions are certainly implied.

There was a confusion in Pope's discussion between simplicity owing to humble life and that owing to language, that confusion which underlay much of the century's speculation on this subject and doubtless contributed to Wordsworth's "revolutionary" notion about the real language of men being the proper language of poetry. In his preface to the *Iliad,* however, Pope clarified this issue by emphasizing the elegance inherent in the concept, saying: "Simplicity is the mean between ostentation and rusticity." By the time Warton had come to do his lengthy essay on Pope, he would still admit that "SIMPLICITY, with elegance and propriety, is the perfection of style in every composition,"[60] yet his attention was focused on other matters. And though simplicity is mentioned in the first volume of this essay, it occurs more frequently in the second volume, which appeared in 1782, and perhaps indicates an increasing interest in this concept. (It was in this volume that Warton quoted Pope's observation, "Arts are taken from nature, and, after a thousand vain efforts for improvements, are best when they return to their first simplicity.")[61] Although Warton does mention simplicity with the highest praise, it is clear that Scott did not get his emphasis on this notion from him. Nor did it come from William Mason's *The English Garden,* which opened with an invocation to "divine Simplicity." And it certainly did not come from Gray, who had once advised Mason on the revision of a poem, "If the sentiment must stand, twirl it a little into an apothegm; stick a flower in it; gild it with a costly expression; let it strike the fancy, the ear, or the heart, and I am satisfied."[62] Rather, for Scott this emphasis on simplicity came most obviously from Beattie, who spent a large part of his critical writing in discussing this idea, and from Langhorne, who in his observation on the merit of Collins shared most of Scott's convictions on the matter. There were other poets Scott admired, such as Shenstone in his *A Prefactory Essay on Elegy,* Glover in his *Leonidas,* Dyer in his *The Fleece* (Scott and Warton championed the last two as the epitome of simplicity),[63] and Collins in his "Ode to Simplicity," who contributed to the general interest on the subject; but the Amwell poet got his ideas, it seems apparent, from Beattie. Beattie was never consistent in the expression of his concept, and like his Quaker friend, he seems to have had considerable difficulty in saying precisely what he meant. But the basic assumption of the following statement, Scott adhered to, even when its author did not:

There is a great deal of cant in the style of poetry, especially of modern poetry. A set of epithets, and figures, and phrases, which a certain set of versifiers bring in upon all occasions, in order to make out their verses, and prepare their rhymes. If a poet has got a good stock of these, and a knack of applying them, and is not very solicitous about energy, consistency, or truth of sentiment, he may write verses with great ease and rapidity; but such verses are not read above once or twice, and are seldom or never remembered. Their tawdry and unnecessary ornaments make them as unwieldy to the memory as a herald's coat is to the body. Besides, where language is much ornamented, there is always a deficiency in clearness, as well as in force; and, though it may please at its first appearance, it rarely continues long in fashion. The favourite authors in every language are the simplest. They have nothing but what is *necessary* or *useful;* and such things are always in request.[64]

It was this same attitude which caused Scott to write in one of his odes that his only desire was to emulate the plans of Virgil, Horace, Akenside, and Shenstone; by so doing, he felt his poems would gain the praises of posterity. Beattie, in his *The Hermit,* also "aimed at simplicity in the expression, and something like uncommonness in the thought,"[65] since Gray had once criticized portions of Part One of *The Minstrel* as being violations of simplicity.[66] Even Johnson pointed out that Swift's "delight was in simplicity. That he has in his works no metaphor, as has been said, is not true; but his few metaphors seem to be received rather by necessity than choice."[67] Complicated as became the term "simplicity," it is perhaps the one term which held no confusion for Scott. He obtained this clarity by sacrificing all nuances and insisting that the word was synonymous with "plainness."[68] It meant "chaste diction, free from tautologous repetitions of the same thoughts in different expressions; free from bad rhymes, unnecessary epithets, and incongruous metaphors."[69]

To illustrate his own conceptions of "classical simplicity," Scott frequently took a liberty in his *Critical Essays* which must have annoyed many readers: he rewrote and rearranged lines and stanzas from the poems under discussion to demonstrate how his theory, if applied, would improve these works. Even John Hoole, Scott's most enthusiastic admirer, was upset at the treatment Gray received in this high-handed fashion, and he complained of Scott: "I think that he has indulged himself too much in his proposed transpositions of several passages in that poem." Though Scott was careful to show in many of these instances that the "improvements" were not really improvements at all, since they lost in imaginative power what they gained in simplicity, he did feel that this was an effective way of demonstrating the validity of his own notions. In "Summer" of his *Seasons,* Thomson had written:

'Tis listening fear and dumb amazement all;
When to the startled eye the sudden glance
Appears far south, eruptive through the cloud,
And following slower in explosion vast,

> The thunder raises his tremendous voice.
> At first heard solemn o'er the verge of heaven,
> The tempest growls; but as it nearer comes,
> And rolls its awful burden on the wind,
> The lightnings flash a larger curve.... [ll. 1128–1136.]

Scott felt this would, with respect to his theory, best appear as

> 'Tis list'ning fear and dumb amazement all:
> When to the startled eye the sudden glance,
> Appears far south eruptive through the cloud;
> And following slow the solemn thunder rolls.
> Long, dark and threatening o'er the verge of heav'n
> The tempest swells, but as it nearer comes,
> And spreads its awful burden on the wind,
> The lightnings flash, &c.

In this revision and compression of Thomson's lines, Scott felt he had presented convincing proof of the defensibility of his basic attitude toward "classical simplicity."

IV

In discussing the judgment and its contribution to poetry, Scott stated, "A poetical mind too seldom thinks with precision; imagination is apt to act without judgment"; here he emphasized the importance of judgment and correctness—judgment being the cause; correctness, the result—in the poet's craft.

> Instruct me them, with view severe,
> To inspect, and keep from error clear;
> Nor spare, though fancy'd e'er so fine,
> One ill-placed thought, or useless line.[70]

Warton said this faculty was usually attained only through long practice and experience in any art,[71] and Scott seems to have shared this conviction. By "judgment," his was the conventional meaning of the rational powers which, untouched by imagination or enthusiasm, would be able to distinguish propriety at all times and would be able to give a poem—although not the heightened emotional charge which could come only from the imagination and its subsidiary powers—the other effects of recollection which constituted the complete poetic experience. This standard definition referred to the power of judgment as that which created a logical structure, prevented the mixing of figures, and made the poem accord with fact (either of the world[72] or of the poet's own poetic imagination).[73] Judgment embodied a knowledge of decorum and good taste. It was the faculty which took the inspirations of the imagination and gave them an acceptable form. Because of the requirements of this power, Scott felt that a correct writer—that is, one who used his judgment effectively—could never write much in quantity; but his productions would be superior for their quality.

Judgment, on its simplest level, was concerned with mechanical accuracy in poems; this concerned poetic structure, metrics, and figures of speech and resulted in the following of certain definite rules about art. Scott's critical assumption here goes back to Pope's popularized concern with following rules being the same as copying nature. Scott, however, emphasized also the old concept of structural unity, where each work embodied within itself the rules by which it was to be judged. Intensive reading of a poem, he would insist, should present the author's purpose and the standards by which his work was to be evaluated.[74] Despite this apparently lenient attitude, Scott felt that consistency was a basic virtue in the structure of a poem; and his principal criticism of Goldsmith's *The Deserted Village* was that it lacked this unifying principle.[75] He was also greatly impressed with the power and influence of sounds—he had once spoken of poetry as existing "where music fraught with useful knowledge flows."[76] Unlike Beattie, who discussed at length how the sound could be made an echo to the sense,[77] Scott suspected this notion, and though he did feel on occasions that there were certain lines which felicitously demonstrated this principle, most direct attempts to achieve this ended in nonsense, either with violations of logical meaning or a faulty use of repetition. Both Johnson and Warton had distrusted such attempts, and Scott was here influenced by them.[78] In his attitude toward metrics, Scott was closely allied with Johnson.

Warton had championed blank verse "for subjects of a higher order, where any enthusiasm or emotion is to be expressed, or for poems of a greater length,"[79] but he admitted that rhyme also had its functions. Scott felt this emphasis should be reversed and said that although blank verse could be defended for specific uses and occasions, poems were best expressed in regular rhymes. But, despite his great admiration for fine versification, Scott insisted that it was not the end in poetry. "The critick's charity is too often induced by it to spare a multitude of poetical sins." His notion of logic and sense and meaning was still basic, and anything which in any way distorted these, no matter how fine it might be in itself, was a flaw in good poetry.

In view of Scott's theory of simplicity, his attitude toward figurative language was completely logical. He occasionally found a "pretty image"; he more frequently uncovered a malformed one. He disliked unnatural or disagreeable conceits, "the frippery of unmeaning epithets, and metaphors, which the *Addisonian* test of painting would render completely ridiculous."[80] His belief in a unified and consistent structure for a work of art naturally caused him to object violently to mixed figures of all kinds and to consider the existence of them in a poem as evidence of a poor judgment at work. He liked the image of "tribulation clothing the child of man" in Dyer's *The Ruins of Rome* and called it a fine orientalism; he was quite fond of discussing such a use of personification. But while he found it one of the most common of poetical figures, and less liable to abuse than the metaphor, he did not feel that it was always used with propriety. Dyer's particular image, however, appealed to his own view of man's earthly state; it also was defended by the type of poem in which it appeared: Oriental poetry was equated with ornamentation, and he defended his own decorated "Oriental Eclogues" because of its species of poetry.[81] English farm poems (his "Amoebaean Eclogues") were something else, of course. Plainness of subject demanded plainness of language.

His greatest objection was made, however, against the metaphor and the simile. Scott's deprecation of the metaphor—he called it "an *ignis fatuus,* that leads many a poet into the bog of nonsense"—followed his theory of "classical simplicity" at the expense of what was his theory of poetry. In a proper figure of speech, especially as regards the simile and metaphor, there must be a real analogy between the particulars which are being compared, if that comparison is to be valid and meaningful. He admitted that where such a proper comparison is made, it "is rational and frequently advantageous. This practice also, by presenting to the reader's mind a new, yet congruous, group of imagery, adds greatly to his pleasure." The assumption here is that of Warton, Beattie, Johnson, and an infinite number of other critics. James Harris approached the problem in a slightly different way when he suggested that the defense of the metaphor is the arrangement of the old and familiar in a new way, and this constitutes its chief pleasure;[82] viewed in this light, the metaphor and simile would be the best example of poetry by Pope's notion of what was often said but never so well expressed, and one would have suspected Scott to have been like Dennis, a defender of this figure, rather than its most outspoken antagonist.

Notwithstanding the beliefs of these critics and the observations he himself made about the pleasure derived from good figures of speech, Scott was inclined to condemn most similes; there were few he could give even qualified praise. In fact, on one occasion he even commended a work for its paucity of similes. He briefly mentioned metonymy—under which category he also placed the synecdoche—and allusion; again, while he could cite instances where they had been effective, his general inclination was to distrust them, as he did most figures, for he felt they were not accurate and were, therefore, violations of his basic assumptions about poetry and truth.

Warton had said that historical accuracy was not essential in poetry, and while Scott agreed with this, he did insist upon scientific accuracy. This was owing to his basic theory that poetry should describe the world of nature in accordance with truth, and he felt Thomson in particular was an admirable example of a man who had directed his attention to nature with scrupulous care. That which was natural was always best, and he praised natural circumstances, natural images, natural descriptions, natural philosophy, and, even, digressions (if they entered the poem naturally). Clearly, Johnson's opposition to numbering the stripes of the tulip did not impress Scott, who felt that in such a minute examination of natural phenomena lay the secret of effective creation. It is easy to see how this emphasis upon nature and the natural could have impressed Wordsworth. This same assumption about the validity of the natural caused Scott to insist that words should be used in their natural order in poetry—a rule which he himself strangely refrained from following, perhaps because, as he once pointed out, transposition could sometimes give strength to a line. Scott was always annoyed by factual inaccuracies in a poem, but he also had high praise for those scientific insights which some poets showed and made them get their natural phenomena properly classified; therefore, he discussed with pleasure the "grey fly" in *Lycidas* and the beetle and the habits of the owl in Gray's elegy. A poet was to deal with truth—the facts of the natural world—and was to rearrange them according to his own thoughts and imagination.

But he was not to alter the basic laws of the universe; even in the world of the imagination, phenomena must abide by the laws of nature. It was only a small step from this to a concern with grammatical accuracy and clarity. He, like Warton, felt that Young was frequently bombastic, and he snorted, "There is a perverse tendency in men to admire what they do not understand. Not only hearers, but readers, are often best pleased with nonsense." This basic assumption would also be pushed further when Wordsworth wrote his famous preface.[53]

When Scott turned his thoughts to the vocabulary of poetry, he did not have any original speculations to make, but he shifted the emphasis of some commentators by discussing vocabulary with respect to repetition. Beattie felt poetic diction was that enormous vocabulary which had been built up over a period of time by poets and consisted of words which should be and could be used only in verse. Scott disagreed with this assumption and felt that poetic diction was not necessarily the result of an attempt at novelty. Rather, it resulted when a poet wished to repeat an idea or a word and, feeling that such repetition was in itself bad, he coined a different phrase which would carry the original meaning in a new form. To solve this problem, Scott said arbitrarily that all repetition was bad, since the reader would already have conceived the idea by its first mention, and repetition of it would serve only to annoy him. He was aware that there existed such a thing as an intended repetition which created an aesthetic effect, and this he termed a "pleonasm," as opposed to the bad repetition or "perissology." Langhorne had liked a pleonasm when he found it, but Scott felt most repetitions were perissologies; at his most tolerant, he called pleonasms "pardonable redundancies" and said that even they could be removed without injury to a poem. In the same manner that he had admitted the possible virtue of some figures of speech, so he conceded the dubious merit of the pleonasm. What the particular language of poetry was to be, Scott did not say. He attacked "rhyming prose," and he felt all prosaisms were evidence of a poetic intention unfulfilled. Perhaps, if a person kept his eye close to nature and was a genius of rare sensitivity, his imagination would help him verbalize in that middle ground which neither rose to poetic diction nor sank to prose. Wordsworth would define this area of language in a fashion which perhaps would have shocked Scott; yet the Quaker's assumptions were carrying him toward the real language of men.

V

The last group of critical remarks to be considered has been called the category of rules; actually, this may not be the best way to describe these various observations, but the totality of them represents what Scott seems to have considered rules or standards for the judgment to follow, in order to bring a poem to correctness. Although many of these observations were established critical dicta which had been given their best expression by Dennis, several were only arbitrary expressions of Scott's own opinions. That which had been said for generations still needed restatement, Scott felt, if it was being ignored. Like Johnson, he seems to have felt that a good thought could not be given too frequent expression.

One of the most important and most approved, critically, of these statements was an insistence on psychological accuracy. Warton had criticized French drama for having its characters speak the sentiments of the author or the spectator rather than those of the character supposedly being portrayed, and Beattie and Priestley were voicing critical commonplaces when they demanded that figures of speech should be properly motivated by the emotional state of the speaker. Scott agreed with these assumptions, and he emphasized that diction should be selected according to the speaker's idiomatic level. The fine gradations of emotion, the varied verbal responses one makes in various states of excitement—all these, he felt, should be chosen with care to effect the author's purpose. Later, Wordsworth himself was to share these same convictions and feel that figures of speech were justified when explicable by the speaker's emotional situation. Scott stressed that such a reading of emotional states into the language of a poem, however, should be restricted to the animate; only in rare cases should the pathetic fallacy be admitted in poetry: "Rural scenes may perhaps be properly said to mourn, because a person who was wont to frequent them is deceased; but not because a shepherdess frowns on her lover, or a lady loses her lap-dog." Poets also frequently described a subject only by saying that it was impossible to be described. Scott held no brief with such nonsense, calling it "a puerile and inadequate expedient"; yet he had toyed with the same device in the conclusion of *Amwell*. Like Warton, he held that a poet should strive to discuss and describe his creations through dealing with particulars and not with generalities. Though minuteness diminished grandeur, particulars were necessary and the only means by which a sense of reality was given to a work of art. He urged that names of places be used in a descriptive poem, as they afforded pleasure, and "specification of position always gives a kind of reality to a supposed scene." However, even details must be selected with care, and the correct choice of particulars was the result only of an accurate and effective judgment.

Anyone making general observations about the nature of poetry must act upon the assumption that his personal taste is a valid basis for generalizations.

> Yet Taste incites me others' works to view,
> And risk a judgment haply not untrue.[84]

Scott realized this and said that in many instances each person must let his own taste guide him. It is clear that he considered his own ideas valid for others; he was laboring with this self-confidence when he flatly asserted that a landscape is best when it shows cultivated ground rather than pasture. "The creation of fictitious persons, and the description of real ones, have generally been esteemed among the principal operations of poetry." In such a creation, one should remember that it is wrong to have a positive introduction of imaginary things, and—here he was standing with Johnson and Warton—comparison with a nonentity cannot elevate a real object. He wanted to see virtue rewarded and vice punished, even though he admitted the world was seldom so just; but seeing this done creates one of the principal pleasures derived from poetry and strives to teach the only acceptable moral position. He, too, liked motion in his scenes and wished his figures set against a proper background so they would stand out; but that same boredom with the static which made Dennis turn from nature as the best subject for poetry, did not occur to Scott.[85] No poem, finally, should ever be "degraded with prosaisms, and obscured with metaphors, encumbered with heterogeneous digressions, and perplexed with conceits and quibbles." To the end, every rule of correct composition would stem from an understanding of his theory of "classical simplicity."

VI

Ten years before Scott's death, one critic wrote:

As Virtuosi, we are quitting the fastidiousness and barbarism of our Gothic ancestors; our eyes are almost reconciled to simplicity; and we even copy the antique. This is the road to nature; and it is to be hoped we shall in time equal those gems and statues and paintings, which we now imitate with so much success and credit.—Our government may become arbitrary and ineffectual; our religion a servile superstition; and our people lose all the spirit and rights of Englishmen. The arts will preserve our existence; they will form a kind of commerce, and furnish our support; they will humanize our manners; implant a sort of veneration of us in all neighbouring states; they will give us, as they have given Rome, some security and credit, instead of that glory and power, which we shall lose, as she did, when we have lost our virtue.[86]

Scott was not so optimistic about the progress of art in his day or the success with which art could preserve a national reputation.[87] One of the reasons he so admired Dyer's *The Ruins of Rome* was for the way it described with dignity and pathos the fatal effects of national luxury. Beattie had shown him how both Horace and Longinus had ascribed the decline of eloquence in their day to a littleness of mind, the effect of luxury and avarice; the manly simplicity of the old writers disappeared as the nation became effeminate and servile.[88] Therefore, Scott saw the society of his own time declining before his eyes. He saw luxury and avarice flourishing everywhere, and when he deplored the state of modern literature, he was also excoriating his society for its social, political, moral, philosophical, and economic ills.

There is latent within his critical writings—as indeed within everything he wrote—the notion that if literature reflects the corruption of the state, cannot an uncorrupted literature purify the state; could not an effect be a cause? It is to do him a considerable disservice to dismiss him with the observation, as one recent critic did, "That he was a whimsical eccentric is emphasized by his repeated harping on the subject of the decline of letters in his day, and, in particular, on the use of the run-on line in heroic verses, which he described as 'a vicious mode of composition.'"[89] Literature had an ameliorative influence; only this belief could justify the devotion of such a large part of his life to it. So he, as one of a band of artists joined together by a retrospective attitude, tried to make Englishmen progress through regression. That the final engraving in the *Poetical Works* should be Blake's plate of a maiden laying a scroll on a pillar "Sacred to simplicity," is significant as emphasizing allegorically and pictorially Scott's basic critical theory. Though Charles Lamb would later ridicule remarks selected at random from the *Critical Essays*,[90] Scott's commentaries, appearing at a significant moment in English critical thought, came to be something besides an age's *divertissement* and impressed one Cambridge student in particular with the justness of their observations.[91] The continued emphasis on simplicity paralleled the growing concern with Gothicism and resulted in that curious blending of the usual and the unusual which was later termed Romanticism.

The theory of "classical simplicity," which suggested that the most uncomplex could also be the most profound, held implications which the formulators and propagandists of it did not live to explore. The young Wordsworth, however, who read the *Critical Essays* with concentration and apparently considered the ramifications of these arguments, went far beyond his source. Even though the full extent of this influence upon his thought cannot be calculated, it was not insignificant. For the *Lyrical Ballads* itself was, in one respect, largely a development and outgrowth of that theory of "classical simplicity," which had been given a renewed attention in the later eighteenth century and had been demonstrated by the Quaker poet of Amwell in his *Critical Essays* and in a number of his poems.

CHAPTER VII

THE CONSISTENT PATTERN

SCOTT'S LIFE may be thought of as being the summation only of several independent careers, but it is clear that in the final analysis they are not separable. Each interest was a facet of his complex personality, and the work in the fields of politics, poor laws, highways, poetry, and criticism was joined together by a basic philosophical belief which he held and by which he lived. Scott believed that man must work in the world if he is to improve it; though improvement itself may never come, still man must strive in this endeavor: otherwise, things will get worse. This basic assumption contradicted the teachings of the Society of Friends, to which he belonged, but it indicated that his life was to be characterized by a deep confidence in his own convictions. The Quaker faith promulgated a belief in and reliance upon the "inner light." Scott accepted this teaching but took his own convictions—not those of the Society—and made of them a plan by which to improve the world.

In all his fields of endeavor, Scott demonstrated an implicit faith in progression through regression. He felt that man had deteriorated from those "partial perfections" of the past and that his falling away from older and nobler patterns had been a primary cause of the world's difficulties. Therefore, he turned to the past for the impetus and inspiration he needed to meet the problems of the present. In politics, he combated the Tory party and its aristocratic assumptions by placing faith in Milton's beliefs and individual personal liberties, the cause of which had been eloquently pleaded by the Commonwealth government. In poor-law and humanitarian reforms, he went to Sir Matthew Hale and William Law for a stimulus and revivified a theory of charitable giving which had been rejected by the Age of Reason.

In highways, he emphasized the Roman model and ideal and defined the perfect road in the same way the conquerors of Britain had. In criticism, he turned to a theory of "classical simplicity," which he felt had been held by Pope and the Augustans, and applied its principles to the works of his own day. In poetry, he imitated the compositions of the Augustans and Milton. In all of these phases of his career, his life seems only to have been the recovery of a past pattern of thought.

But Scott's adoption of older forms was not a simple imitative process. Though he never was aware of the fact, he seldom successfully applied an older pattern without reshaping it and making of it something personalized and unique. His political theories represented Commonwealth ideas mixed with a quality of despairing hope which was removed from both the seventeenth- and eighteenth-century notions of progress. His humanitarian reforms took some of Hale's basic assumptions, mixed them with Law's rather impractical views of the nature of man, crossed them with Mandeville's ideas about human motivation, and blended them into that curious amalgam of the idealistic and the practical, a paradox which was at the basis of his philosophy. Even when he wrote on roads, he was not like other eighteenth-century writers who could declaim the glories of transportation. His reëmphasis upon a plan which was essentially Roman was paradoxically colored by the conflict between a desire to build fine roads and a desire to cut off all communication between the country and the town.

In poetry and criticism, however, his mixture of the old and the new was most apparent. Although he stated categorically that his basic theory of "classical simplicity" was Augustan and Popean, he never really appeared to know what Pope's theory was. In fact, one of his greatest attacks was launched against satire; and satire was Pope's forte! His theory of "classical simplicity," it seems, drew much from the obvious excellence of

Pope's clarity, but added to it notions which Pope himself would have deplored. In his concern with the simple subject, the country prospect, and the particularized detail, Scott had moved a great distance from the Augustan theory of general nature; he had been influenced by Thomson, Warton, and Beattie and the beginnings of the Romantic movement.

It was when he operated as a poet that the difficulty Scott had with his adaptation of the past became most apparent. In his poetry was clearly illustrated that dichotomy between the man who wished to be like his ancestors and the man who was not afraid to be himself. It was to be his peculiar nature that he could retain both aspects of his personality from the beginning of his life until the end, and he could simultaneously write mediocre poetry in the former tradition and acceptable work in the genres which he was not afraid to adapt to the demands of his own inspirations. The body of his poetry is the best illustration of this paradoxical and contradictory aspect of his nature.

To read and know John Scott, therefore, is to know both a man and an age. As no man can be separated from the currents of his time but must be swept up by them into the eddies and whirlpools of public thought and concern, so Scott was caught in the streams of natural affairs and became a part of that gigantic flood which was the Enlightenment. All of his ideas were predicated upon the concerns of man; there was nothing of the idle dreamer or troglodyte about him. On the other hand, merely to be a part of an age is a claim which is hardly sufficient to justify remembrance. A man must have a value inherent in himself if he is to be remembered. John Scott was a man of considerable talent and ingenuity and should have retained a modest amount of fame for his accomplishments. Called by the Webbs the foremost of eighteenth-century writers on local government, he seems assured of permanent importance in economic circles. In politics and literature, however, he has lacked a place: not because he has been examined and rejected, but because he has been ignored and his relationship with Johnson and with Wordsworth, forgotten. Investigation of his political theories, however, will reveal him as an astute writer who could have defeated many of Johnson's assertions, had the doctor not taken a cavalier attitude and refused to quarrel. In poetry, especially, Scott has justifiable claims to remembrance. The finer odes and the poem on his country village should ensure something other than oblivion. Originally called John Scott, and then John Scott of Amwell, or John Scott the Quaker—not to be confused with all of the other John Scotts of literature—the poet was, by his name itself, relegated to a position which suggested literary insignificance. For those who read the poet's most distinguished work, however, the name means something else. By them, he is remembered for his microcosm of uncommon beauty which he abandoned to create a similar order for the macrocosm of chaotic England. By them, the Friend can never be recalled but as John Scott of *Amwell*.

NOTES

NOTES TO CHAPTER I

[1] Samuel Johnson, *Letters, with Mrs. Thrale's Genuine Letters to Him*, ed. by R. W. Chapman (Oxford, 1952), III, 176.

[2] *Ibid.*, p. 185.

[3] *Ibid.*, p. 222.

[4] *Ibid.*, p. 191.

[5] *Boswell's Life of Johnson*, ed. by G. Birkbeck Hill and L. F. Powell (Oxford, 1934), IV, 338.

[6] [John] Hoole, "An Account of the Life and Writings of the Author," in John Scott, *Critical Essays on Some of the Poems, of Several English Poets* (London, 1785), pp. [i]–viii. Unless otherwise indicated, all information on Scott's life is drawn from this account.

[7] Johnson, *Letters*, III, 225.

[8] After Scott's death in 1783, his wife and daughter continued to live at the Amwell estate. Maria De Horne Scott was buried November 12, 1786, when the daughter was about nine. On March 14, 1787, Samuel Scott apparently walked among his brother's "shrubberies" for the last time, and on that day he helped a cousin select volumes for Scott's daughter from the library at Amwell. The daughter married Joseph Hooper, and in 1839 she owned the manor of Bartrans on the east side of Braughing Hundred in Standon parish. She also owned the manor of Halfhide, or Westmill, in Braughing Hundred in Ware. She died around 1860, and Amwell House passed into the hands of the Tite family. In 1906, the house became the Ware Grammar School. Meanwhile, the grotto became a separate property, with a house built near it in the nineteenth century. This house and the grotto itself are now the property of John C. Hanbury, Esq., of Ware.

[9] Even as early as 1778, Scott's reputation as a writer was falling behind his reputation as a man of good works. Cf. John Langhorne's review of the 1778 highway book, in the *Monthly Review*, LVIII (May, 1778), 380: "This ingenious Gentleman, well known to the world by his poetical reputation, and not less known in his amiable and benevolent character, seems to be a powerful rival (in point of fame) to THE MAN OF ROSS;—a rival, who, notwithstanding, like the hero of Virgil, will open his arms for his friends, and shoot his arrow into the air.

"In such an age as this, too much cannot be said in favour of a worthy and public-spirited man; for the poet's observation is certainly applicable to the times—'An age, / When dissipation reigns, and prudence sleeps.'"

[10] *Boswell's Life of Johnson*, II, 166.

[11] *Ibid.*, V, 240.

[12] Samuel Johnson, *Lives of the English Poets*, ed. by G. Birkbeck Hill (Oxford, 1905), II, 116.

[13] Johnson, *Letters*, III, 243.

[14] *Boswell's Life of Johnson*, III, 21.

[15] *Ibid.*, II, 338, 351.

[16] *European Magazine*, II (September, 1782), 195.

[17] Samuel Scott, *A Diary of Some Religious Exercises and Experience* (London, 1809). The deathbed account is all that is mentioned (pp. 93–95), although there were references made afterward to the memoirs and the surviving relatives of Scott (pp. 96, 151, 162, 187, 202). Though Samuel admitted to having kept earlier diaries, the published one began on June 1, 1780, and was primarily a record of his own religious thoughts.

[18] *Ibid.*, p. iii.

[19] *Ibid.*, p. 224.

[20] *Ibid.*, p. 119.

[21] *Ibid.*, p. 140.

[22] *Ibid.*, p. ix.

[23] Johnson, *Lives of the English Poets*, II, 79.

[24] *Boswell's Life of Johnson*, I, 490.

[25] Reginald Hine, *Charles Lamb and His Hertfordshire* (London, 1949), pp. 253, 270. Cf. also *London and Its Environs Described* (London, 1761), VI, 256–257: "Here is a very considerable market for corn, and so great is the malt trade here, and in the neighborhood, that 5000 quarters of malt and other corn are frequently sent in a week to London, by the barges, which return with coals."

[26] Hine, *Lamb*, p. 12.

[27] John Scott, "Ode III. To Childhood," in his *Poetical Works* (London, 1782), pp. 174–175.

[28] Scott, *Critical Essays*, pp. 307–308.

[29] *Johnsonian Miscellanies*, ed. by G. Birkbeck Hill (Oxford, 1897), II, 378, 397.

[30] Scott, *Diary*, p. 172.

[31] Letter of Joseph Cockfield to the Reverend Mr. Weeden Butler, January 1, 1767, in John Nichols, *Illustrations of the Literary History of the Eighteenth Century* (London, 1828), V, 772–773.

[32] John Scott, "Winter Prospects in the Country. An Epistle to a Friend [John Turner] in London, 1756," in *A Collection of Poems, in Four Volumes. By Several Hands*, [ed. by George Pearch] (London, 1783), IV, 109.

[33] Scott, *Critical Essays*, p. 244. Cf. also p. 146: "By attention to solemn musick, particularly that of bells heard at a distance, he [Scott] has found his thoughts first regulated to a pleasing calm, then employed on a variety of serious and pathetick images, and at length oppressed in a manner that became painful."

[34] Johnson, *Lives of the English Poets*, II, 315.

[35] *Johnsonian Miscellanies*, II, 8.

[36] Scott, *Poetical Works*, p. 24. In his *Observations on the Present State of the Parochial and Vagrant Poor* (London, 1773), pp. 80–81, he said: "There is, indeed at present, a very detrimental conflux of people from the provinces to the metropolis; where the morals, health, and lives of thousands, are annually offered spontaneous victims at the altars of folly, avarice, and ambition: could an eligible means of repressing this conflux be discovered, the discovery would be a most important and desirable acquisition." And for his *Moral Eclogues* (London, 1778), pp. 2–3, he wrote:

> For us the country boasts enough to charm,
> In the wild woodland or the cultur'd farm.
> Come, CYNTHIO, come! in town no longer stay;
> From crouds, and noise, and folly, haste away!
>
> .   .   .   .
>
> Come, CYNTHIO, come! if towns and crouds invite,
> And noise and folly promise high delight;
> Soon the tir'd soul disgusted turns from these—
> The rural prospect, only, long can please!

NOTES TO CHAPTER II

[1] On the title page of the quarto there is an engraving by Wale of a reclining matron with three cherubs bearing to her the produce of the harvest. It was apparently a common engraving and appeared two years later on the title page of *The Muse's Recreation, in Four Poems* (London, 1762), a publication of Joseph Johnson, who had nothing to do with Scott's publications himself, though he was in partnership for a time with Payne, the friend of Scott and the man to whom one of the poet's odes was addressed.

Notes

[2] *Monthly Review,* XXIII (July, 1760), 70. The review itself covered pages 68–73.

[3] Anna Seward, *Letters: Written Between the Years 1784 and 1807* (Edinburgh, 1811), V, 202–203.

[4] William Shenstone, *Letters,* ed. by Duncan Mallam (Minneapolis, 1939), p. 398.

[5] "Elegy IV. Written at the Approach of Winter," in John Scott, *Poetical Works* (London, 1782), pp. 43–46.

[6] Samuel Johnson, *Lives of the English Poets,* ed. by G. Birkbeck Hill (Oxford, 1905), III, 224.

[7] *Ibid.,* I, 75. Cf. Scott's letter to Elihu Robinson, May 25, 1782, in Friends Library, London: "But on this Subject the Opinion of Dr. Johnson in *Lives of the Poets* is with me decisive—My own Sentiments previously—to reading his work were exactly Similar to his respecting Devotional Poetry, and I was not vain enough to think of succeeding where every man before me had failed."

[8] Johnson, *Lives of the English Poets,* I, 49–50.

[9] Robert Clutterbuck, *The History and Antiquities of the County of Hertford* (London, 1821), II, 76. For a study of Hoole's life, cf. Arthur Sägesser, *John Hoole, His Life and His Tragedies* (Bern, [1917]).

[10] Raymond D. Havens, *The Influence of Milton on English Poetry* (Cambridge, U.S.A., 1922), p. 673.

[11] Joseph Warton, *An Essay on the Genius and Writings of Pope* (4th ed., corr.; London, 1782), I, 5.

[12] For an interesting study of this subject and one from which the information of this paragraph is drawn, cf. Robert A. Aubin, "Grottoes, Geology, and the Gothic Revival," *Studies in Philology,* XXXI (July, 1934), 408–416. Scott's grotto is not mentioned, however. Miss Manwaring's account of Scott's cave-carving compulsions (Elizabeth W. Manwaring, *Italian Landscape in Eighteenth Century England* [Oxford, 1925]) is misleading. Cf. p. 153: "In all this discussion of gardening and shifting of taste, the situation of the amateur, especially if of limited means, was distressing. Poor John Scott of Aimwell [Miss Manwaring persists in so labeling the poet throughout her book] developed his few acres, about 1765, according to the mode as then understood, and showed them proudly to his guest, Dr. Johnson. . . ." Admittedly, Scott's fortune was not one of the greatest in England; yet it was large enough to impress all of his acquaintances, and there is no record of anyone's feeling that the Amwell estate was not life in the grand manner—especially for a Quaker.

[13] R. T. Andrews, "Scott's Grotto, Amwell," *East Herts Archaeological Society. Transactions,* I (1899), 15–31.

[14] Johnson, *Lives of the English Poets,* III, 350–351.

[15] *Ibid.,* p. 135.

[16] Thomas Gray, *Correspondence,* ed. by Paget Toynbee and Leonard Whibley (Oxford, 1935), III, 1065.

[17] In 1819, Thomas Campbell in his *Specimens of the British Poets; with Biographical and Critical Notices, and an Essay on English Poetry* (London, 1819), VI, 432, wrote as though the grotto were no longer in existence. But in 1822, R. A. Davenport, in his *The British Poets* (Chiswick, 1822), LXX, 9, said that the grotto was still a center of attraction for tourists. It still exists, but I am informed by its owner, John C. Hanbury, Esq., that it is in disrepair.

[18] Havens, *Influence of Milton,* pp. 685–686. Both Hoole and Langhorne wrote irregular sonnets.

[19] William Watson, *An Account of a Series of Experiments, Instituted with a View of Ascertaining the Most Successful Method of Inoculating the Small-Pox* (London, 1768), p. 39.

[20] Letter of Joseph Cockfield to the Reverend Mr. Weeden Butler, April 15, 1766, in John Nichols, *Illustrations of the Literary History of the Eighteenth Century* (London, 1828), V, 763.

[21] Letter of April 25, 1766, *ibid.*, pp. 764–765.

[22] [John Scott], *Observations on the Present State of the Parochial and Vagrant Poor* (London, 1773), p. 88.

[23] Letter of Joseph Cockfield to the Reverend Mr. Weeden Butler, March 25, 1767, in Nichols, *Literary History*, V, 775.

[24] Letter of January 28, 1768, *ibid.*, p. 778.

[25] *Ibid.*, p. 777.

[26] Letter of April 4, 1768, *ibid.*, p. 782.

[27] Letter of July 11, 1768, *ibid.*, p. 783.

[28] Letter of August 8, 1768, *ibid.*, p. 784.

[29] *Ibid.*, p. 787.

[30] Letter of November 7, 1766, *ibid.*, pp. 789–790.

[31] "Ode XII. To a Friend," in Scott, *Poetical Works* (London, 1782), pp. 198–199.

[32] *Boswell's Life of Johnson*, ed. by G. Birkbeck Hill and L. F. Powell (Oxford, 1934), I, 212.

[33] Letter of Joseph Cockfield to the Reverend Mr. Weeden Butler, December 5, 1768, in Nichols, *Literary History*, V, 790; letter of December 22, 1768, *ibid.*, p. 791.

[34] *Ibid.*, p. 792.

[35] Originally the poem had begun:

> —Though kindly silent thus my friend remains,
> I read enquiry in his anxious eye;
> Why my pale cheek the frequent tear distains,
> Why from my bosom bursts the frequent sigh.—
>
> Foe to the world's pursuit of wealth and fame,
> Thy THERON early from the world retir'd,
> Left to the busy throng each boasted aim,
> Nor aught, save peace in solitude, desir'd.

Besides changing the first two lines from the third to the second person (thereby increasing the personal quality of the elegy), Scott inserted a transitional quatrain between the two stanzas:

> Long from these scenes detain'd in distant fields,
> My mournful tale perchance escap'd thy ear:
> Fresh grief to me the repetition yields;
> Thy kind attention gives thee right to hear!

Structurally, this transitional stanza added to the poem because what followed then was a narration (in disguised language) of Scott's love affair with Sarah Frogley, his marriage to her, and her early death. In revision, Scott also was able to cut out a line like: "Where is that blooming form my soul admir'd?" and alter it to: "Where is that form, that mind, my soul admir'd." He also changed the concluding stanza from,

> 'Tis but to wake to nobler thought the soul,
> To urge us ling'ring from earth's fav'rite plain,
> To Virtue's path our vague steps to controul,
> Affliction frowning comes, thy minister of pain!

to,

> 'Tis but to wake to nobler thought the soul,
> To rouse us ling'ring on earth's flowery plain,
> To Virtue's path our wand'rings to controul,
> Affliction frowning comes, thy minister of pain!

This revision was doubtless motivated by the *Monthly Review*'s criticism of the poem: "Should the Author's anguish of mind permit him ever to revise this little piece, and give it any farther polish and finishing, we should be glad to see, in a second edition, that the last line but one hath undergone the file: To virtue's path our vague steps to controul." *Monthly Review,* XLI (December, 1769), 475–476.

[36] Nichols, *Literary History,* V, 799–800.

[37] Letter of Joseph Cockfield to the Reverend Mr. Weeden Butler, January 23, 1771, *ibid.,* p. 802.

[38] Perhaps the best description of Langhorne's poetry was written by Thomas Campbell in 1819: "His Muse is elegantly languid. She is a fine lady, whose complexion is rather indebted to art than to the healthful bloom of nature." *Specimens of the British Poets,* VI, 365. It is unfortunate but true that the same fine lady was peering over Scott's shoulder when he wrote a number of his poems.

[39] John T. Langhorne, "Memoirs of the Author," in John Langhorne, *Poetical Works* (London, 1804), I, 21.

[40] "Elegy I. Written at the Approach of Spring," in Scott, *Poetical Works,* p. 28.

[41] Letter of Joseph Cockfield to the Reverend Mr. Weeden Butler, September 18, 1769, in Nichols, *Literary History,* V, 799.

[42] To be sure, he gave as his reasons for this omission not Quaker piety but the fact that "neither by birth nor fortune I have any claim" to one. Letter of March 19, 1768, *ibid.,* p. 781.

[43] Samuel Scott, *A Diary of Some Religious Exercises and Experience* (London, 1809), p. 3.

[44] *Ibid.,* p. 2.

[45] *Ibid.,* pp. 15–16.

[46] Letter of Joseph Cockfield to the Reverend Mr. Weeden Butler, September 16, 1771, in Nichols, *Literary History,* V, 807.

[47] *Boswell's Life of Johnson,* II, 10.

[48] Letter of Joseph Cockfield to the Reverend Mr. Weeden Butler, March, 1769, in Nichols, *Literary History,* V, 794.

NOTES TO CHAPTER III

[1] The fulsome adoration which Wilkes received is seen in the frontispiece to *A Narrative of the Proceedings against John Wilkes* (London, 1768), where, beneath his portrait, was printed: "N. B. The Portrait of Mr. Wilkes, cut round the circle serves for a Watch Paper." Wilkes himself encouraged this moblike adoration; in his own anonymously printed *English Liberty Established, or a Mirrour for Posterity* (London, 1768), he had these lines printed beneath a picture of him standing before his inquisitors: "Warmed with the love of freedom & his Country, / He hears their threats unmov'd. / And with superior greatness smiles." In both of these works, Wilkes's name was linked with the Magna Charta and the names of John Hampden and Algernon Sidney.

[2] William P. Courtney and D. Nichol Smith, *A Bibliography of Samuel Johnson* (Oxford, 1925), p. 115.

[3] William Forbes, *An Account of the Life and Writings of James Beattie* (new ed. in 2 vols.; London, 1824), I, 149.

[4] Samuel Scott, *A Diary of Some Religious Exercises and Experience* (London, 1809), p. 12.

[5] *Ibid.,* p. 147.

[6] *Ibid.,* p. 100.

[7] Courtney and Smith, *Bibliography,* p. 114.

[8] Boswell shared the same conviction; cf. *Boswell's London Journal, 1762–3,* ed. by

Frederick A. Pottle (New York, 1950), p. 227: "Surely a regular limited royal govern-ment is the best and the most conducive to the happiness of mankind. A republic is in my opinion a most confused, vulgar system, whereas a monarchy inspires us with gay and spirited ideas."

[9] John Scott, *Critical Essays on Some of the Poems, of Several English Poets* (London, 1785), pp. 32–33.

[10] It would be misleading to suggest, however, that Scott was able to maintain a consistent impartiality. He minimized Wilkes's impiety and immorality by stressing the fact that the evidence used against the editor of the *North Briton* had been seized ille-gally. See [John Scott], *The Constitution Defended, and Pensioner Exposed; in Remarks on The False Alarm* (London, 1770), p. 5.

[11] *Ibid.*, p. 30.

[12] *Ibid.*, p. 5. Scott felt Wilkes had been unjust in indiscriminately censuring the Scots, and he said that he was certain Wilkes must later have repented of this injustice done by him (p. 20).

[13] *Ibid.*, p. 3. Much the same idea had been the theme of John Scott's earlier "Sonnet. On Arbitrary Government," in *A Collection of Poems, in Four Volumes. By Several Hands,* [ed. by George Pearch] (London, 1783), IV, 116:

> Boast not your state, slaves of despotic sway,
> > Where wanton Gallia, 'midst her vine-clad hills,
> > Her olive bowers, her myrtle-shaded rills,
> Her mild air's fan, her genial sun's survey:
>
> Nor ye, where Asia like a queen sits gay,
> > 'Midst her rich groves where odorous balm distils,
> > And the charm'd eye th' Elysian landscape fills,
> And hand in hand young Spring and Autumn play:
>
> Each boon to you your haughty lords deny,
> > And at their will your frail lives you resign:
> > Behold, and 'midst your flowery scenes repine!
> Under bleak Albion's cloud-envelop'd sky,
> > Her meanest sons secure their own,
> > And bow to Heaven and Liberty alone.

[14] [Scott], *Constitution Defended*, p. 2.

[15] *Ibid.*, p. 26.

[16] "Not only Petitions now so offensive to Dr. J——n, but even Remonstrances, were once not disapproved; on the contrary, the people were upbraided with their acqui-escence.

> "Thro' Freedom's sons no more *Remonstrance* rings,
> Degrading Nobles and controuling Kings;
> Our supple tribes repress their Patriot throats,
> And ask no questions but the price of votes.
> > > > > "Vide. The Vanity of Human Wishes.
> > > > "By S. Johnson, Dodsley's Collection, vol. 14.

"Verily it attracteth tears into the aged eyes of Martinas once again to remark the debility of intellect in a friend, whose elaborate Dictionary, and well-devised conjec-tural Annotations on the labours of that learned Clerk, Master William Shakespeare, have heretofore afforded unto him, right delectable, and profitable amusement: But truth constraineth me to declare, that my friend, in this his indiscriminate censure, of those whom the propitious ray of golden fortune, hath not rendered conspicuous among their fellows, unwittingly departeth from his former opinions holden forth in a most excellent little tract of his, entitled The Rambler, wherein in No. 68, I read as followeth: However vanity or insolence may look down with contempt on the suffrage of men, undignified by wealth, and unenlightened by education, it very seldom happens, that they commend or blame without justice. Vice and Virtue are easily distinguished, *oppression, according to Harrington's aphorism, will be felt by those that cannot see it;* and perhaps, it falls out very often, that in moral questions, the philosophers in the *Gown* and in the *Livery,* differ not so much in their sentiments, as in their language, and have equal power of discerning *right,* though they cannot point it out to others with equal address." *Ibid.,* pp. 26–27.

[17] Samuel Johnson, *Lives of the English Poets,* ed. by G. Birkbeck Hill (Oxford, 1905), III, 446.

[18] *European Magazine,* II (September, 1782), 195.

[19] *The Victoria History of the Counties of England,* ed. by William Page. *A History of Hertfordshire* (London, 1912), III, 391–392. After Maria De Horne Scott Hooper's death (she was the poet's only child), this estate was sold to Robert Hanbury, after whose death in 1884, it descended to his son, R. C. Hanbury, whose son, E. S. Hanbury, was the owner in 1912.

[20] C. Fell Smith, "John Scott," *Dictionary of National Biography,* LI (1897), 42–43.

[21] John Nichols, *Illustrations of the Literary History of the Eighteenth Century* (London, 1828), II, 661.

[22] *James Beattie's London Diary, 1773,* ed. by Ralph S. Walker (Aberdeen, 1946), p. 46.

[23] *Ibid.,* p. 48.

[24] *Boswell's Life of Johnson,* ed. by G. Birkbeck Hill and L. F. Powell (Oxford, 1950), V, 18.

[25] *Ibid.,* III, 292.

[26] *Johnsonian Miscellanies,* ed. by G. Birkbeck Hill (Oxford, 1897), I, 286.

[27] Samuel Johnson, *Letters, with Mrs. Thrale's Genuine Letters to Him,* ed. by R. W. Chapman (Oxford, 1952), I, 407–408. Mr. Chapman sought the source of Johnson's echoed "Dryads and Fairies" in Scott's *Amwell,* "but was disappointed." *Amwell,* of course, was not published until two years *after* Johnson wrote his letter, and the phrase is not found in it. This speculation gives birth to another: did Scott read Johnson his manuscript poetry on the 1773 visit? Though Johnson appears to have enjoyed visiting Amwell, he once attacked the country gentleman who spent money entertaining guests (*Boswell's Life of Johnson,* IV, 221–222), and he is reported to have said, "Were I a country gentleman, I should not be very hospitable, I should not have crowds in my house." *Ibid.,* p. 204.

[28] *Ibid.,* II, 458.

[29] *Johnsonian Miscellanies,* II, 118.

[30] They disagreed also with Scott on the sensibility of the poor, the advantages of a general standard tax, the theory of imprisonment as opposed to capital punishment, and the advisability of allowing the poor to drink tea.

[31] It would be difficult to compute the total number of pamphlets which dealt with the subject of poor relief. Eden, in his bibliography, listed 118 which appeared between 1673–1773. (Sir Frederic Morton Eden, *The State of the Poor* [London, 1797], III, ccclxxi–ccclxxx.) Dorothy Marshall, *The English Poor in the Eighteenth Century* (London, 1926), pp. 284–285, listed several works not mentioned by Eden. Both Eden and Marshall restricted themselves to a consideration solely of those pamphlets directly concerning poor-relief systems, whereas the Webbs (Sidney and Beatrice Webb, *English Local Government: English Poor Law History: Part I. The Old Poor Law* [London, 1927], p. 158), by considering any tract which dealt with economics, used nearly a

thousand pamphlets for the period between 1670–1834. Because of the particular nature of John Scott's attitude, I have had occasion to use courtesy literature and sermons which treat the concept of benevolence as seen in the humane gentleman. The number, therefore, of works which treat either wholly or in part the problem of the poor is prodigious.

[32] It was probably this aspect which most impressed the Webbs who, in listing the pamphlets which advocated some system other than a parochial one for the maintenance of the poor, singled out Scott's pamphlet as "an able work" in their only critical comment on the list. Webb, *Poor Law,* p. 271.

[33] Scott acknowledged his indebtedness to Hale and referred with highest praise to the jurist's pamphlet. See [Scott], *Observations on the Present State of the Parochial and Vagrant Poor* (London, 1773), pp. 32–33.

[34] Scott's authorship had been announced in the advertisements included in his *Poetical Works* of 1782, and it had been referred to in a review of that volume. Cf. *European Magazine,* II (September, 1782), 196 and II (November, 1782), 448–449.

[35] Eden, *State of the Poor,* I, 359: "... the present age, whatever its characteristic vices may be, is an age of alms-giving. The evil, perhaps, most to be complained of, is, that benevolence is exercised without discrimination or selection, and that idleness is encouraged by what Lord Kames calls 'an overflow of charity in the good people of England.' " Scott would have found this viewpoint untenable, believing instead that the result of charity could only be virtuous. The basic cause of disagreement was, of course, that Eden viewed results in terms of the character of the recipient; Scott, the donor.

[36] *European Magazine,* II (September, 1782), 196.

[37] [Scott], *Observations on the Poor,* pp. 117–118: "... 'but too many of the indigent, when the present necessity is over, will injure the very hand that has been extended for their assistance; a behaviour, which, far from exciting the complacence of the injured, must necessarily excite their detestation!'

"But thou, who indulgest disgust at the ingratitude of thy dependants, pause a moment, and say, if thou dost well to be angry; remember they are men, and that thou art a man also."

[38] Scott was aware of the provisions in the 43 Elizabeth for equalizing the poor tax by allowing one parish to tax an adjacent one to help support an excessive number of paupers. He correctly saw, however, that these were seldom enforced and were useless, as the overseer was more inclined to let his charges starve than to conquer his pride and seek assistance from others. *Ibid.,* p. 69.

[39] Jonas Hanway, *Letters on the Importance of the Rising Generation* (London, 1767), I, 5–75. He attributed the high mortality rate among infants to the workhouses.

[40] Henry Fielding, *A Proposal for Making an Effectual Provision for the Poor* (London, 1753), *passim.*

[41] Thomas Alcock, *Observations on the Defects of the Poor Laws* (London, 1752).

[42] In Scott's own Hertfordshire, apprehended vagrants (forty-five were taken in 1773, the year in which Scott published his pamphlet) were employed in spinning and in beating hemp. The profits derived from this employment were paid to the masters of the houses of correction, and no money was ever paid to the vagrant for his labor. *Reports from Committees of the House of Commons* ([London?], 1803), IX, 290.

[43] Richard Burn, in his *The History of the Poor Laws: With Observations* (London, 1764), had also referred to the precarious situation of the poor foreigner in England. One of the primary sources of Scott's pamphlet was Burn's famous book, and it seems clear that Scott's discussion of foreigners had its source here; indeed, there was little Scott could add to Burn's argument, and he was content to quote large portions of it. The significance of Scott's remarks, however, lies not in a statement of the plight of

these foreigners, but in his humanitarian discussion of the reasons which made them come to England originally. His purpose was clear: to circumvent the traditional English hatred of the foreigner as the intruder; to do this successfully, Scott had to show that the foreigner, in coming to England, had been motivated by those qualities of character which ranked highest with Englishmen: a desire to have religious freedom, and a desire to produce service to the world as a skilled craftsman.

⁴⁴ [Scott], *Observations on the Poor*, p. 51. Cf. also p. 124: "State lotteries may justly be accounted another cause of poverty: the poor as well as the rich are ambitious; and, if they save for nothing else, will sometimes save for the hope of a sudden advance in their station."

⁴⁵ Clement Ellis, *The Gentile Sinner, or England's Brave Gentleman Character'd in a Letter to a Friend* (4th ed.; Oxford, 1668), p. 140: "The course he takes to *air* his *Bags,* and keep them from *moulding,* is to *distribute* freely to *all* that are in *need*. If he take some paines to become *richer* then others, it is only to put a *cheat* upon that which men miscall *Fortune,* and to manifest he hath a *power* so great as hers: that is, to make himself *poor* again at his pleasure: and to show that *charity* can entertaine as *rich* servants as *she*. . . . He esteems it a very high *Honour,* that God hath vouchsafed to make him *one* of the *Stewards* in *His* great *Family:* and he is nothing *ambitious* of *his Epithete,* to his *Name,* or *reward* of his *pains* who is recorded in the *Gospel* for his *injustice*."

⁴⁶ [Scott], *Observations on the Poor*, p. 14.

⁴⁷ *Ibid.,* p. 15: "The charity of the ecclesiastics was so absolutely necessary to the support of the poor that on the dissolution of the religious houses they soon became very numerous and destitute." Scott did not make the mistake common to his age of believing that poor relief before the reign of Elizabeth had been left to the church alone. Instead, he followed Burn's argument that the church, although a partner in the relief program, was not the sole source, as legislation had existed since the days of Richard II for the treatment of the poor. Cf. Eden, *State of the Poor*, I, 344–345.

⁴⁸ "Amoebaean Eclogue II. Rural Business; or, The Agriculturists," in John Scott, *Poetical Works* (London, 1782), p. 120.

⁴⁹ *Boswell's Life of Johnson,* IV, 217.

⁵⁰ *Ibid.,* II, 126.

⁵¹ William Bell, *A Dissertation on the Following Subject: What Causes Principally Contribute to Render a Nation Populous?* (Cambridge, 1756), p. 13; *An Infallible Remedy for the High Prices of Provisions* (London, 1768), p. 7; *Boswell's Life of Johnson,* III, 56.

⁵² Scott did qualify his condemnation of novels to avoid including moral tales which "on account of their tendency, are proper for public perusal." [Scott], *Observations on the Poor*, p. 128.

⁵³ John Cooke, *Unum Necessarium* (London, 1648), pp. 18–23; John Cary, *An Essay on the State of England* (Bristoll, 1695), pp. 152–164; Daniel Defoe, "Giving Alms No Charity and Employing the Poor a Grievance to the Nation," in *Defoe's Writings.* Vol. XIII. *The Shortest Way with the Dissenters and Other Pamphlets* (Stratford-upon-Avon, [1927–1928]), pp. 185–186; [Daniel Defoe], *The Great Law of Subordination Consider'd* (London, 1724), p. 82; [Thomas Wilson], *Distilled Spirituous Liquors the Bane of the Nation* (London, 1736), *passim;* Henry Fielding, *An Enquiry into the Causes of the Late Increase of Robbers* (London, 1751), p. 18; [Nicholas Hardinge], *Reasons for Establishing and Maintaining a Workhouse in the Town of Kingston upon Thames* ([London?], 1751), p. 1; *Considerations, Humbly Offered to Parliament* (London, 1758), *passim; An Inquiry into the Management of the Poor* (London, 1767), pp. 19–20; [John Arbuthnot], *An Inquiry into the Connection Between the Present Price of Provisions, and the Size of Farms* (London, 1773), p. 51. For a detailed study

of the drinking habits of Englishmen, seen geographically, cf. Eden, *State of the Poor,*
I, 534–547.

⁵⁴ John Webb, "Letter to the Editor, June 1, 1815," *Lady's Magazine,* XLVI (July,
1815), 315–316.

⁵⁵ *Johnsonian Miscellanies,* I, 205.

⁵⁶ A not unusual statement was the following: "Touching the poore that crie hard
for foode, and finde small supply: the reason is, for that they doe not complaine vnto
God of their grieuous sinnes (the verie maine cause of all their calamities:).... When
God by his messengers, called vpon them to leaue their euill wayes, and serue him
better, they would not heare to follow the same: Therefore doth God nowe shut vp
his eares, and others also, when they cry for foode." [Henry Arthington?], *Provision
for the Poore, Now in Penurie* (London, 1597), p. [1].

⁵⁷ "Ode XXI. Written after a Journey to Bristol," in Scott, *Poetical Works,* p. 226.

⁵⁸ Jonas Hanway phrased this attitude with due nicety: "Charity in the character of
Britannia shews a tenderness for the meanest of her Sons who are of use." This exists
in Hanway's holograph in the Huntington Library copy of his *Miscellanies* (n.p., 1765).
For a similar sentiment, cf. William Berriman, *The Excellency and Reward of Charity*
(London, 1725), pp. 11–12.

⁵⁹ *Boswell's Life of Johnson,* I, 68.

⁶⁰ John Scott, *Digests of the General Highway and Turnpike Laws; with the Schedule
of Forms, as Directed by Act of Parliament; and Remarks. Also, an Appendix, on the
Construction and Preservation of Roads* (London, 1778), p. 345: "That *Friend of Man,*
Mr. HOWARD, at the Peril of his Life, has explored the Secrets of Iniquity in our
Prison-houses. He has done his Duty—No more can be required of *him:* but if a few
Gentlemen of Spirit, Ability, and Humanity, in every County, were to follow his
Example, and examine the *Prison* Workhouses of their respective Counties, I believe
Conduct would be brought to Light, that could scarcely be supposed to exist even
among Savages."

⁶¹ [Scott], *Observations on the Poor,* pp. 64–65; cf. also p. 134: "I will not say that
the frequency of murder is owing to the frequency of our executions; but such spectacles certainly harden the human heart: those who see life taken and resigned in so
careless a manner, will not have a proper value for their own lives or the lives of
others."

⁶² He credited Fielding for this idea.

⁶³ Scott felt that it was never the intention of the government to have the penalty of
death for "venial transgressions." Rather, he believed that this law was established
coexistent with a dispensing power of reprieve given to a judge, so that a great villain,
who had committed heinous crimes and—through lack of evidence—had gone un-
punished, might be apprehended for some peccadillo and then given his total deserts.

⁶⁴ [Society of Friends], *Extracts from the Minutes and Advices of the Yearly Meeting
of Friends* ([London], 1783), pp. 89–90, 193. Scott differed from the Quakers only in
his insistence that charity was its own reward and that there was no necessity to look
to a heavenly reward for such acts. He emphasized the fact (cf. his *Observations on the
Poor,* p. 53) that "the people called quakers" not only contributed to the general parochial assessment for the relief of the poor but that they maintained at their own
expense and in a decent and respectable manner the poor who were members of the
Society of Friends. Eden in his *State of the Poor,* I, 588–589, also praised the Quakers
for their great charity, but he insisted that the belief that no Quaker was supported by
his parish, was a polite fiction. Eden said that Quakers who were idle and extravagant
were expelled from the Society; therefore, although there would be no Quakers receiving parochial aid, there would be those on the relief rolls who had been members
of the Society of Friends.

NOTES TO CHAPTER IV

[1] Although both the *Monthly Review* and the *Critical Review* reviewed this work, extensive search has failed to reveal an extant copy, and no commentator on the condition of the highways mentioned it. Even the Webbs, who read Scott's works with intense interest, did not mention it as ever having existed. All that we know about its contents and subject matter must therefore be drawn from these two reviews of it.

[2] William P. Courtney and D. Nichol Smith, *A Bibliography of Samuel Johnson* (Oxford, 1925), p. 117.

[3] Especially is this true of Johnson's most famous dictum on patriots, "Patriotism is the last refuge of a scoundrel," which was made April 7, 1775. *Boswell's Life of Johnson*, ed. by G. Birkbeck Hill and L. F. Powell (Oxford, 1934), II, 348.

[4] In the first three editions of the *Dictionary* (1755, 1756, and 1765), Johnson had defined the word "patriot" in this fashion:

"Patriot—n.s. One whose ruling passion is the love of his country.

Patriots who for sacred freedom stood.   *Tickel*
      The firm *patriot* there,
Who made the welfare of mankind his care,
Shall know he conquer'd.   *Addison*
Here tears shall flow from a more gen'rous cause,
Such tears as *patriots* shed for dying laws.   *Pope*"

[5] Sir John Hawkins, "Anecdotes and Sayings of Johnson," in *Johnsoniana, or Supplement to Boswell*, collected by Piozzi, Hawkins, Tyers, Hoole, *et al.* (London, 1836), p. 132.

[6] *Modern Patriotism, a Poem* (London, [*ca.* 1725]), p. 4, and *The History of the Rise, Progress, and Tendency of Patriotism* (London, 1747), pp. 13–15, are typical examples.

[7] *An Essay towards a Catalogue of Patriots, Real and Pretended* (London, 1769).

[8] [Scott], *The Constitution Defended, and Pensioner Exposed; in Remarks on The False Alarm* (London, 1770), p. 25.

[9] The Johnsonian theory of traditionalism was seen in *The False Alarm:* "Governments formed by chance, and gradually improved by such expedients, as the successful discovery of their defects happened to suggest, are never to be tried by a regular theory. They are fabricks of dissimilar materials, raised by different architects, upon different plans. We must be content with them as they are; should we attempt to mend their disproportions, we might easily demolish, and difficultly rebuild them." Samuel Johnson, *Works*, ed. by Robert Lynam (London, 1825), V, 378.

[10] For the genesis of this opinion, cf. [Scott], *The Constitution Defended*, p. 10 (footnote of Scriblerius): "That passion which much prevaileth in the heart of man, vulgarly ycleped self-love, hinteth unto me, that this same plea may be advanced in justification of every act of violence, which it may seem meet unto government in the fullness of its power to exercise."

[11] Johnson did not mention here divine right as such, but in the quality of reverence he advocated toward monarchy, simple respect seems charged with almost religious awe: "... to insult a king with a rude remonstrance, only because there is no punishment for legal insolence, is not courage, for there is no danger; nor patriotism, for it tends to the subversion of order, and lets wickedness loose upon the land, by destroying the reverence due to sovereign authority." Johnson, *Works*, V, 429. For the same idea, cf. *The False Alarm:* "All other parties, however enraged at each other, have agreed to treat the throne with decency; but these low-born railers have attacked not only the authority, but the character of their sovereign, and have endeavoured, surely without effect, to alienate the affections of the people from the only king, who, for

almost a century, has much appeared to desire, or much endeavoured to deserve them." *Ibid.*, p. 390.

[12] Samuel Scott would not have agreed with this. Good deeds done to compensate for secret sins are "filthy rags." Samuel Scott, *A Diary of Some Religious Exercises and Experience* (London, 1809), pp. 65–66.

[13] "Letter to the Editors, August 6, 1782," *British Magazine and Review,* I (August, 1782), 126: "Whatever be my religious *persuasion,* it is well known that I am no bigot, nor wanting in liberality of sentiment and personal respect for those of *others.*" He seems to have forgotten here his attitude toward the Catholics, which apparently never changed.

[14] This terminology had been first used by Scott in his sonnet "To Britain," which was written in 1766. The same word was also used in his poor-relief pamphlet (*Observations on the Present State of the Parochial and Vagrant Poor* [London, 1773], p. 78).

[15] [John Scott], *Remarks on The Patriot. Including Some Hints Respecting the Americans: with an Address to the Electors of Great Britain* (London, 1775), p. 42. This same philosophy was also developed in [Henry] Brooke, *The Fool of Quality* (rev. ed.; London, 1776), III, 204–272, a book which Scott greatly admired.

[16] Both the *Critical Review* and the *Monthly Review* gave reviews of Scott's pamphlet, but neither of them seems to have felt that Scott's tract was of much significance, as it had no meaning independent of Johnson's *The Patriot.* Both reviews, however, pointed out the ingenious and just reasoning of Scott.

[17] *Johnsonian Miscellanies,* ed. by G. Birkbeck Hill (Oxford, 1897), II, 47.

[18] *Boswell's Life of Johnson,* II, 351–352.

[19] Margaret Forbes, *Beattie and His Friends* (Westminster, 1904), p. 123.

[20] *Private Papers of James Boswell from Malahide Castle,* ed. by Geoffrey Scott and Frederick A. Pottle. Vol. XI. *The Journal of James Boswell, 1775–6* ([New York], 1931), p. 229.

[21] Perhaps the highest praise the poem ever received was accorded by Nathan Drake in his *Literary Hours; or, Sketches, Critical, Narrative, and Poetical* (3d ed.; London, 1804), III, 533: "From the era of Denham to the present day, *Local Poetry* has been assiduously cultivated; and though difficult to render popular, from the confinement to which the poet is subjected, some pieces have acquired and deservedly maintained no inconsiderable reputation. Among those which have been written in blank verse, the *Amwell* of Scott and the *Lochleven* of Bruce, hold, in my opinion, the most distinguished rank. If the former be more digressive and varied, the latter is more pathetic and pictoresque, and occasionally approaches the sublime. Neither of these pleasing productions, likewise, fatigue the attention by extreme length; a circumstance of essential consequence in loco-descriptive poetry, which, even in the hands of a master, is but too apt to offend by reiterated attempts to describe what, without having previously visited the scenery, can seldom impress the ideas of locality, or appear otherwise than vague and general sketches from Nature."

[22] Robert A. Aubin, *Topographical Poetry in XVIII-Century England* (New York, 1936), p. 95.

[23] *Ibid.,* p. 96.

[24] Samuel Johnson, *Lives of the English Poets,* ed. by G. Birkbeck Hill (Oxford, 1905), I, 77–78.

[25] Cf. Aubin, *Topographical Poetry,* pp. 3–96, for the source of my discussion.

[26] Raymond D. Havens, *The Influence of Milton on English Poetry* (Cambridge, U.S.A., 1922), p. 246.

[27] Line 208 (John Scott, *Poetical Works* [London, 1782], p. 73) originally read: "Fixes his eye on future joy, that flies," but this was altered to "Directs his eye to distant Joy, that flies." The awkward metrics of the original verse probably caused the change; but even in revision, Scott refused to sacrifice alliteration.

[28] Aubin, *Topographical Poetry,* p. 62. The use of footnotes for supplementary material soon became a consuming passion with Scott, and his later poems abound in historical and botanical observations.

[29] Havens, *The Influence of Milton,* p. 252.

[30] "In 1765 Jago had made Edgehill and the prospect from it the theme of the most elaborate local poem which had yet appeared in our language. About the same time, though the poem was published some years later, John Scott had made Amwell the subject of a poem which was no unworthy anticipation of what Cowper was to do for Upton." J. Churton Collins, "The Descriptive Poetry of the Eighteenth Century," in *Poets' Country,* ed. by Andrew Lang (London, 1907), p. 144. Mr. Collins was not always so pleased with *Amwell,* however; cf. p. 209 where he cites one passage as "an excellent illustration of the Nature-painting characteristic of the eighteenth century, when this poetry became elaborated: not a touch of imagination, not a touch of fancy, and without any appeal to either; body without soul, accident without essence."

[31] Denham had also praised Fanshawe's version of Guarini, and Johnson liked Denham's portrait of Fanshawe. Johnson, *Lives of the English Poets,* I, 77.

[32] John Scott, *Critical Essays on Some of the Poems, of Several English Poets* (London, 1785), p. 125.

[33] Charles Burlington, *The Modern Universal British Traveller* (London, 1779), p. 246: "In the course of the New River are 43 sluices, and over it are 215 bridges. On its approaching the reservoir, called New River Head, there are several small houses erected at a considerable distance from each other on its banks, into which the water runs, and is conveyed by pipes to the nearer and more easternly parts of the metropolis. On its entering the above reservoir it is there ingulphed by 58 main pipes, each of seven inches bore; and here also an engine, worked by horses, throws a great quantity of water up to another reservoir situated on much higher ground, from which the water runs in pipes to supply the highest ground in the city and its liberties. Many years ago 30,000 houses were thus supplied by this water, and since that time several main pipes have been laid to carry it into the liberties of Westminster." John Scott is alleged to have been the author of the poem which stands engraved on a stone by the New River:

> Amwell, perpetual be thy stream,
> Nor e'er thy spring be less,
> Which thousands drink who never dream
> Whence flows the boon they bless.
>
> Too often thus ungrateful man
> Blind and unconscious lives,
> Enjoys kind Heaven's indulgent plan,
> Nor thinks of Him who gives.

[34] Cf. "Amwell," in Scott, *Poetical Works,* p. 77, in which he used the phrase "How picturesque" three times in a similar fashion.

[35] De Horne apparently died some time after May 26, 1769, when he was reported being near death. Cf. Letter from Joseph Cockfield to the Reverend Mr. Weeden Butler, May 26, 1769, in John Nichols, *Illustrations of the Literary History of the Eighteenth Century* (London, 1828), V, 796. Turner, according to Hoole, died June 30, 1769.

[36] For an account of Hassall, cf. Reginald Hine, *Confessions of an Un-Common Attorney* (London, 1945), pp. 74–75, and Reginald Hine, *Charles Lamb and His Hertfordshire* (London, 1949), pp. xxiv, 103–107.

[37] Horace Walpole found this a "grand and beautiful image which struck me extremely." Letter of Horace Walpole to the Reverend Mr. William Mason, April 8, 1776, in Horace Walpole, *Letters,* ed. by Mrs. Paget Toynbee (Oxford, 1904), IX, 343.

[38] John Scott, *A Letter to the Critical Reviewers: Occasioned by Their Account of Scott's Poetical Works, in Their Review for July 1782* (London, 1782), p. 10.

[39] Letter from John Scott to Elihu Robinson, October 1, 1776, in the possession of Mr. and Mrs. Donald F. Hyde of Somerville, New Jersey.

[40] *Gentleman's Magazine,* XLVIII (March, 1778), 112.

[41] Letter from John Scott to James Beattie, October 24, 1778, in the Beattie Collection, University of Aberdeen, Scotland.

[42] Samuel Scott was also a member of the Watton trust, but it is to be doubted that he was an asset to the board; he refused to help discharge a toll-gatherer, even when the man convicted himself. Scott, *Diary,* pp. 47–48.

[43] Scott's work on highways may have been closely related to his development of the grotto. Cf. R. T. Andrews, "Scott's Grotto, Amwell," *East Herts Archaeological Society. Transactions,* I (1899), 23: "It is not very difficult to conjecture where the chalk from the excavated chambers and passages [of the grotto] was deposited, for taking those which are at the present day clearly wholly within the cliff, 250 cubic yards would cover the quantity removed, and so what with the mound round the council chamber and other artificial mounds, this amount could easily have been disposed of, even had none been sent out elsewhere to form or repair roads in the town of Ware, or for Mr. Scott's new high road between Ware and Hertford, which it is said he was instrumental in making."

[44] "Utility of Scot's Digest," *Gentleman's Magazine,* L (January, 1780), 20.

[45] [Scott], *Observations on the Poor,* pp. 4, 10, 13, 15, 44, 54; he referred to the editions of 1762, 1769, and 1770. Scott called Burn's *Justice of the Peace* a "truly valuable Work" (John Scott, *Digests of the General Highway and Turnpike Laws; with the Schedule of Forms, as Directed by Act of Parliament; and Remarks. Also, an Appendix, on the Construction and Preservation of Roads* [London, 1778], p. 249). Burn, in his *History of the Poor Laws,* pp. 277–280, had touched briefly upon the subject of highways as an important one, and he had given passing reference to some of the most obvious faults of the existing systems. Langhorne also recognized Scott's indebtedness to Burn. Cf. *Monthly Review,* LVIII (May, 1778), 379.

[46] W. T. Jackman, *The Development of Transportation in Modern England* (2 vols.; Cambridge, 1916), paid little attention to Scott and considered him as merely one of a long line of eighteenth-century commentators.

[47] Sidney and Beatrice Webb, *English Local Government: Statutory Authorities for Special Purposes* (London, 1922), p. 205.

[48] *Ibid.,* p. 210.

[49] Sidney and Beatrice Webb, *English Local Government: The Story of the King's Highway* (London, 1920), p. 132.

[50] *Ibid.,* p. 49.

[51] *Critical Review,* XLVI (September, 1778), 234. When attacked on this point, Scott called his humorous bit the weakest paragraph in his *Digests,* and he complained of this criticism as being illiberal. Letter to James Beattie, October 24, 1778, in the Beattie Collection, University of Aberdeen, Scotland.

[52] Scott, *Digests,* p. 247.

[53] He followed here the proposal of Malachy Postlethwayt in his *The Universal Dictionary of Trade and Commerce* (2d ed.; London, 1757), II, Pt. II, 617.

[54] Tobias Smollett, *The Expedition of Humphry Clinker* (Oxford, 1925), II, 79.

[55] [Arthur Young], *A Six Months Tour through the North of England* (2d ed.; London, 1771), I, 349.

[56] Scott, *Digests,* pp. 247, 344. Cf. [Scott], *Observations on the Poor,* p. 18. Daniel Defoe wrote a famous tract with the same assumption: Andrew Moreton, *Every-body's*

Business, Is No-body's Business (4th ed.; London, 1725). Better known to Scott, however, was probably Izaak Walton's *Compleat Angler,* which also complained, "That which is everybody's business is nobody's business."

[57] This was not an uncommon attitude. Cf. Daniel Bourn, *A Treatise upon Wheel-Carriages* (London, 1763), p. 34: "RATHER might it not be wished, that the ordering and controul of this great affair, should be wholly invested in the hands of gentlemen of the greatest weight and influence? whose aims are as distinguished as their personages, designs as noble as their blood, and whose public spirit and abilities tally with and equal their fortunes. These are they to appoint, to put the wheels in motion; it is for mechanics and artificers to fulfill and execute. We may with equal justice expect our battles to be fought without officers, as any considerable undertaking to be well executed without governors, and those too of importance and authority."

[58] *Boswell's Life of Johnson,* III, 353.

[59] Jane Austen, *Pride and Prejudice,* ed. by R. W. Chapman (3d ed.; Oxford, 1932), p. 15.

[60] *Boswell's Life of Johnson,* V, 322.

NOTES TO CHAPTER V

[1] Letter from John Scott to James Beattie, October 24, 1778, in the Beattie Collection, University of Aberdeen, Soctland.

[2] *Ibid.*

[3] *Ibid.*

[4]
> *"Vivere naturae si convenienter oportet,—*
> *—Novistine locum potiorem rure beato?*
>
> "HOR. Epist. Lib. I. ep. x. 1. 12.
>
> *"At secura quies, et nescia fallere vita,*
> *Dives opum variarum; at latis otia fundis,*
> *Speluncae, vivique lacus; at frigida Tempe,*
> *Mugitusque boum, mollesque sub arbore somni*
> *Non absunt. Illic saltus, ac lustra ferarum,*
> *Et patiens operum parvoque assueta juventus,*
> *Sacra deûm, sanctique patres: extrema per illos*
> *Justitia excedens terris vestigia fecit.*
>
> "VIRG. Georg. II. l. 467."

When these poems were reprinted in the *Poetical Works,* the first of the two mottoes was omitted.

[5] William Forbes, *An Account of the Life and Writings of James Beattie* (new ed. in 2 vols.; London, 1824), II, 40.

[6] *Ibid.,* p. 65.

[7] Joseph Warton, *An Essay on the Genius and Writings of Pope* (4th ed., corr.; London, 1782) I, 3.

[8] The log for visitors is now in the possession of John C. Hanbury, Esq., of Ware. On its 110 pages there are approximately three thousand names, suggesting that during the time of Scott the grotto was open to anyone who cared to see it. The falling off of the grotto's popularity as a tourist attraction may be due to Scott's son-in-law, Joseph Hooper, of whom a clipping in the book says: ". . . though it does not accord with his system of retirement to admit of too frequent visits, yet he is not adverse to gratifying occasionally the curiosity of persons of taste and discernment."

[9] John Webb, "Letter to the Editors, June 1, 1815," *Lady's Magazine,* XLVI (July, 1815), 316.

[10] *Ibid.*

[11] *James Beattie's Day-Book, 1773–1798,* ed. by Ralph S. Walker (Aberdeen, 1948), p. 107.

[12] Letter from James Beattie to the Duchess of Gordon, April 25, 1781, in the Beattie Collection, University of Aberdeen, Scotland.

[13] Letter from John Scott to James Beattie, January 25, 1782, *ibid.*

[14] *Ibid.*

[15] *Ibid.*

[16] Samuel Johnson, *Lives of the English Poets,* ed. by G. Birkbeck Hill (Oxford, 1905), III, 433: Gray "had a notion not very peculiar, that he could not write but at certain times, or at happy moments; a fantastick foppery, to which my kindness for a man of learning and of virtue wishes him to have been superior."

[17] Letter to James Beattie, January 25, 1782, in the Beattie Collection, University of Aberdeen, Scotland.

[18] Letter of May 10, 1782, in Forbes, *Life of Beattie,* II, 93–94.

[19] H[erman] Liebert, *Johnson's Last Literary Project* (New Haven, 1948), p. 5. This volume is now in the Yale University Library.

[20] *Boswell's Life of Johnson,* ed. by G. Birkbeck Hill and L. F. Powell (Oxford, 1934), II, 229–230.

[21] Letter from John Scott to Elihu Robinson, May 25, 1782, in Friends Library, London.

[22] *London Chronicle,* LI (June 13 to June 15, 1782), 569.

[23] *Critical Review,* LIV (July, 1782), 47.

[24] *Boswell's Life of Johnson,* V, 274. Cf. also Johnson, *Lives of the English Poets,* I, 340, 400; III, 147. Scott disagreed, however. Cf. his *A Letter to the Critical Reviewers* (London, 1782), p. 23: "Some may possibly think the world is improperly troubled with this matter; and that a contemptuous silence had been better suited to your impertinence; but here I think differently. My Book was offered to the Publick as a rational and inoffensive amusement; you ill-naturedly endeavoured to prejudice the Publick against it, and your endeavours call upon me to plead in its vindication. The plan of contemptuous silence I could not approve; it might have been erroneously construed into timidity. Besides, I am well convinced, that it is from the contempt of Authors, and the indolence of Readers, that you are principally indebted for the little importance you hold in the World of Letters." Cf. also his "Letter to the Editors, November 26, 1782," *European Magazine,* II (November, 1782), 449: "This may be termed by some, vanity and egotism; but called upon as I am to plead in my own defense, I am not ashamed to speak the truth, and to speak it boldly. To do so I am sure is more manly than the practices by which some writers raise themselves into popularity. What little reputation I can boast, has been gained openly and fairly; I have not wrote, nor procured others to write puffing paragraphs, to recommend my poetry, in the public papers."

[25] Scott, *A Letter to the Critical Reviewers,* p. 23.

[26] *Ibid.,* pp. 4, 6.

[27] The difference between the two journals was once commented on by Johnson: "The Monthly Reviewers (said he) are not Deists; but they are Christians with as little christianity as may be; and are for pulling down all establishments. The Critical Reviewers are for supporting the constitution, both in church and state. The Critical Reviewers, I believe, often review without reading the books through; but lay hold of a topick, and write chiefly from their own minds. The Monthly Reviewers are duller men, and are glad to read the books through." *Boswell's Life of Johnson,* III, 32.

[28] Cf. [Scott], *Observations on the Poor,* p. 66, where he referred to "the words of the ingenious authors of the Monthly Review," and *A Letter to the Critical Reviewers,* p. [2],

where he said: "Those who wish to see justice done him [Scott] by liberal, impartial, and ingenious Criticks, are referred to the Account of his Poems given by the Gentlemen of the Monthly Review, in their Number for September last."

[29] Scott, *A Letter to the Critical Reviewers,* pp. 5, 7.

[30] *The Calamities and Quarrels of Authors,* ed. by Benjamin Disraeli (New York, 1868), I, 218–224.

[31] Johnson, *Lives of the English Poets,* III, 147.

[32] *British Magazine and Review,* I (November, 1782), 366. I have been unable to locate Scott's newspaper rebuttal to the *Critical Review's* reply to his pamphlet.

[33] *Critical Review,* LX (November, 1785), 346.

[34] "Letter to the Editors, November 26, 1782," *European Magazine,* II (November, 1782), 449.

[35] *Ibid.,* p. 448: "He says, that, 'I do not rank in the higher classes of our poets.' To rank in the first class of our poets, I should suppose it necessary to have produced an Epic or a set of good Tragedies: this I have not done, and of course can have no right to the honour. But the higher classes of our poets is an indefinite expression, to which every man may affix his own ideas; and he may rank writers in those classes whose company I should not be very proud of."

[36] John Scott, *Poetical Works* (London, 1782), p. [92].

[37] Scott, *A Letter to the Critical Reviewers,* p. 7.

[38] "Observations on the Oriental Eclogues," in *The Works of the British Poets,* ed. by Robert Anderson (London, 1795), IX, 534.

[39] Scott, *A Letter to the Critical Reviewers,* p. 8.

[40] John Scott, *Critical Essays on Some of the Poems, of Several English Poets* (London, 1785), p. 332.

[41] Disraeli, *The Calamities and Quarrels of Authors,* I, 224.

[42] Scott, *A Letter to the Critical Reviewers,* p. 8.

[43] Scott, *Critical Essays,* p. 361.

[44] *Boswell's Life of Johnson,* II, 453.

[45] Letter of Joseph Cockfield to the Reverend Mr. Weeden Butler, February 10, 1766, in John Nichols, *Illustrations of the Literary History of the Eighteenth Century* (London, 1828), V, 760.

[46] Martha Pike Conant, *The Oriental Tale in England in the Eighteenth Century* (New York, 1908), p. 54.

[47] Scott, *Poetical Works,* p. [124].

[48] *Ibid.*

[49] Letter from John Scott to Elihu Robinson, May 25, 1782, in Friends Library, London.

[50] Johnson, *Lives of the English Poets,* II, 67.

[51] Scott, *A Letter to the Critical Reviewers,* p. 18.

[52] Cf. "Amwell," in Scott, *Poetical Works,* p. 83, where he had spoken of his poetical sketch of the character of Thomas Hassal: "The character here given of him must be allowed, strictly speaking, to be imaginary; but his composition, in the said register, appeared to me to breathe such a spirit of piety, simplicity, and benevolence, that I almost think myself authorized to assert that it was his real one."

[53] Letter to James Beattie, May 10, 1782, in Forbes, *Life of Beattie,* II, 92.

[54] Warton, *Essay on Pope,* II, 391.

[55] Scott, *A Letter to the Critical Reviewers,* p. 18.

[56] *Ibid.,* pp. 11–12.

[57] *Ibid.,* p. 15. Actually, however, in "The Mexican Prophecy," the stanzas were of varied lengths, though a standard meter was used. The poem's last line was a pentameter, which properly should not have appeared in the regular ode.

[58] Warton, *Essay on Pope,* I, 64.

[59] Scott, *A Letter to the Critical Reviewers,* pp. 11–12.

[60] Scott, *Poetical Works,* p. 246.

[61] "Ode I. To Leisure," "Ode V. A Landscape," "Ode VII. Written in Winter," "Ode IX. Leaving Bath, 1776," "Ode XVI. Viewing the Ruins of an Abbey. To a Friend," "Ode XX ['This scene how rich from Thames's side']," "Ode XXI. Written after a Journey to Bristol," "Ode XXIV. The Tempestuous Evening," "Ode XXV. The Melancholy Evening," "Ode XXVI. The Pleasant Evening."

[62] "Ode III. To Childhood," "Ode IV. Hearing Music," "Ode VI. To a Friend, on His Marriage, and Removal into the Country," "Ode VIII. To a Friend [Lettsom]," "Ode X. To J. Payne, Esq. Accountant-General of the Bank of England," "Ode XI. To a Friend [Charles Frogley] Apprehensive of Declining Friendship," "Ode XII. To a Friend [Joseph Cockfield]."

[63] "Ode II. The Evening Walk," "Ode XIII ['I hate that drum's discordant sound']," "Ode XVII. Privateering," "Ode XVIII. To Hospitality," "Ode XXIII. To Disease," "Ode XXVII. After Reading Akenside's Poems."

[64] "Ode XIV. Written after Reading Some Modern Love-Verses," "Ode XV. The Muse; or, Poetical Enthusiasm," "Ode XIX. The Apology," "Ode XXII. To Criticism."

[65] "Ode XIX. The Apology," in Scott, *Poetical Works,* pp. 218–219.

[66] Scott, *Critical Essays,* p. 271.

[67] "Ode V. A Landscape," in Scott, *Poetical Works,* p. 178.

[68] "Ode XXIV. The Tempestuous Evening," *ibid.,* p. 233.

[69] "Ode XXV. The Melancholy Evening," *ibid.,* p. 235.

[70] "Ode XXVI. The Pleasant Evening," *ibid.,* p. 238.

[71] "Ode XIII," *ibid.,* p. 201.

[72] Although I have not made a thorough investigation of the extent to which this ode was reprinted, the following places reveal some idea of its popularity: *Biographical and Imperial Magazine,* IV (August, 1790), 132; Joseph Ritson, *A Select Collection of Songs, with Their Original Airs,* ed. by Thomas Park (2d ed.; London, 1813), II, 203; Campbell, *Specimens of the British Poets,* VI, 432–433 (doubtless it was in reference to this poem that Campbell wrote [p. 431]: "His own verses are chiefly interesting, where they breathe the pacific principles of the quaker; while his personal character engages respect, from exhibiting a public spirit and liberal taste, beyond the habits of his brethren"); [Effingham Wilson], *The Lacon of Liberty* (London, 1844); *The Oxford Book of Eighteenth Century Verse,* ed. by D. Nichol Smith (Oxford, 1926), pp. 556–557. The most enthusiastic comment on the ode was made by Robert Anderson in his "Life of Scott" in *The Works of the British Poets,* XI, 728: "But there is not, perhaps, in the whole compass of his poetry, any thing more expressive of his philanthropical affections and comprehensive benevolence, than the following little *Ode.* It is truly British, and truly humane." Around 1840, Charles Knight in his *Glimpses of the Past* referred to this as Scott's "one well-known poem"; it was recollecting this ode which caused him to investigate the life of Scott and include him in his work.

[73] *British Magazine,* I (December, 1782), 459. The Latin version is listed as being done by "a friend of the author."

[74] *Specimens of the Later English Poets* (London, 1807), III, 214.

[75] "Paraphrase of Dr. Johnson's Epitaph on Thomas Hanmer," in Samuel Johnson, *Works,* ed. by Robert Lynam (London, 1825), VI, 410.

[76] Letter from John Scott to James Phillips, May 23, 1783, in Gibson Collection, Friends Library, London.

[77] Letter from John Scott to James Beattie, June 6, 1783, in the Beattie Collection, University of Aberdeen, Scotland.

[78] Oswald Doughty, *English Lyric in the Age of Reason* (London, 1922), p. 194.

[79] Scott, *Critical Essays,* p. 246.

[80] Letter to James Beattie, June 6, 1783, in the Beattie Collection, University of Aberdeen, Scotland.

[81] Letter from John Scott to James Beattie, August 29, 1783, in Forbes, *Life of Beattie,* II, 107.

[82] All of the information on Scott's deathbed actions and attitudes is drawn from [Samuel Scott], *Some Memoirs of the Last Illness of John Scott* ([London, 1785]).

[83] Samuel Scott, *A Diary of Some Religious Exercises and Experience* (London, 1809), p. 96: " 'Gather up the fragments that remain that nothing be lost,' was the command of our great master; consistent with which, I esteem it my duty to preserve, and make known to some, the dying expressions of the deceased; as a testimony to the cause of Christianity, and the power of Christ."

NOTES TO CHAPTER VI

[1] Though in his poor-law tract there had been references made to the moral problems created by salacious literature ([Scott], *Observations on the Present State of the Parochial and Vagrant Poor* (London, 1773), pp. 126–129), Scott's first work devoted solely to literary criticism was what is presumed to have been his anonymously published letter on the Rowley controversy in the August, 1777, *Gentleman's Magazine.* In his *Poetical Works* (London, 1782), he for the first time publicly acknowledged his critical theories in several minor poems and in the lengthy "Essay on Painting."

[2] Letter to James Beattie, June 6, 1783, in the Beattie Collection, University of Aberdeen, Scotland.

[3] Scott began his volume by saying, "... from personal respect, I am sorry to differ in opinion [from Johnson]" (p. 1). But he later was more indignant, when he wrote: "The Temple of Fame, lately erected under the title of The Works of the English Poets, affords a striking instance of caprice in the matter of admission to literary honours. Had Criticism, rational impartial criticism, kept the gate of this temple, several names which now appear within its walls, would certainly never have appeared there" (p. 247). In his letters to Beattie, Scott was even more frank: "He [Johnson] is a good Prose Writer, a Good Moralist, and a Good Poet, yet strange to tell! he is either a very incompetent Judge of Poetry or else he suffers his prejudices to operate against and overpow'r his Judgment." Letter of June 6, 1783, in the Beattie Collection, University of Aberdeen, Scotland. Cf. also his letter of August 29, 1783, in William Forbes, *An Account of the Life and Writings of James Beattie* (new ed. in 2 vols.; London, 1824), II, 106: "It is strange so good a writer, both in prose and verse, should be so ill a critic; and that a man, whose private character is so benevolent, should, as an author, indulge such contemptuous acrimony."

[4] James Allison, "Joseph Warton's Reply to Dr. Johnson's *Lives,*" *Journal of English and Germanic Philology,* LI (April, 1952), 186–191.

[5] For this opinion, Scott has been labeled "Denham's most independent critic"; the criticism itself "was emphatically the exception in his century, but by 1820 the march of mind was leaving Denham a position among the more or less forgotten minor classics." Robert A. Aubin, *Topographical Poetry in XVIII-Century England* (New York, 1936), pp. 40, 37.

[6] Letter to James Beattie, August 29, 1783, in Forbes, *Life of Beattie,* II, 106–107.

[7] John Scott, *Critical Essays on Some of the Poems, of Several English Poets* (London, 1785), p. 96.

[8] Joseph Warton, *An Essay on the Genius and Writings of Pope* (4th ed., corr.; London, 1782), I, 50–51.

[9] Samuel Johnson, *Lives of the English Poets,* ed. by G. Birkbeck Hill (Oxford, 1905), I, 78.

[10] Raymond D. Havens, *The Influence of Milton on English Poetry* (Cambridge, U.S.A., 1922), p. 427.

[11] Warton, *Essay on Pope,* I, 346–347.

[12] Scott, *Critical Essays,* p. 7.

[13] *Ibid.,* p. 185; cf. Vicesimus Knox, *Essays, Moral and Literary* (London, 1778), I, 92.

[14] In his edition of Collins: *The Poetical Works of Mr. William Collins. With Memoirs of the Author and Observations on His Genius and Writings.*

[15] Curiously enough, Scott's defense of Goldsmith and Collins was not everywhere understood. Cf. Thomas Campbell, *Specimens of the British Poets; with Biographical and Critical Notices, and an Essay on English Poetry* (London, 1819), VI, 431: "His [Scott's] critical essays contain some judicious remarks on Denham and Dyer; but his verbal strictures on Collins and Goldsmith discover a miserable insensibility to the soul of those poets."

[16] Warton, *Essay on Pope,* I, 42.

[17] "Ode XXII. To Criticism," in Scott, *Poetical Works,* pp. 228–229. Professor Hooker has suggested that the critic's function so defined was perhaps influenced by a desire not to appear ill-tempered and eager to pounce upon any fault. Scott's assumption about the critic's duty had previously been emphasized by Dennis, Dryden, Addison, and a host of other writers. Cf. Edward Niles Hooker (ed.), *The Critical Works of John Dennis* (Baltimore, 1939–1943), I, 439–440.

[18] Cf. his letter to Elihu Robinson, May 25, 1782, in Friends Library, London, where he spoke of the *Poetical Works* as "giving to the Publick a Rational and Inoffensive Amusement, in which (what can be said of the works of too few Poets) *Taste* might be gratified without the Contamination of Morals."

[19] [Scott], *Observations on the Poor,* pp. 127–129.

[20] "Epistle II. Winter Amusements in the Country. To a Friend in London," in Scott, *Poetical Works,* p. 272:

> While Fancy's powers the eventful novel frame,
> And Virtue's care directs its constant aim;
> As Fiction's pen domestic life portrays,
> Its hopes and fears and joys and griefs displays;
> By GRANDISON's or CLINTON's story mov'd,
> We read delighted, and we rise improv'd.

Cf. also [Scott], *Observations on the Poor,* p. 128: "The *Grandison* of *Richardson,* the *Rasselas* of *Johnson,* the *Almoran and Hamet* of *Hawkesworth,* the *Fool of Quality* by *Brooke,* and perhaps one or two more, in this respect merit an honourable exemption from censure."

[21] Forbes, *Life of Beattie,* I, 383.

[22] "Letter to the Editors, November 26, 1782," *European Magazine,* II (November, 1782), 448–449. Cf. also John Scott, *A Letter to the Critical Reviewers* (London, 1782), pp. 6, 10.

[23] Scott, *Critical Essays,* p. 342.

[24] Warton, *Essay on Pope,* II, 12.

[25] Johnson, *Lives of the Poets,* I, 22–23.

[26] *Ibid.,* III, 224.

[27] Scott, *Critical Essays,* pp. 243–244.

[28] William Wordsworth, "An Evening Walk," in *Poetical Works,* ed. by Ernest de Sélincourt (Oxford, 1940), I, 20. Nowell Smith has shown how Wordsworth took the

phrase "prospect all on fire," used in *An Evening Walk,* from Moses Browne's *Sunday Thoughts,* a poem which Scott quoted with high praise in his criticism of Thomson. *Ibid.,* p. 321. Cf. Scott, *Critical Essays,* pp. 349, 351, where Scott singled out this particular expression for especial approval. Cf. also Marjorie Letta Barstow, *Wordsworth's Theory of Poetic Diction* (New Haven, 1917), pp. 57, 109; she feels that Scott's emphasis on drawing new images from nature and on having them clear and distinct, doubtless influenced Wordsworth.

[29] "Letter to the Editor, June 19, 1777," *Gentleman's Magazine,* XLVII (August, 1777), 364: Scott here defended the value of the Rowley poems not with regard to their authorship or their antiquity, but with regard to their intrinsic merits.

[30] Scott, *A Letter to the Critical Reviewers,* p. 16.

[31] Scott, *Critical Essays,* p. 174: "The human mind always dwells with complacence on the ideas of rural solitude, and cottage innocence: we afford a ready indulgence to the deception which annexes to those ideas, the idea of unmixed happiness; though experience convinces us that no such happiness is really existent. There is another favourite satisfaction which we derive from the contemplation of greatness elevating humble merit. A poem which describes these subjects in the most agreeable colours, cannot fail to interest the reader."

[32] *Ibid.,* p. 143.

[33] Edward N. Hooker, "Introduction to the Series on Wit," in Augustan Reprint Society, Series One: *Essays on Wit* (November, 1946), pp. 1–6.

[34] Jean H. Hagstrum, *Samuel Johnson's Literary Criticism* (Minneapolis, 1952), pp. 155–158.

[35] Scott, *Critical Essays,* p. 224.

[36] Johnson, *Lives of the English Poets,* I, 19.

[37] *Ibid.,* III, 233.

[38] Hagstrum, *Johnson's Criticism,* p. 173.

[39] Scott, *Critical Essays,* p. 188.

[40] Hooker, *Works of Dennis,* II, cxxv.

[41] "First Epistle of the Second Book of Horace," ll. 340–347.

[42] Scott, *Critical Essays,* p. 248.

[43] *Ibid.,* pp. 2–3.

[44] Johnson, *Lives of the English Poets,* III, 251.

[45] "An Essay on Poetry and Music, as They Affect the Mind," in James Beattie, *Essays on the Nature and Immutability of Truth* (Dublin, 1778), II, 6.

[46] *Ibid.,* pp. 258–259.

[47] Warton, *Essay on Pope,* I, 48.

[48] *Ibid.,* p. 12.

[49] *Ibid.,* II, 165.

[50] Johnson, *Lives of the English Poets,* I, 51.

[51] Warton, *Essay on Pope,* I, 90.

[52] Scott, *Critical Essays,* pp. 65–66: "Originality in poetical composition has been much too indiscriminately applauded. Priority of production may perhaps be allowed to add value, where all other circumstances are equal; but the query, whether a mere hint be preferable to a complete design, a rude outline to a finished picture, is a query which will be answered in the affirmative, only from the mouth of ignorance or partiality."

[53] "Essay on Painting," in Scott, *Poetical Works,* pp. 307–308.

[54] Scott, *A Letter to the Critical Reviewers,* p. 16. Cf. also his "Letter to the Editors, November 26, 1782," *European Magazine,* II (November, 1782), 449: "Enthusiasm, I means rational enthusiasm, (not that false fire which produces rant and bombast) is perhaps one principal characteristic of my compositions."

[55] John Langhorne, "Observations on the Oriental Eclogues," in *The Works of the British Poets,* ed. by Robert Anderson (London, 1795), IX, 536.

[56] Raymond D. Havens, "Simplicity, a Changing Concept," *Journal of the History of Ideas,* XIV (January, 1953), 4–5. This entire article is an admirable study of the concept of simplicity.

[57] *Ibid.,* p. 13.

[58] *Ibid.,* p. 25.

[59] Langhorne, "Observations on the Odes, Descriptive and Allegorical," in Anderson (ed.), *The Works of the British Poets,* IX, 539.

[60] Warton, *Essay on Pope,* I, 146.

[61] *Ibid.,* II, 178–179. Pope wrote this in a paper he gave to Mr. Spence.

[62] William Mason, *Poems of Gray. To Which Are Prefixed Memoirs of His Life and Writings* (2d ed.; London, 1775), I, 258.

[63] Warton, *Essay on Pope,* I, 36; II, 401.

[64] Forbes, *Life of Beattie,* II, 13.

[65] *Ibid.,* I, 86.

[66] *Ibid.,* I, 188–193.

[67] Johnson, *Lives of the English Poets,* III, 51.

[68] Scott, *A Letter to the Critical Reviewers,* p. 7.

[69] *Ibid.,* p. 12.

[70] "Ode XXII. To Criticism," in Scott, *Poetical Works,* p. 230.

[71] Warton, *Essay on Pope,* I, 102.

[72] He criticized Milton for having the flowers of spring and summer blooming indiscriminately together in *Lycidas.* Cf. his "Essay on Painting," in Scott, *Poetical Works,* pp. 308–309:

> No rude incongruence should thy piece disgrace,
> No motley modes of different time and place;
> By Grecian chiefs no Gallic airs be worn,
> Nor in their hands be modern weapons borne;
> Nor mix the crested helm and coat of mail
> With the vast curl'd peruke, or pointed tail.

[73] He felt Milton also erred in not making up his mind whether the day-star was a person or a heavenly body. Scott said that the distinction between these two kinds of circumstance was between the natural and the poetic. Earlier (*Observations on the Poor,* p. 126), he had condemned puppet shows and pantomimes for their "monstrous incongruities and insufferable indecencies."

[74] "Letter to the Editors, August 6, 1782," *British Magazine and Review,* I (August, 1782), 127.

[75] Scott, *Critical Essays,* p. 251: "The Deserted Village would have pleased me better, if all the circumstances relative to Auburn the inhabited, had been grouped in one picture; and all those relative to Auburn the deserted, in another. The Author's plan is more desultory; he gives us, alternately, contrasted sketches of the supposed place in its two different situations."

[76] "Sonnet I. Apology for Retirement. 1766," in Scott, *Poetical Works,* p. 313.

[77] "Essay on Poetry and Music," in Beattie, *Essays on Truth,* II, 265–278.

[78] Johnson, *Lives of the English Poets,* III, 230–231; Warton, *Essay on Pope,* I, 152–153. But cf. I, 364, where Warton praises Milton "who always accommodates the sound to the sense."

[79] Warton, *Essay on Pope,* II, 154.

[80] Scott, *A Letter to the Critical Reviewers,* p. 7.

[81] *Ibid.,* p. 10.

[82] James Harris, *Works* (London, 1801), II, 385.

[83] Wordsworth, *Poetical Works*, II, 397–398.

[84] "Essay on Painting," in Scott, *Poetical Works*, p. 278.

[85] Hooker, *Works of Dennis*, II, cii–ciii.

[86] [David Williams], *Essays on Public Worship, Patriotism, and Projects of Reformation* (London, 1773), pp. 36–37.

[87] Letter to James Beattie, June 6, 1783, in the Beattie Collection, University of Aberdeen, Scotland: "... the prevailing Taste in Polite Literature at least in Poetry is wretched: Classical simplicity is resigned for Gothic Affectation and Writers who in the Time of Addison and Pope would have been honoured with a Place in the *Bathos* or the *Dunciad* are applauded and held up as Standards of Excellence by the Superficial and ignorant Periodical Criticks of the Day."

[88] "Essay on Poetry and Music," in Beattie, *Essays on Truth*, II, 186–187.

[89] James Gray, "Beattie and the Johnson Circle," *Queen's Quarterly*, LVIII (Winter, 1951–52), 530.

[90] Charles Lamb, "Ritson *versus* John Scott the Quaker," in *Works of Charles and Mary Lamb*, ed. by E. V. Lucas (London, 1903), I, 218–226. This was a short article which Lamb wrote as a hoax, but which he later acknowledged as his. It consisted of quotations from Scott's *Critical Essays*, followed by notes supposedly written in Ritson's hand in the margin of the volume, attacking the critical point made. The humor was directed at Scott's rather pedantic remarks, without any attempt being made to ascertain the critical system which underlay Scott's work.

[91] A less favorable view was presented by J. W. H. Atkins, *English Literary Criticism: 17th and 18th Centuries* (London, 1951), p. 354, where the *Critical Essays* falls into the category of those works "which witnessed to widespread and varied critical activities without adding much to the critical advance...."

BIBLIOGRAPHY

BIBLIOGRAPHY

The bibliography is divided into three sections: the works of John Scott, the known letters of Scott, and the periodical reviews of his work and life. All entries are arranged chronologically.

The Works of John Scott

[Scott, John]. *Four Elegies: Descriptive and Moral*. London, 1760.

——. *Elegy, Written at Amwell, in Hertfordshire, MDCCLXVIII*. London, 1769.

——. *The Constitution Defended, and Pensioner Exposed; in Remarks on The False Alarm*. London, 1770.

——. *Observations on the Present State of the Parochial and Vagrant Poor*. London, 1773.

Scott, John. *A Digest of the Present Act for Amendment of the Highways: With a Calculation of the Duty, Composition, and Contribution for Every Rent from £1 to £400 Per Annum. For the Use of Surveyors, &c. Also a List of Forfeitures and Penalties, with a Schedule of Forms and Remarks*. London, 1773. [I was unable to discover any extant copy of this tract.]

[Scott, John]. *Remarks on The Patriot. Including Some Hints Respecting the Americans: with an Address to the Electors of Great Britain*. London, 1775.

Scott, John. *Amwell: A Descriptive Poem*. London, 1776.

——. ——. 2d ed. London, 1776.

——. ——. Another ed. Dublin, 1776.

——. *Digests of the General Highway and Turnpike Laws; with the Schedule of Forms, as Directed by Act of Parliament; and Remarks. Also, an Appendix, on the Construction and Preservation of Roads*. London, 1778.

[Scott, John]. *Moral Eclogues*. London, 1778.

Scott, John. *Poetical Works*. London, 1782.

——. *A Letter to the Critical Reviewers: Occasioned by Their Account of Scott's Poetical Works, in Their Review for July 1782*. London, 1782.

——. *Critical Essays on Some of the Poems, of Several English Poets. With an Account of the Life and Writings of the Author; by Mr. [John] Hoole*. London, 1785.

——. *Poetical Works*. 2d ed. London, 1786.

——. ——. 2d ed. [Actually, this is the 3d ed.] London, 1795.

The Works of the British Poets, with Prefaces, Biographical and Critical, ed. Robert Anderson. Vol. XI. London, 1795.

The Cabinet of Poetry, ed. S. J. Pratt. Vol. VI. London, 1808.

The Works of the British Poets, Collated with the Best Editions, ed. Thomas Park. Vol. XXXIX. London, 1808.

The Works of the English Poets, from Chaucer to Cowper, ed. Alexander Chalmers. Vol. XVII. London, 1810.

Specimens of the British Poets; with Biographical and Critical Notices, and an Essay on English Poetry, ed. Thomas Campbell. Vol. VI. London, 1819.

The British Poets, ed. R. A. Davenport. Vol. LXX. Chiswick, 1822.

The Works of the British Poets, with Lives of the Authors, ed. Robert Walsh, Jr. Vol. XXXII. Philadelphia, 1822.

The Known Letters of Scott

October 1, 1776. From John Scott at London to Elihu Robinson. In the possession of Mr. and Mrs. Donald F. Hyde, Four Oaks Farm, Somerville, New Jersey. [Examined by typescript.]

June 19, 1777. From "A Detester of Literary Imposition, but a Lover of good Poetry" [John Scott] at London to the Editor, *Gentleman's Magazine,* XLVII (August, 1777), 361–365.

March 18, 1778. From John Scott at Amwell to the Editor, *Gentleman's Magazine,* XLVIII (March, 1778), 112.

[May, 1778]. From John Scott at Amwell to the Editor, *Gentleman's Magazine,* XLVII (May, 1778), 203.

October 24, 1778. From John Scott at Amwell to James Beattie. C. 319: The Beattie Collection, University Library, King's College, University of Aberdeen, Aberdeen, Scotland. [Examined by microfilm.]

January 25, 1782. From John Scott at Amwell to James Beattie. C. 370: Beattie Collection. [Examined by microfilm.] An inaccurately transcribed and abbreviated portion of this letter is quoted by Margaret Forbes, *Beattie and His Friends* (Westminster, 1904), p. 182.

March 30, 1782. From John Scott at London to James Beattie. C. 376: Beattie Collection. [Examined by microfilm.]

May 10, 1782. From John Scott at London to James Beattie. Letter CLVII: William Forbes, *An Account of the Life and Writings of James Beattie* (new ed. in 2 vols.; London, 1824), II, 90–94.

May 25, 1782. From John Scott at London to Elihu Robinson. Portfolio 30 #9: Friends Library, Friends House, Euston Road, London, England. [Examined by microfilm.]

August 6, 1782. From John Scott at Amwell to the Editors, *British Magazine and Review,* I (August, 1782), 126–127.

November 26, 1782. From John Scott at Amwell to the Editors, *European Magazine, and London Review,* II (November, 1782), 448–449.

May 23, 1783. From John Scott at Amwell to James Phillips. Gibson Collection: Vol. IV. 187: Friends Library, London, England. [Examined by microfilm.]

June 6, 1783. From John Scott at London to James Beattie. C. 405: Beattie Collection. [Examined by microfilm.] An inaccurately transcribed and abbreviated portion of this letter is quoted by Margaret Forbes, *Beattie and His Friends,* p. 195.

August 29, 1783. From John Scott at Amwell to James Beattie. Letter CLXIII: William Forbes, *An Account of the Life and Writings of James Beattie,* II, 105–109.

PERIODICAL REVIEWS OF SCOTT'S WORK AND LIFE

[Review of *Four Elegies: Descriptive and Moral*]. *London Magazine,* XXIX (April, 1760), 224.

———. *Monthly Review,* XXIII (July, 1760), 68–73.

[Review of *Elegy, Written at Amwell, in Hertfordshire, MDCCLXVIII*]. *Monthly Review,* XLI (December, 1769), 475–476.

[Review of *The Constitution Defended, and Pensioner Exposed; in Remarks on The False Alarm*]. *London Chronicle,* XXVII (April 28–May 1, 1770), 409–410.

———. *Critical Review,* XXIX (May, 1770), 389.

———. *London Magazine,* XXXIX (May, 1770), 268.

———. *Monthly Review,* XLII (May, 1770), 405.

[Review of *Observations on the Present State of the Parochial and Vagrant Poor*]. *London Magazine,* XLII (March, 1773), 149.

———. *Monthly Review,* XLVIII (April, 1773), 322–324.

———. *Critical Review,* XXXVI (August, 1773), 151–154.

———. *Town and Country Magazine,* V (September, 1773), 490.

[Review of *A Digest of the Present Act for Amendment of the Highways*]. *Monthly Review,* XLIX (December, 1773), 498–500.

———. *Critical Review,* XXXVII (January, 1774), 74.

[Review of *Remarks on The Patriot. Including Some Hints Respecting the Americans*]. *Critical Review*, XXXIX (January, 1775), 76.

––––––. *Monthly Review*, LII (February, 1775), 184.

––––––. *London Magazine*, XLIV (April, 1775), 203–204.

[Review of *Amwell*]. *Critical Review*, XLI (April, 1776), 318.

––––––. *Monthly Review*, LIV (May, 1776), 383–388.

––––––. *Gentleman's Magazine*, XLVI (July, 1776), 318–319.

"Card to the Vindicator of Dr. Beattie," *Gentleman's Magazine*, XLVIII (April, 1778), 152.

[Review of *Digests of the General Highway and Turnpike Laws*]. *Monthly Review*, LVIII (May, 1778), 379–380.

––––––. *Critical Review*, XLVI (September, 1778), 233–234.

[Review of *Moral Eclogues*]. *Critical Review*, XLVI (December, 1778), 473.

––––––. *Gentleman's Magazine*, XLIX (January, 1779), 36.

––––––. *Monthly Review*, LX (April, 1779), 301–302.

"Utility of Scot's Digest," *Gentleman's Magazine*, L (January, 1780), 20.

[Review of *Poetical Works*]. *London Chronicle*, LI (June 13–15, 1782), 569–570.

––––––. *Critical Review*, LIV (July, 1782), 47–50.

––––––. *British Magazine and Review*, I (August, 1782), 123–126.

––––––. *European Magazine*, II (September, 1782), 193–197.

––––––. *Monthly Review*, LXVII (September, 1782), 183–190.

––––––. *Gentleman's Magazine*, LII (October, 1782), 489.

[Review of *A Letter to the Critical Reviewers*]. *British Magazine and Review*, I (November, 1782), 366.

––––––. *Critical Review*, LV (January, 1783), 77–78.

[Obituary of Scott]. *European Magazine*, IV (December, 1783), 479.

––––––. *Gentleman's Magazine*, LIII (December, 1783), 1066.

––––––. *Town and Country Magazine*, XV (December, 1783), 672.

[Review of *Critical Essays on Some of the Poems, of Several English Poets*]. *Critical Review*, LX (November, 1785), 345–350.

––––––. *Monthly Review*, LXXVII (July, 1787), 25–31.

[Reprinting of "I hate that drum's discordant sound"]. *Biographical and Imperial Magazine*, IV (August, 1790), 132.

Webb, John. "Letter to the Editor, June 1, 1815," *Lady's Magazine*, XLVI (July, 1815), 315–316.

INDEX

INDEX